METHODS AND MACROS

AutoCAD

Computer Graphics Technology and Management Series

Series Consulting Editor: Carl Machover
Edited by: David M. Gauthier

AutoCAD: Methods and Macros

by Jeff Guenther, Ed Ocoboc, and Anne Wayman

VersaCAD Tutorial: A Practical Approach to Computer-Aided Design

by Carol Buehrens

METHODS AND MACROS

AutoCAD

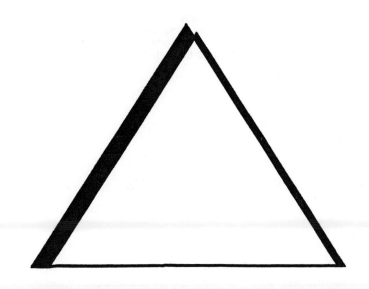

Jeff Guenther, Ed Ocoboc
and Anne Wayman

COMPUTER
GRAPHICS
TECHNOLOGY
AND
MANAGEMENT
SERIES

TAB Professional and Reference Books

Division of TAB BOOKS Inc.
P.O. Box 40, Blue Ridge Summit, PA

The following are trademarks of the companies as listed:

ADE is a trademark of Autodesk, Inc.
AutoLISP is a trademark of Autodesk, Inc.
AutoCAD is a trademark of Autodesk, Inc.
AutoSHADE is a trademark of Autodesk, Inc.
AutoWord is a trademark of Technical Software, Inc.
CAD.Camera is a trademark of Autodesk, Inc.
dBASE III is a trademark of Ashton-Tate Corporation
IBM is a trademark of International Business Machines Corporation
Lotus is a trademark of Lotus Development Corp.
MS-DOS is a trademark of Microsoft Corporation
Newkey is a trademark of FAB Software
Norton Utilities is a trademark of Peter Norton Computing, Inc.
PC-DOS is a trademark of International Business Machines Corporation
Primavera is a trademark of Primavera Systems, Inc.
PrimaVision is a trademark of Primavera Systems, Inc.
PrimaCAD is a trademark of Primavera Systems, Inc.
Prokey is a trademark of RoseSoft
SideKick is a trademark of Borland International
SuperKey is a trademark of Borland International
TouchPen is a trademark of Sun-Flex Company
UNIX is a trademark of AT&T Bell Laboratories
WordStar is a trademark of MicroPro International Corp.

FIRST EDITION
SECOND PRINTING

Copyright © 1988 by Jeff Guenther, Ed Ocoboc, and Anne Wayman.
Printed in the United States of America

Library of Congress Cataloging in Publication Data

Guenther, Jeff.
AutoCAD : methods and macros / by Jeff Guenther, Ed Ocoboc, and
Anne Wayman.
p.   cm.
ISBN 0-8306-0189-9   ISBN 0-8306-2989-0 (pbk.)
1. AutoCAD (Computer program language)   I. Ocoboc, Ed.
II. Wayman, Anne.   III. Title.
T385.G84 1988
620′ .00425′0285—dc19   87-28933
                                                          CIP

Questions regarding the content of this book
should be addressed to:

Reader Inquiry Branch
TAB BOOKS Inc.
Blue Ridge Summit, PA 17294-0214

Contents

Dedications

To my wife, Kate, and my boys, John and Adam.
                                                    JG

To my wife, Debbie, who has put up with the whirr of a computer in the late, and wee hours; to my daughter Jessica, and son Mike, both saw me during the writing, and to my parents, Yaye and Ed, and to my in-laws, Chuck and Kay.
                                                    EO

To Tyler Sperry, now editor of *Dr. Dobbs Journal*, who has put up with late night and early morning pleas for help; the formerly all-male Encinitas Computer Club, who answered so many questions nine years ago, and to my Ultimate Source.
                                                    AW

Introduction,
or How To Read
and Use This Book

The following are some general notes about how this book is designed. Most people will never read this page, and will be forever baffled by much of the material.

Virtually every command available in AutoCAD is discussed herein. The more complex commands are covered in greater detail. For most commands, you will be led down into the nooks and crannies of the command to its very end. Occasionally, where the procedure becomes blatantly obvious from the prompt, no further space is wasted: for example, many commands end in a "Yes/No (Y/N)" prompt. Does the average reader really need to be told to enter Y or N if he (or she) wants to proceed or retreat?

It is very important to read the prompts as you work with AutoCAD. Although there are audible beeps to accompany most error messages, the beeps can be suppressed when you configure AutoCAD. The prompts keep you aware of where you are at all times, what AutoCAD is expecting, what is happening—but only if you *read the prompt!*

Help is available for most commands via the HELP command. See the AutoCAD Glossary Section for more information under "HELP." Anything that is not clear about the operation of a command will often become easy to understand with HELP.

Throughout this book, the word *enter* is used to indicate that information is to be passed to AutoCAD by the operator. This involves, usually, typing in something from the keyboard *and* pressing the "Return" key. (On some keyboards, the Return key says "Enter" on it, or some other term.) The space bar will also act as a [Return] in AutoCAD, except when doing text entry.

To give a *null response* means to press the [Return] key without typing in anything or selecting any points.

Most commands produce prompts requesting further data or choices. Any options that have the first letter capitalized can be selected by entering that letter.

The word *select* here usually means to locate a point on the drawing using a button on the mouse or other pointing device. Often the directions refer to locating a point with the puck, since the best pointing device is a digitizing tablet and puck, although any standard input device will work. It is assumed, except as noted, that the user will have some kind of pointing device other than the keyboard. The price of mice is so low that there is almost no excuse for not having one. Keyboard entry is slow and frustrating.

Keys are shown by enclosing their label in square brackets: e.g., [CTRL] for the *Control* key, [Return] for the *Return* key, and so forth. Three keys usually are used in combination with another key: [CTRL], [SHIFT], and [ALT]. For example, [CTRL]

Legend for Command Charts

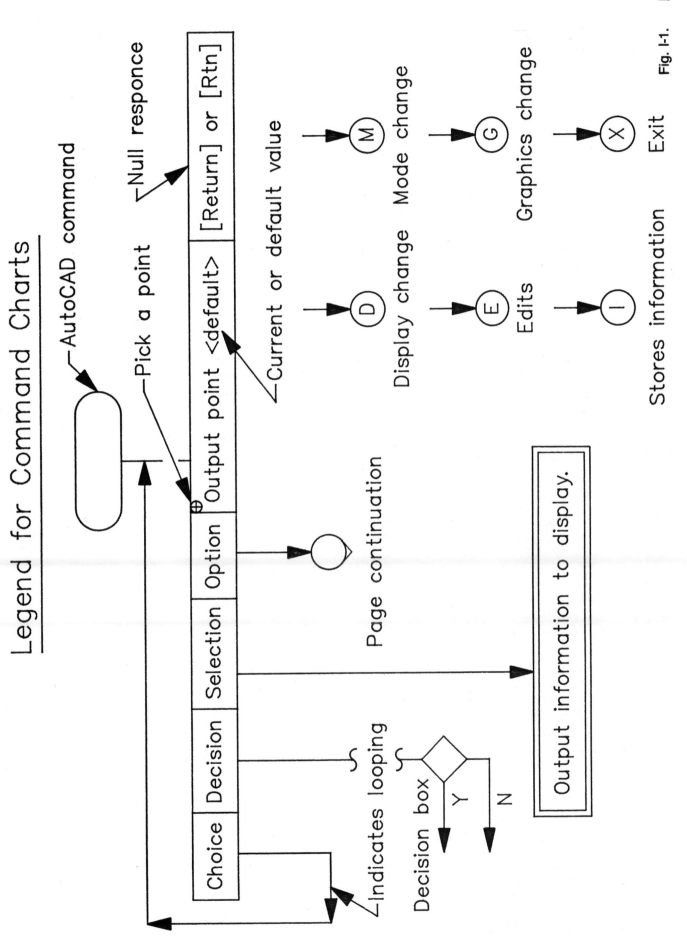

Fig. I-1.

C indicates that the Control key is to be held down, the C key pressed and released, and then the Control key released.

You should already be familiar with your system's procedures. If not, you will find it helpful to read a few books on computer terms, DOS, and so forth, before plunging ahead into AutoCAD.

For the more complex commands, a Command Tree Chart has been provided to show you the options within the various levels of the command. Refer to these charts when you are first trying out a command and whenever you are using parts of a command that you haven't worked with for a while. The convention used for the Command Tree Charts is shown in Fig. I-1.

The command is enclosed in a box with round ends. Multiple choice options are shown together in rectangular boxes. If there is a default choice that can be selected by giving a null response, it is shown in pointy brackets. Choosing a [Return] response otherwise is shown in brackets: [Return] or [Rtn].

An item all by itself in a box indicates that you are to provide AutoCAD with the input data listed. Often these boxes will contain a dot whose meaning is defined below.

Yes or No options are usually shown in a diamond, as are some of the two-choice options. Output of information from AutoCAD to the display is shown in rectangular double-line boxes.

Making any particular choice is shown by an arrow originating from the box enclosing it. Arrows entering any multiple choice option rectangle put you back into the entire box; you can choose any of the options available, not just the one where the arrow enters.

A dot at the upper left corner of a box indicates that you can enter a point with your mouse or other pointing device to provide the information needed to implement that part of the command. Alternatively, keyboard entry is usually possible for such input.

The kind of output from each operation is indicated by a circle containing one of these letters:

> *D* = The display is altered
> *G* = Graphics are added
> *E* = Erasure or other editing has been done
> *I* = Information has been passed to or from AutoCAD
> *X* = Exits back to the Command: prompt
> *M* = A drawing mode has been altered.

It is assumed that you have all three ADE's (Advanced Drafting Extensions). If you don't, you might want to purchase them from your AutoCAD dealer. See the ADE entry under the AutoCAD Glossary Section for a list of what features are included in each ADE.

Section 1

Basic Techniques

This section is designed to get you started with AutoCAD. The first chapter, Up, Up and Away, will take you, step-by-step, through your first drawing. We put this first because most users will have their computer system set up. If, however, your computer isn't up and running, or if you haven't even bought one yet, you'll want to start with the second chapter, Configuring AutoCAD.

Chapter three, What If It Doesn't Work, is important only if you've got a problem after you've configured AutoCAD. Its Question and Answer format will make it easy to find exactly the information you need.

Once you're up and running, you'll want to spend some time with the fourth chapter, Planning Drawings for Efficiency. Chapter five teaches you how to make the most of Macros and Menus, and Chapter six deals with Scripts. The information here is based on hard-won experience and will save you hours of frustration and wasted time.

The seventh chapter, Third Party Software, gives you an overview of the kinds of additional software you might want to buy to enhance your use of AutoCAD.

Additional help is available as spelled out in the eighth chapter, Resources.

Chapter nine discusses Plotting and the tenth chapter covers Attributes.

1

Up, Up and Away

The quickest way to get a feel for using AutoCAD is to create a drawing. To get started, we'll create a sign that looks like the one on page 4.

If you have not configured AutoCAD for your computer and printer or plotter, you'll need to refer to Chapter 2 (Configuring AutoCAD) before you start the drawing.

CREATING A SIMPLE DRAWING

Once you're configured, begin AutoCAD at the C> prompt by entering: *ACAD*.

When we use the term, 'Enter' or 'Entering' we intend for you to type in the command name or move your crosshairs to the appropriate point and press the ENTER or RETURN key.

There are two steps to start a new drawing:

1. From the AutoCAD Main Menu, choose "Create a New Drawing."

   Enter: *1*

2. The Main Menu will remain, and the words, "New Drawing File Name" will appear at the bottom of the screen.

   Enter: *BETTER*

   Note: File names can be entered in upper or lower case or a combination.

A blank screen with the AutoCAD menu on the right will appear. At the lower left will be the word, COMMAND: To draw the rectangular box outlining the sign, do the following steps:

1. Enter: *GRID*

   This displays a grid of dots for your reference—it's not part of the drawing and won't be plotted.

   Enter: *0.5*

3

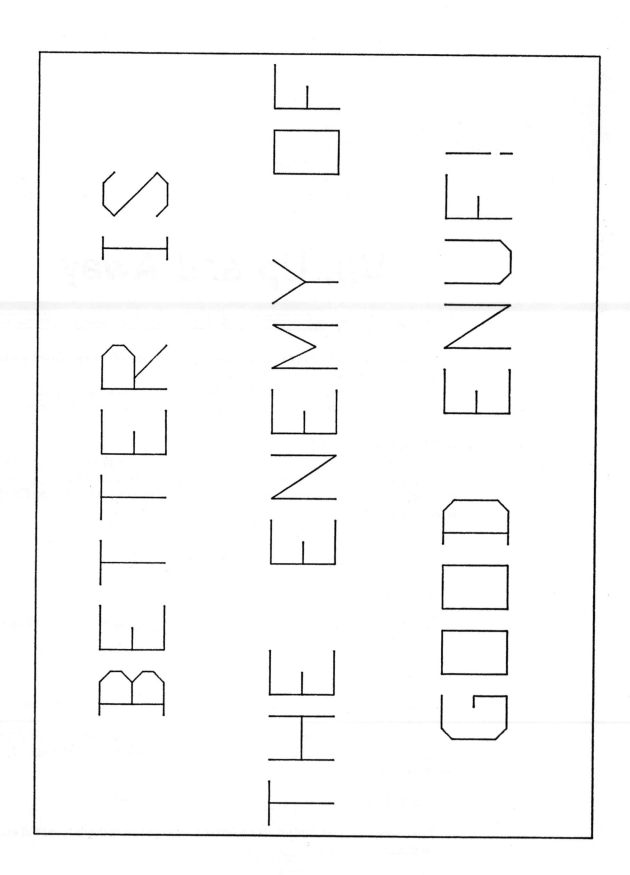

BETTER IS THE ENEMY OF GOOD ENUF!

2. Enter: *SNAP*

SNAP speeds up drawing by forcing what you draw to line up with the grid.

Enter: *0.5*

This creates SNAP's invisible rectangular grid to 0.5 drawing units.

3. Enter: *LINE*

A line is the basic drawing entity. It is created by locating a point at each end.
We will draw four lines, making a box around the sign. You may type the coordinates for an end point and press RETURN to fix the point OR move the crosshairs to the end point and press the spacebar or RETURN to fix each point.
If you have a mouse or tablet, you can hit the "pick" button to select the point.
Create three lines of the box using the following four endpoints:

1,1
10,1
10,7
1,7

You now have the first three lines of your drawing displayed on the screen.

4. Enter: *C*

Here, C is the CLOSE subcommand and will add the fourth line to your box, closing it.

To enter the text, do the following:

1. Enter: *TEXT*

TEXT is the command that lets you put the text or words in a drawing.
The screen will display:

Starting point (or A,C,R,S, or M):

Choosing a "Starting point" with the cursor causes your text to be left justified, "A" aligns the text between two points, "C" centers the text, "R" right justifies the text, and "S" lets you choose the font or style of your text.

2. Enter: *C*

The screen will display the following prompts one at a time:

Center point:
Height <0.20>:
Rotation angle <0>:
Text

The items in the < > brackets are defaults, that is, the values AutoCAD will use if you hit RETURN without entering anything.

3. At *'Center point:'* enter: *5.5,5.5*
This sets the center point of your text.

4. At *'Height <0.20>:'* enter: *0.75*
   This sets the height of your text to ¾ of an inch.

5. At 'Rotation angle <0>:' press RETURN to accept the defaults.

6. At *'Text:'* type: *BETTER and press RETURN three times.*

   The triple RETURN picks up the center command, the letter height and the rotation angle.

7. At *'Text:'* type: *IS THE* and press *RETURN* three times.

8. At *'Text:'* type: *ENEMY OF* and press *RETURN* thrice.

9. At *'Text:'* type: *GOOD ENUF!* and press *RETURN* once.

10. Enter: *END*

   This ends and saves your drawing and returns you to the Main Menu.
   The next step is to plot or print your drawing. If you're using a dot matrix printer, skip to "PRINTING;" do the following if you're using a plotter:

Plotting

1. Turn your plotter on and load the paper.

2. From the Main Menu, choose item 3, 'Plot a Drawing.;
   The screen will display:

   Specify the part of the drawing to be plotted by entering: Display, Extents, Limits, View, or Window <D>:

   Enter: *L*
   (We will discuss the other options later in Chapter 9, Plotting.)

   The screen will display the basic plot specifications that were set up in your configuration of AutoCAD. At the end of the list is the question:

   Do you want to change anything? <N>

   Press *RETURN* or *N* to accept the default.

   The screen will display:

   Position paper in plotter
   Press RETURN to continue or S to Stop for hardware set up.

3. Insert the plotter pen.

4. Press *RETURN.*

   Your drawing will begin to plot.

Printing

   Using a dot matrix printer is similar to using a plotter, but there are some differences.

Follow the steps for plotting, with these exceptions:

In step 1, turn on your printer and load the paper.

In step 2, choose item 4, "Printer Plot a Drawing>" Enter *BETTER* when prompted for the file name.

Skip step 3, and press *RETURN*; your drawing will begin to print.

2

Configuring AutoCAD

AutoCAD was written so it can be used with a variety of equipment. In order to make use of the program, you must tell it exactly which display, digitizer, printer and/or plotter you're using. This is called configuring.

The AutoCAD configuration program is also used to let you set the operating parameters and defaults that work best for you.

Configuration is done the first time you set up AutoCAD for use on a particular station, or whenever you change to a different type of hardware. Once you've run the configuration program, you're all set—until you get a new piece of equipment, or you want to change the defaults and/or operating parameters.

Remember, after you have completed the configuration, you'll need to put a copy of the acad.cfg file on a set of backup disks, so that you can restore the setup if you lose your working files. Also, if you intend to change your configuration, you may want to keep a copy of the original configuration on a separate disk.

When you start up AutoCAD, it checks to see if it's been configured. If it hasn't, it will automatically present you with the Configuration Menu. If AutoCAD has been configured, but you want to change the configuration, simply choose option 5, 'Configure AutoCAD,' from the Main Menu.

The Configuration menu looks like this:

Configuration menu
0. Exit to Main Menu
1. Show current configuration
2. Allow I/O port configuration
3. Configure video display
4. Configure digitizer
5. Configure plotter
6. Configure printer plotter
7. Configure system console
8. Configure operating parameters.
Enter selection <0>:

Notice the 0 in the default angle brackets. In this case, pressing the space bar or the ENTER key would return you to the Main Menu. There is a default presented each

time you are prompted to choose a task. The tasks and options are described below in more detail:

0. Exit to Main Menu. When you choose zero, you'll first be asked if you want to keep any changes you have made in the configuration. Choosing No will return you to the Main Menu and leave the old configuration in place. Entering Y for Yes will cause the changes to be written to the acad.cfg file.

1. Show current configuration. This option allows you to double check the current configuration.

2. Allow I/O port configuration: 'I/O' refers to Input/Output. The ports on your computer are where you physically attach devices like the printer, plotter, digitizing tablet, mouse, puck, etc.

If you have only one serial port, you probably don't need to worry about this option. If you have two serial ports, then you have a 50-50 chance that you're coupled to the right port. If your digitizer doesn't work, chances are you've got the wrong port set. The same thing applies to plotters. Specific information about particular equipment port configuration will be handled in the other options.

If you choose this option, the screen will display:

Do you wish to do I/O port configuration? <N>

You can accept the default at this point. If you answer Yes, your current I/O port configuration will be displayed.

3. Configure video display: Your computer might allow a variety of graphics displays. When you choose this option, AutoCAD will list the displays available. You will be asked to choose which you want to use. Enter the number corresponding to your equipment, then provide further information about your hardware if prompted to do so. (Note: If your graphics system is not among those listed, you might be able to get drivers for it from your AutoCAD dealer or from the system manufacturer. This is an area for caution.)

You will also be given the opportunity to enable or disable the Status Line and the Menu/Prompt Areas. If, like most users, you're using a single screen, you'll probably want to leave both enabled.

If squares look like rectangles and circles look like ovals on your screen, you need to correct the aspect ratio of the display. During the video display configure option, you will be offered a chance to do so. The screen will display:

If you have previously measured the height and width of a "square" on your graphics screen, you may use these measurements to correct the aspect ratio. Would you like to do so? <N>

For now, if this is the first time you have configured the system, take the default, No. If you later find that you need to make adjustments, get into the Drawing Editor and create a drawing called "square.dwg", consisting of about a 6″ by 6″ square. Write down the horizontal and vertical measurements of the square as they actually appear on your screen. Then exit back to the Main Menu and reconfigure the display. Take Y for Yes at the prompt above, and then enter the measurements as prompted. Call up the square again in the Drawing Editor and check it.

4. Configure digitizer. The list of tablets and mice that are supported by AutoCAD, or for which the manufacturer provides AutoCAD drivers, continues to grow. Most of these devices require slightly different drivers. When you choose this option, a list of supported digitizers will be displayed. Enter the number corresponding to your equipment, then provide further information as prompted: number of buttons, model number, etc. If you can't find your pointing device among those listed, try to find out from your dealer or from the manufacturer which of the others listed has the same driver. You may be able to fool AutoCAD into thinking it has the other digitizer hooked up.

5. Configure plotter. This selection allows you to match AutoCAD with your plotter. A list of plotters will be displayed. Select your plotter or the nearest work-alike. You will then be asked to answer various questions, such as model number, and so forth. For single pen plotters, you will also be asked: Do you want to change pens while plotting? <N> Pen changes are a method of using more than one color or pen size on a single pen plotter. A *Yes* answer will cause AutoCAD to stop plotting when it has plotted everything corresponding to the first color, allowing you to change pens.

What To Do If Your Plotter Makes Egg-Shaped Circles

Once you have chosen a plotter, AutoCAD assumes the plotter works the way the manufacturer intended it to work. Sometimes, however, there are discrepancies similar to the aspect ratio for displays, and AutoCAD allows you to calibrate the program to make the proper adjustments.

When you first configure AutoCAD for your plotter, don't calibrate it. After you have finished configuring your system, get into the Drawing Editor and draw an 8-inch square, then plot and measure it. Write down both the horizontal and vertical lengths. Get into the configuration menu and choose option 5, Configure plotter. The screen will display:

Would you like to calibrate your plotter ? <N>

If you have previously measured the lengths of a horizontal and a vertical line that were plotted to a specific scale, you may use these measurements to calibrate your plotter.

Enter Y. AutoCAD will then ask for your actual measurements and what the correct measurements should have been. Repeat this process until you are satisfied with the accuracy of the square. If you are careful, once through will do it.

6. Configure printer plotter. Like video displays, digitizers, and plotters, printers also come in a large variety, and AutoCAD must be told what sort of printer you're using. When you make this selection, a list of printers will be displayed. Make the appropriate choice.

The "ADI plotter" is also offered for selection in this section. This is not a real plotter but is a way to create printer plot files for later processing. This choice allows you to write your drawings to a .prp file in AutoCAD's DXB format, ASCII, or binary format.

The remainder of the configure routine for printer plotters is similar to pen plotters.

7. Configure system console. This part of the configuration step is not necessary for most PC's. If you have a machine that has settable console parameters, AutoCAD will provide the necessary prompts to allow selecting the right settings for your application.

8. Configure operating parameters. This selection allows you to set certain parameters for the way AutoCAD responds. The suboptions for the operating parameter menu are as follows:

0. Exit to configuration menu
1. Alarm on error

Activating this choice results in AutoCAD sounding a beep whenever you make an invalid entry.

2. Initial drawing setup

This option allows you to choose your own default prototype drawing, which AutoCAD will use to set all parameters for every new drawing you start. Remember, you can override this default when you create a new drawing from the Main Menu. (See Main Menu in the AutoCAD Glossary Section.) The screen will display:

Enter name of default prototype file for new drawings or . for none <current>:

A single period means you want no default prototype drawing.

3. AutoLISP feature

If you have the ADE-3 package you can enable or disable AutoLISP at this point. The screen will display:

Do you want AutoLISP enabled? <current>:

Enter *Yes* or *No*. Keep in mind that using AutoLISP means AutoCAD will use more memory. If you don't have enough memory to use AutoLISP, you will receive a message to that effect and AutoLISP will be disabled for that drawing.

CONFIGURATION ERROR RECOVERY

If you make an error during the configuration process, there are four ways to recover:

§ CTRL C will cause AutoCAD to ignore the choices made in the current section and return you to the most recent menu.

§ When you exit the configuration program, you'll be asked if you want to save the new configuration. If you answer No, the standard defaults will be re-established.

§ The information generated by the configuration program is kept in a file called acad.cfg. When you update the configuration, the original data is kept in a file called acad.bak. If you need to, you can delete the acad.cfg file, rename the acad.bak as acad.cfg and begin again.

§ If, as suggested, you're working from backup disks, you can use your master disks to recover and start again.

It's also a good idea to keep a backup of your working AutoCAD disk away from your computer. You can recover your acad.cfg file from the backup working disk if necessary.

3

What if It Doesn't Work

If you bought your copy of AutoCAD and much of your hardware from a value-added reseller, you know where to go for help when your system doesn't work, or when it does strange and wonderful things, or goes beep in the night. But many CAD users today bought their stuff from a little shop that used to be a Chinese laundry, where the systems come out of a huge crate from Timbukthree bearing brands like "KimChee AT," "Turbo BenWa," and "Golden Pagoda Jr." The reseller sticks a little label reading "Shadetree Technologies" over the manufacturer's brand and sets the stuff out on the counter. The documentation may contain phrases like: "The system is always in turbo mode, even using a reprogrammed BIOS." That is, when you get any documentation at all.

Wherever you got your system, you will find that the more *you* can diagnose your own problems, the faster your system will be back on line. Your supplier will help you, usually, and most suppliers will give you pretty good warranty service, but you will still find it expedient to run a few tests *before* calling for help. Remember, too, the less bucks the supplier made from the sale, the less time he can afford to spend helping you. Help him by doing your homework and by recording any error messages you get when you encounter problems. The following diagnostic section won't do everything for you, but it will give you a place to start and will probably solve 50 percent of your trouble. A few of the more common hardware and software faults are listed below, along with a few suggestions of what to do or what to try.

There are some general hints which apply to most situations:

§ About 50 percent of all computer problems involve bad cabling: shorts or broken solder joints inside the cable connectors, loose connectors, bent pins, incorrectly constructed cables, cables connected to the wrong ports, loose screws.

§ If you suspect you have a bad component, try swapping it with one you know is good. If the problem doesn't go away, chances are the original component is not at fault.

§ Usually, history is a clue as to what is going on. Did someone else just get through using the PC? Did the "computer menace" from down the hall come to you an hour or so ago and ask for some unformatted floppies? Did "Tom Terrific" recently tell you he just got a great new program off a bulletin board? Did the "corporate hacker" ask to borrow the DOS book and a screwdriver yesterday afternoon? Did you install another board in the last day or two? Did you have

KLEIN BOTTLE STORAGE

a power failure recently? Think of what is new in the last few days or hours and try to conceive how there might be a connection with what is going wrong right now.

§ If you think everything has been properly installed and still can't get the system to work, read whatever documentation you do have. Most users, it seems, never get around to *really* reading the manuals.

§ Errors in manufacturers' instructions are quite common. Review the documentation to see which data could be causing the problem, if it were in error.

§ Static occasionally gets blamed for errors and other problems. You can buy static mats, static grounding bars, static spray, anti-static glare screens, anti-static underwear, and so forth. How much protection is enough? There is no answer. How much money is enough? Static is a very real problem, but you don't have to spend a thousand dollars to eliminate 99 percent of static-caused faults.

§ Check to see if your version of AutoCAD requires BUFFERS=20 and FILES=20 in your config.sys file.

Below are some specific problems and solutions:

Nothing Happens When I Turn on the Switch

Look at the pilot light on your keyboard or CPU. Is it on? Check to see if the thing is plugged in. If it is, check every switch and connection between the outlet and your CPU, especially your surge protector. Check also whether someone has turned off the power to the outlet, or whether a circuit breaker has turned it off. Take a lamp and plug it into the outlet and into the surge protector to check for power. Don't forget to turn the lamp on.

Surge protectors do fail, sometimes in the process of stopping a major spike from reaching your system.

I Get a Flashing Cursor and That's All

Put a DOS disk in A drive and reboot [CTRL][ALT][DELETE]. If the system comes up satisfactorily, try to access C drive. If you can get the C> prompt, do a directory on C and see if the File Allocation Table or the DOS files have been trashed.

If the DOS files have been lost, copy them from A to C.

If the FAT area has been garbled, you may have to reformat the drive.

If you can't access C drive at all, you most likely have a bad drive or a bad controller board. Shut off the power, open the case and try disconnecting and reconnecting the cables on the drive and on the controller board. This will sometimes get things moving again. Don't change the orientation of the cables unless you have some valid reason to believe they have been incorrectly installed.

I Get Power on at the System, But Nothing at all on the Display

Check to see if the brightness and/or contrast have been turned down on the display. Check also for a burned out fuse in the display.

I Can't Get AutoCAD Up From the C> Prompt

Do a directory on the subdirectory you are in and see if AutoCAD is really in there. If not, do a directory on the other subdirectories until you find where the program is. (This is sometimes the problem on multi-user systems, rarely, but not unheard of, on single-user systems.)

If you are certain you are in the right directory, but can't find the program, whip out your Peter Norton (Norton Utilities) and use the NU program to see if some twerp has erased your copy of AutoCAD. Norton can also look for the ACAD files and find them wherever they are hiding on your hard drive, if you don't know.

Check to see if you have a graphics board in your system which will work with AutoCAD.

I Can't Get the Digitizer to Work

Do you get the cursor crosshairs on the screen? Try hitting the F10 button to get them up.

If you have changed any switch settings on your digitizer, try turning the digitizer off and on again. Check the switch settings on your digitizer. Check also to see if your digitizer cable is correct and working properly—See the Hardware Options section of the Appendix.

Look at the indicator lights on the digitizer to see if they show normal function. Install a spare puck, if you have one. If that doesn't do it, try reconfiguring AutoCAD from the Main Menu (Selection 2). Option 2 of the reconfiguration menu will allow you to change the I/O port configuration. Then take Option 4 to configure the digitizer. Change the digitizer to the other COM port.

I Can't Get the Mouse to Work Right

If the mouse works poorly, you may have configured for the wrong brand. Check again. Also, make sure that the mouse was *not* activated in DOS unless called for by AutoCAD.

Do you get the cursor crosshairs on the screen? If not, try reconfiguring AutoCAD from the Main Menu (Selection 5). Option 2 of the reconfiguration menu will let you change the I/O ports. Then take Option 4 to configure the mouse. Change the mouse to the other COM port.

Check the mouse power supply, if it is a separate component. Is it plugged in? Try turning the mouse off and on again, if it has a switch. Check to see if your mouse cables are properly connected—See the Hardware Options section of the Appendix.

It Takes Forever to Do a Zoom or Pan

See "The Case of the Creeping Zoom" in Chapter 4 (CAD Efficiency). Make sure you have a coprocessor chip and that the dip switch on the motherboard has been properly set to access the coprocessor. This switch is usually number 2 on the dip switch three inches further in from the edge of the motherboard, near the coprocessor. See the documentation for your system, if any.

The Printer Won't Print

Run the built-in printer diagnostic test. See if the ribbon or paper is jammed. Look for pieces of tape in the mechanism. This also could be a cabling problem. Check to see if the cable connection at the back of the PC is tight and is screwed in firmly. If you are trying to do printer plots, exit AutoCAD and see if the printer will take a simple DOS print command. Printing out your autoexec.bat file as a sample document is a good test.

If you have more than one parallel port, try changing to the other one and print the sample document.

Usually printers are shipped with a manual. Check the manual and see if the dip switches are still at the factory settings. See also Appendix G.

If you can get the printer to work in DOS, but not in AutoCAD, run through the reconfigure option from the Main Menu to be sure you have selected the right type of printer and that the AutoCAD drivers are installed.

Often, the printer port is on the Hercules graphics card. If strange things have also been happening on your display, try a new graphics card.

The Plotter Won't Plot

Check the power and data cables as mentioned above. Note that the plotter cable can sometimes be swapped end for end, depending on what kinds of ports are used. A "backwards" cable will not work, in many cases. After you have checked the cables and tried to plot again, run the plotter diagnostic to see if it will plot at all.

Try changing the COM port for the plotter, similar to the procedure above for the digitizer. Older versions of AutoCAD don't let you interrupt a plot. If you have a big drawing, it may take a long time before you get control again. Make up another very small drawing, say, a single circle in the middle of the drawing limits. Try to plot this, rather than your working drawing, to save time.

The Plotter Puts Peculiar Lines Through My Drawing

This kind of thing has been blamed on everything from static to sunspots. One victim swore it was due to the radio station on the roof. I'm not so sure about the latter, but here are some other theories:

§ The IBM AT has been known to give these stray vectors with some plotters. AutoCAD has patched drivers for these cases. Contact AutoCAD or your dealer if you have a version 2.15 or 2.18 with this problem running on an AT.

§ Make sure that you don't have your plotter plugged into a circuit that also has an electric motor drawing current from it. Possible "noisy" loads include microwave ovens, motor-driven tools, large hot plates, fans, refrigerators, and air conditioners.

§ Look for plotter data cables strung along the floor, tangled up with power cords. It is remotely possible to get cross-talk from one to the other. Separate the cables and/or install shielded cables, if all else fails.

§ Look at your drawing and be very sure that objects, especially text, are not right at the edge of the plotting area. AutoCAD sometimes runs into the allowable plot border and goes looking for the missing vector on the other side of the planet, leaving a line behind it.

I'm Drawing, But Everything I Draw Disappears

You have turned off the layer you're working on.

I'm Erasing, But Everything I Erase Reappears Later in the Same Place

This is almost as perplexing as drawing on a layer that has been turned off. Reappearing objects are usually blocks that have been INSERTed two or more times on top of each other. When you ERASE one, the others are still there, waiting for a REDRAW, to rise up and laugh at you.

Two solutions: window erase wherever possible, getting everything at once, or, after an erasure by pointing at single objects. REDRAW to make sure that you don't have another bunch of drawings underneath the layer.

My Menus Don't Work Right Any More

AutoCAD updates seldom take into consideration the mega-hours users have put into developing menus. If your menus were created under an older version, there is a high probability that the AutoCAD command structure has changed, making your macros obsolete.

The worst change was when Autodesk unnecessarily changed Centered text to mean centered on the baseline, instead of centered on the text itself. In the next update, Autodesk belatedly created Middle text to replace the old Centered text.

Autodesk also changed some commands, such as ERASE, so that when you select objects by one method, you have to hit [Return] to continue with the rest of the command. If you don't hit [Return], you are still in object selection mode and can use another selection method to pick other entities. This is a useful feature but you must correct old macros for it by putting in another semicolon at the end of every selection step.

Occasionally, the compiling of a menu.mnu file into a menu.mnx file will create problems. Delete the .mnx file and check the .mnu file in a text editor before letting AutoCAD recompile the file.

The System Locks Up On Me With No Warning

This has been known to happen fairly often with older versions of AutoCAD, before 2.05. It sometimes was associated with inserting one drawing into another, where both drawings contained many duplicate definitions of the same blocks. After *ignoring* about 20 duplicate definitions, the system would get amnesia and ignore the operator, too.

Pirate copies of software have a reputation for doing extremely obnoxious things, the most common of which is locking up. The reasons vary, but the cure is obvious.

Another cause of mysterious locking up is getting a gremlin in your PC hard drive. Gremlins, it seems, like to eat the bits stored on hard drives. The solution is to try reloading the entire program onto the drive. You can prevent future recurrences by running Norton Utilities' DiskTest routine on the drive.

The System Locks Up When I Try To Zoom Extents

Do a STATUS command. Look at the drawing extents and see if they are realistic. If not, WBLOCK the useful part of the drawing away to a new drawing file and continue with that file.

I Get An Error Message While Drawing And Then I Can't Draw

Make sure you have enough room on your hard drive for your drawing *and* a backup. If that doesn't do it, try reconfiguring AutoCAD from the Main Menu.

4

Planning Drawings
for Efficiency

The beauty of AutoCAD is not in its ability to make lines on paper quickly. In fact, a good designer can put pencil lines on paper faster than any CAD system. A drafter can use templates and rub-ons faster than that, and a so-so clerk with an erasable transparency can often do even better.

The real power in any CAD system, including AutoCAD, is in its ability to rapidly replicate high-quality drawings and portions of drawings. CAD can also do difficult constructions more accurately than hand-drafting, but these applications are relatively rare.

Most respectable service bureaus will not claim a productivity ratio greater than one to one. In other words, their CAD drawings take as long as their hand drafting, or longer.

CAD can help you generate specialized drawings with a productivity ratio as high as eight to one *if* most or all of the following statements apply:

§ Special, custom menus have been created for the application.
§ Large numbers of repeated blocks are used or a significant number of similar drawings can be cloned from a single master drawing.
§ The operator has considerable experience with that type of drawing.
§ The drawing is proofed on the screen and is only plotted once.
§ The drawings are planned before starting CAD.

Given a challenging CAD assignment, few can resist the urge to sit right down at the workstation and start doinking down lines without a plan. You probably won't be able to resist, either. But remember, as you window erase your first hour's work, we told you so.

The way to avoid wasting work is to *plan ahead*! Take ten or fifteen minutes before you start CAD drawing to decide how the drawing should be made. Ask yourself questions like these:

§ Do I already have a similar drawing which can be cloned and edited to make this drawing?

§ Should I use a non-standard drawing size? Should I stand this drawing on end?

§ What standard blocks do I have on file which can be used now?

§ What recurring parts of this drawing can be blocked, or arrayed, or copied or mirrored?

§ Should this be laid out by hand first?

§ Could the preliminary hand sketch be digitized?

§ Would it be faster to draw this dude by hand and forget CAD?

§ How should I split this drawing into layers?

§ Is this drawing actually a form? If so, should it be done as a Lotus spreadsheet instead of as a drawing?

§ Should this drawing be done in stages, with on-screen review by interested parties *before* plotting?

§ Should revisions to this drawing be made in pencil on the latest plot, saving replotting until all changes are made?

§ What fonts should I use?

§ Should this drawing be split up into two or more drawings? If so, should it be recombined later?

§ Who should do this CAD assignment?

§ Should I create a custom menu for this task? If not, which existing menus should I use?

§ What line-styles and colors should I use? Should I use traces?

§ Should I do part of this drawing and then clone it for use in another?

§ In what order should the parts of this drawing be done? Should the text come first or last?

§ What grid and snap should be used?

§ Should I go to the beach instead?

§ How many ZOOM's and PAN's will I have to use? How close in will I have to ZOOM?

§ Should I get a typist to help me enter the text?

THE CASE OF THE CREEPING ZOOM

"Egad!" you cry, burying your nose between the 'g' and the 'h' on your keyboard. "It's been fifteen minutes since I started a ZOOM All and it's not done yet!"

The creeping zoom has struck again. Early versions of AutoCAD and early hardware are slow. If you are in such a fix, and can't afford to buy the latest AutoCAD updates (which are not exactly cheap) or the latest Turbo-whiz 286, 386, 486, or whatnot, you will have to substitute brains for bucks. Here's how:

§ Turn on QTEXT, if you've got it. (Version 2.0)

§ WBLOCK the completed parts of the drawing away to a file and reINSERT that file when you are all done. This can be done more than once, if necessary. Just be sure to reINSERT with an asterisk, so you can edit the reinserted material.

§ Use the STATUS command to check the number of entities. Compare the STATUS data with that of similar drawings to see if you have more entities in your drawing than is reasonable. Occasionally a drawing will get loaded up with multiple inserted blocks, drawings, arrays, layers, and so forth that contain enough items to slow regeneration down. If the number of entities looks suspicious, END the drawing and look at the file size in DOS for confirmation.

§ Turn off the GRID if you don't need it, or at least make it very coarse. This will save a few seconds in each ZOOM All.

§ Cut down on the number of times you need to ZOOM in on drawing features:

a. Instead of doing a ZOOM All to see where something is and then Window ZOOMing in on it, start the ZOOM All and cancel it with a [CTRL] C as soon as you see where you want to go. Then do the Window ZOOM.

b. Alternatively, make use of the VIEW command to create the necessary close-in views. This will permit you to jump directly to a view, instead of doing any ZOOM All first.

c. Similarly, if you know the approximate coordinates of everything in your drawing, you can do a ZOOM W and give the actual coordinates of the corners of a window surrounding an object using the keyboard instead of the cursor.

d. Object snaps can sometimes be used to lock onto blocks and other entities from a distant ZOOM.

e. Rewrite your menus to function from a ZOOM All position. This can be done by building in OSNAP modes, by providing ZOOM W's as described above in step c, or by letting your macros request absolute coordinates for insertion of items.

f. Use PAN instead of ZOOM if you are only moving a short distance.

§ Freeze any layers which have many entities and which are not going to require further editing.

§ Turn off unused layers. This will not speed up regeneration in itself, but will make it easier to use various snap modes from a far out ZOOM by getting extraneous objects off the screen.

§ Exit to DOS and create a RAM disk to hold pieces of the drawing. This will cut down file access time a little.

§ Buffer two or three commands together and take a break while the machine catches up with you. For example, you can enter ZOOM [Return] A [Return] QTEXT [Return] OFF [Return] END [Return] 0 [Return], and then go to lunch while the drawing gets backed up.

§ Turn off REGENAUTO to prevent unnecessary regenerations of the drawing.

§ Turn fast zoom on with VIEWRES (Version 2.5).

§ Turn FILL off.

If the above steps still do not speed up your ZOOM's and PAN's to an acceptable level, you probably will have to invest some money in hardware or software improvements.

If you can't afford a new machine, you may want to buy a speed-up board, or other hardware for higher productivity. The first thing to add, if you don't already have one, is an 8087 coprocessor chip. RAM disks are also helpful, as are hardware pan and zoom cards, like the Photon 800™ and the Nth Engine™. A hard drive speeds up disk access but is not a cure-all for slow systems, since disk access time is a small fraction of drawing time.

STANDARDS

If you want to operate your CAD installation efficiently, you should have the following:

High Quality Materials. Floppy disks, hardware, operator chairs, pens, ink, media, there is no point in trying to save money when buying these commodities; anything you save will be spent several times over when low-quality-goods rise up and bite you in the pocketbook. Some people say "You only get what you pay for." But "You get no more than you pay for," is closer to the truth. Sometimes you get a lot less.

The Best Operators You Can Get. Some CAD purchasers assume that because CAD can give you high productivity ratios, that every designer or drafter will automatically crank out more and better drawings. This is not quite the case. CAD does give every operator more power. A fast drafter will use that power to draw twice as much, or more. A diddler will use that power to diddle twice as much, or more.

Standards and Procedures. You should establish firm procedures for handling incoming work. Tasks on hand should be planned in detail before beginning drawing. Future tasks should be forecast and scheduled to the extent possible.

Archiving. Document naming procedures should be set up so as to minimize the chance of losing a drawing. Archives should be managed to ensure that there are at least two current copies of every drawing which may have a future use. Standard blocks must be drawn and archived along with other drawings.

Quality Control. Every completed drawing should be examined for adherence to standards, completeness, accuracy, general quality and productivity.

THE WORKING ENVIRONMENT

AutoCAD is an efficient, powerful program, but it is only as good as its operator. In addition to proper training, operator efficiency can be greatly enhanced by the proper working environment.

This can be a tricky area because AutoCAD operators come in different sizes, with individual tastes and preferences. It's also necessary to consider costs. With these caveats, it will pay dividends to keep the following in mind when you set up AutoCAD work stations.

Lighting

One of the most important goals of proper lighting is to avoid screen glare. Light bouncing off the screen not only prevents the operator from seeing all the fine details in a drawing, but will increase the operator's fatigue immensely. Fine mesh screens fitted over the CRT go a long way toward solving this problem and are well worth the relatively minor investment. The anti-glare screens which incorporate static grounding add extra protection.

The cool-white fluorescents used in many offices have been shown not only to increase fatigue, but to actually generate extra tension in computer operators. Research indicates these problems are the result of the limited light spectrum emitted by the cool-white bulbs. The best solution is to replace the cool-white bulbs with bulbs that emit a full spectrum of color. Although these bulbs cost a bit more per unit, they create a more natural light which allows longer sessions at the computer.

If you can't replace the cool-white fluorescents, you can mitigate the problem by adding either incandescent or natural light. So called drafter's lamps are inexpensive and each operator can position them to suit personal preference on the work station.

Natural light can be a blessing or a curse. It's a blessing when it doesn't cause glare and a curse when it does. Natural light can be filtered with some sort of thin curtain material; if the curtain can be opened and closed, optimum light levels can be achieved.

CRT Display

Even the best monitors will produce some operator fatigue if stared at long enough. The mesh screens mentioned above will help to some degree.

Color screen displays can be valuable in identifying drawing elements when you're working with AutoCAD, but can create problems with operator fatigue. The screen flicker is often increased for some color systems, and the multiple hues can also be tiring. Proper lighting is even more important with color displays than with monochrome CRTs.

Monochrome screens come in two colors: green or amber. There is some data to indicate that amber screens are easier on the eyes than the green. Amber screens are the European standard for monochrome.

Some of the newer black and white displays offer high resolution with reasonable cost and fatigue levels.

No matter what sort of display you're using, it can probably be turned down. Lowering the intensity of the display can help lessen eyestrain and operator fatigue, if not reduced too low.

The Work Station

How the AutoCAD operator sits in relationship to the keyboard, tablet and screen is extremely important. Since operators come in various sizes and work stations are more or less fixed, adjustable seating is the answer. Both the height of the seat and the back should be easily and independently adjustable.

Another possibility is the *back chair*. It looks strange because the user appears to be kneeling rather than sitting. But the kneeling position forces the user to sit up straight which reduces fatigue. These chairs are now available in adjustable models and some even swivel. The price has come down and they're well worth considering.

Keyboard Placement. Ideally, the height of the keyboard should be adjustable. Failing that, the keyboard should be placed so it allows operators to rest the heels of their hands, particularly if they're doing lots of keyboard entry.

CRT Placement. The placement of the screen is important too. It should allow sitting operators to look straight ahead at the CRT. Adjustable screen stands or holders allow proper, individual CRT placement.

Workplace Attitude

Long hours at the computer may look efficient, but studies show that standing, stretching and moving around often actually increase production. Encourage your operators to take brief breaks whenever they need them.

5

Macros and Menus

The use of plain English for AutoCAD permits easy entry of commands from the keyboard. Even more efficiency can be obtained by the use of *macros*. Macros are pre-recorded commands or command sequences which can be selected by the use of a mouse or TouchPen™ or tablet, or in some cases, from the keyboard. Only a single keystroke is needed to activate each command or series of commands. This not only saves typing, but eliminates mistakes. Also, a cleverly constructed series of macros (called a *menu*) can guide the operator to follow only established standards and methods. A few examples of macros are shown below:

Macro	Function
line;	Starts the LINE command.
zoom;a;	Zooms to the limits of the drawing.
zoom;a;end;	Zooms, then ends the drawing.

Note that the semicolon is used in place of the [Return] key. When AutoCAD encounters a space or a semicolon in a macro, it assumes that a [Return] is intended at that point. (There are a couple of exceptions to this: A space at the end of a text string is interpreted as a space, and at the end of a macro, a space which is preceded by a backslash (\), a semicolon (;), or a plus sign (+) does *not* act like a [Return]. When in doubt, use a semicolon!)

If you want certain locations or parameters to be entered by the operator, a backslash in the macro will cause it to pause until information is entered via the mouse or keyboard, or other input device. More examples:

erase;\;	Erases a single object and stops.
line;	Starts a line. Operator must end it.
line;\ \;	Draws a single line and ends it.
*circle;\ *	Draws a circle.

With one exception, a backslash pauses for only a single input. That exception is the SELECT command, where a backslash suspends operation of the macro until the operator has input as many items as needed and hit [Return].

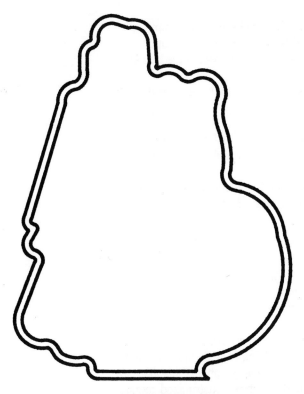

This is an example of a polyline (interior figure) and an offset (outside figure).

Does anybody know what this object is?

Macros can be almost any length. If a macro requires more than one line, the commands on the second line may not be picked up by AutoCAD. Should this be the case, end the first line with a plus sign (+) and continue the macro on the next line; there is no limit to the number of lines a macro may run, except good sense.

*[NEW DRAWING]INSERT stdblox 0,0 1 1 0;LAYER new 0,1,2,3,4;set 1;;GRID on; +
SNAP .25;ORTHO on;*

The macro above would be used when starting a new drawing. Commands are shown in capitals here for clarity; you may use upper or lowercase. Spaces are interpreted by AutoCAD as [Return]s, except as noted above; semicolons also indicate [Return]s.

Note that the macro name [NEW DRAWING] only serves as a label for the screen. It does not execute, because it is enclosed in brackets. Only the first eight characters of the label will show on the screen: NEW DRAW. The macro inserts a drawing which contains certain standard blocks, turns on five layers, starts drawing on layer 1, and turns on the grid, quarter-inch snap, and ortho mode.

In case you're wondering why there are two semicolons before the GRID command, the LAYER command takes two [Return]s to exit. The LAYER command is used twice above: once to create new layers and then, without leaving the command, again to set the working layer to layer 1.

ASCII control characters may be used in macros. The most useful of these is the [CTRL] C, which cancels a command which has not been completed. The [CTRL] key is replaced in the macro by the caret (^). It is sometimes a good idea to begin a macro with ^C to ensure that AutoCAD is not still waiting for input for a previous command. A menu which is being debugged should include ^C all by itself in a *cancel* command to kill other macros which don't work correctly.

Another handy ASCII control character is the backspace: ^H. This permits making menu items for the entry of text that do not end in a space (which would terminate the macro). For example, suppose you want a series of macros to put numbers on piping:

[1/8 text]TEXT; \ .125;0;   Starts the text command and waits for the text.
[DrnkgH2O]DWo^H   Types in DWo, backspaces over the o, and then
                                         waits for more text.

[1]1o^H	Adds a 1 and then waits for more input.
[2]2o^H	Adds a 2 and then waits for more input.
(etc.)	(Other macros provide the rest of the numerals as needed.)
[CSteel]-150#CS;	Finishes the line number and ends the command.

The macros listed above could be used to add a line number 1/8 inch high, horizontally, such as: DW1122-150#CS. Other similar items in this menu would include additional prefixes and suffixes (-300#CS, -125#CI, etc.)

For very advanced users, AutoLISP functions may be included in macros for performing complex constructions. This is beyond the scope of this book, but will be covered in a later volume.

MENUS

Menus are sets of macros, usually constructed to work together to speed up a particular AutoCAD application. AutoCAD comes with a standard multipurpose menu which is designed to place virtually all AutoCAD commands within reach of the screen, tablet, and puck buttons.

One minor problem with the AutoCAD screen menu is that commands are buried two and three layers deep in the menu structure. If you are doing very diverse drawings, you may find this menu useful. It is low in efficiency for specialty applications like plot plans, electrical ladder diagrams, and so forth, which should have customized menus.

The AutoCAD standard tablet menu is better than the screen menu for most applications, because it has 79 choices (commands and other input options) available at one time, instead of 20 or fewer for the screen menu. This menu is still not optimum for special applications, because of the lack of insertion commands for standard application blocks. You can customize it, however, by adding macros for the 9 by 25 area at the top. This will give you a total of 324 items available, including the screen menu accessible from the monitor area of the tablet.

There are five types of menu:

Menu Type	Accessed via	Max. No. of Macros At One Time
Screen	Screen cursor	20 macros on screen at one time
Tablet	Tablet puck	616, with crowding
Function Box	Function box	240, depending on mfr.
Button	Tablet puck	9 to 16, depending on mfr.
Keyboard	Keyboard	30 to 120, or more

SCREEN MENUS

The right hand side of the AutoCAD display is reserved for the screen menu. It will show a maximum of 20 items at one time. The last line on the menu is NEXT; selecting NEXT calls the next 20 items of the menu if it has more than one page. You may have as many 20-item pages as you wish. The first page of the screen menu is always the one displayed when the menu is loaded with the MENU command.

Only the first eight letters of each screen menu item are shown on the screen. Each item can be given a title which will not affect the operation of the macro it calls; simply enclose the title in square brackets, thus: [InsrtGizmo]. The first eight characters of the title will be displayed: InsrtGiz. This should be sufficient for most purposes.

The screen menu can be accessed from the keyboard or by use of a mouse or tablet.

Keyboard Entry. Pressing the [Insert] key will shift the cursor to the menu area. Up and down cursor keys will control the cursor within the menu. The highlighted item will be executed by pressing the [Insert] key again. To leave the menu area without selecting an item, hit [Delete].

Pointing Devices. Move the mouse or puck to the right until one of the items is highlighted. The pick button (usually the middle button on a mouse or puck, or the zero button on a 12-button puck) will select the highlighted item when pressed.

Commands can still be typed in, even when a menu has been installed. Notice as you type, though, that AutoCAD is looking for similarities between what you type and the screen menu. The closest match will be highlighted; pressing [Insert] will select that item without having to complete what you are typing.

TABLET MENUS

The surface of a digitizing tablet can be configured to hold four menus, in addition to the area reserved for graphics and screen menu access. Overlays or *templates* showing what each menu item is can be taped to the digitizer surface. Each rectangular area corresponding to a macro can hold a short (and small) keyword or, better, a symbol for what the item does. To select from the tablet menu, place the puck (or stylus) over the desired item and hit the pick button.

Unlike screen menus, tablet menus require that you tell AutoCAD exactly where the menus are. This is done with the TABLET command. See the AutoCAD Glossary Section for details on the TABLET command. The various macros which make up each tablet menu must be arranged in rectangular groups.

BUTTON MENUS

Unless configured otherwise, the first items in the first page of a screen menu may be accessed from the buttons on a puck. A twelve button puck will give you anywhere from nine to twelve items which can be called from the puck. A three button mouse will sometimes let you access the first two items, which is not very good but is still useful. (Note that if you change pages, the buttons can still select the first items from the first page, assuming you can remember what they were.)

The cursor does not have to be in the menu area on the screen, it may be anywhere on the screen to access these first macros. And if the macro you invoke with a button calls for input of a point, AutoCAD will supply the location where the cursor lay when the button was pressed.

You can also define button menus which are independent of the screen menus. This requires that you remember how the buttons are defined, or have a piece of paper nearby with the button menu items listed.

KEYBOARD MENUS

There are several programs around that allow you to define keyboard macros. The best known of these are SuperKey™, by Borland, ProKey, and Newkey. With some practice and a little effort, you can set up your system to automatically boot up with a sequence of macros to do, for example, a ZOOM All when you strike [ALT]F1, a ZOOM Previous for [ALT]F2, half inch SNAP for [ALT]F3, etc., etc.

WRITING MENUS

A well-written menu is a thing of beauty to watch in action. It can increase the productivity of an AutoCAD installation by a factor of two, and maybe more for some applications. Many CAD operators can't type very well, and the time saved there is significant. Cleverly constructed menus can also compel the operator to follow standards closely and minimize errors. Good menus can make difficult constructions easy.

A single menu file can hold macros for the screen, the tablet, the puck, and a function box. You just have to tell AutoCAD where each section starts by using labels prefixed with three asterisks (***) followed by the name of the menu device for that section. The following is an example of a menu file:

```
***SCREEN
[BigLimits]LIMITS;0,0;36,24;
```

```
[SmallLimits]LIMITS;0,0;11,8.5;
[Gizmo]INSERT;gizmo;\1;1;0;
***BUTTONS
ERASE;\;
INSERT;gizmo;\2;2;0;
ERASE;L;;
QUIT;Y;
***TABLET1
INSERT;gizmo;\2;1;0;
INSERT;gezeets;\1;2;0;
INSERT;thingmabob;\1;1;45;
***TABLET2
ZOOM;P;
REDRAW;
ERASE;W;\ \;;
OOPS
STATUS
LINE;\ \;
***TABLET4
MENU;CLOUD;LAYER;S;9;;
MENU;HEAVEN;LAYER;S;7;;
***AUX1
TEXT;C;\.125;0;\;
TEXT;A;\ \.25;\;;
TEXT;\.5;30;\;;
```

The menu above has sections for an auxiliary function box, screen, button, and three out of the four possible tablet menus.

The first section is a screen menu which allows you to (a) set your drawing size to 36 by 24 or to (b) 8 ½ by 11 paper. The third macro in that menu (c) inserts a block called "gizmo" without changing its shape or rotating it.

The second section is a button menu which will allow you to; erase whatever lies under the cursor when the number 1 button is pressed, insert a twice-normal-size gizmo at the cursor location when button 2 is pressed, erase the last object drawn (button 3), or wipe out your drawing with a single keystroke with no possibility of recovery (button 4). (Don't ever put such a macro in one of your menus. It is shown here to demonstrate that there is danger, as well as power, in macros.)

The third section has insertion macros to put fat gizmos, skinny gezeetses, or slantwise thingmabobs into your drawing.

The fourth section is fairly obvious, except for the LINE command, which draws only a single line and then stops.

The fifth section can call either of two menus and simultaneously changes the layer.

The sixth section is a function box menu for doing centered eighth-inch text, quarter-inch aligned text, or half-inch left-justified text rising at a 30 degree angle.

AutoCAD can also use *submenus*. These are menu sections which can be called up without loading a new menu. The reason for having submenus is that a screen or puck can only hold a limited number of items relative to the total number that may be needed for a particular application. (Although Autodesk says this applies to tablets as well, the need for submenus on a tablet seems remote. The density of most tablet menus, the need to replace the overlay, and the ease with which you can call an entirely different menu make submenus an unnecessary complexity for tablets. For that reason, the remarks will be tailored to apply to screen menus, although they may be applicable to other menu types as well.)

A submenu is to be labelled with a unique name (using AutoCAD's naming convention: 31 characters or less, etc.) prefixed by two asterisks (**). The following is an example of a menu with two submenus, as it appears in the .mnu file and as it appears on the screen initially:

```
***SCREEN
[zoom all]ZOOM;A;                              zoom all
[zoom in]ZOOM;5X;                              zoom in
[zoomprev]ZOOM;P;                              zoomprev
[zoom ext]ZOOM;E;                              zoom ext
[grid on]GRID;ON;                              grid on
[grid off]GRID;OFF;                            grid off
[flange ]INSERT;flange;\1;1;90;                flange
[clevis ]INSERT;clevis;\1;1;90;                clevis
[whatnot]INSERT;WHATNOT;\1;1;90;               whatnot
[whatsit]INSERT;WHATSIT;\1;1;90;               whatsit
[Blocks]$S=BLOX                                Blocks
[BkwdsBlx]$S=BACKWARDS                         BkwdsBlx
**BLOX 7
[widget]INSERT;WIDGET;\1;1;0;
[dlybbr]INSERT;DEELYBOBBER;\1;1;0;
[doodad]INSERT;DOODAD;\1;1;0;
[gadget]INSERT;GADGET;\1;1;0;

[BkwdsBlx]$S=Backwards
[BACK UP]$S=
**Backwards -7
[Bwidget]INSERT;WIDGET;\-1;1;0;
[Bdlybbr]INSERT;DEELYBOBBER;\-1;1;0;
[Bdoodad]INSERT;DOODAD;\-1;1;0;
[Bgadget]INSERT;GADGET;\-1;1;0;

[Blocks]$S=BLOX
[BACK UP]$S=
```

The two submenus are "Blox" and "Backwards." A selected submenu will cover up part or all of the superior menu, starting with the first line, unless told otherwise. Here, the Blox submenu has been told to appear starting with line 7 from the top of the screen, covering only the flange and clevis macros. The Backwards submenu will appear starting seven lines from the bottom of the screen, and won't cover any items in the starting menu.

"Blox" active:	"Backwards" active:
zoom all	zoom all
zoom in	zoom in
zoomprev	zoomprev
zoom ext	zoom ext
grid on	grid on
grid off	grid off
widget	flange
dlybbr	clevis
doodad	whatnot
gadget	whatsit
	Blocks
BkwdsBlx	Bwidget
BACK UP	Bdlybbr
	Bdoodad
	Bgadget
	Blocks
	BACK UP

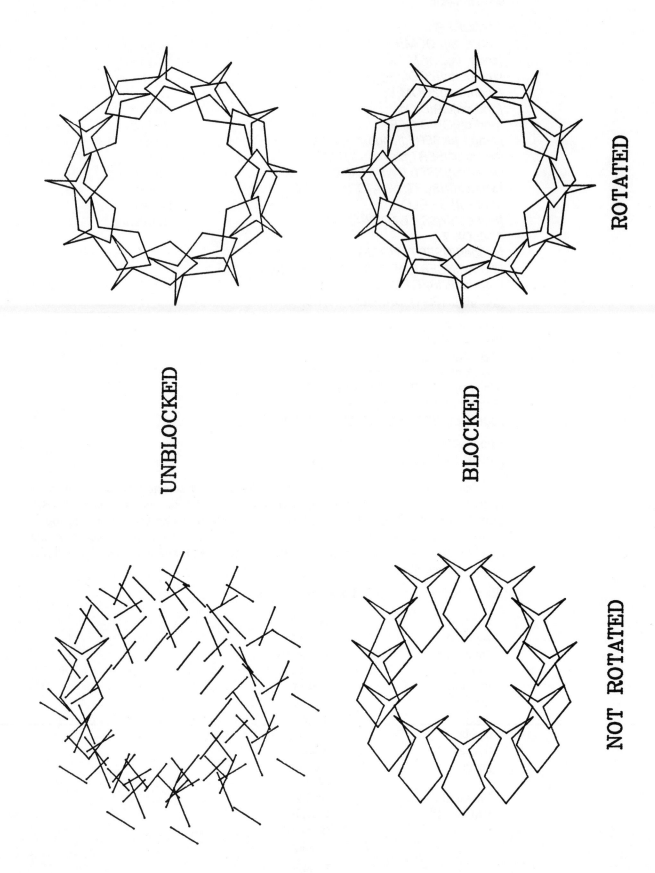

UNBLOCKED

BLOCKED

ROTATED

NOT ROTATED

CIRCULAR ARRAYS

The Blox submenu allows choosing four items for insertion. The Backwards menu inserts the same four items, except puts them in backwards (note the minus sign in front of the X width factor). Both of the submenus can call each other or return to the superior menu. The line $S = {blank} deactivates any screen submenu, just as $S = somethingorother would call a screen menu named somethingorother. The blank lines in the submenus are put there to control how the display looks.

The list is a sample of menu commands that call up submenus:

$S = screenstuff	Calls **screenstuff submenu to the screen
$B = buttonstuff	Calls **buttonstuff submenu to buttons
$T1 = tabletstuff	Calls **tabletstuff submenu to tablet area 1
$A1 = aux1stuff	Calls **aux1stuff submenu to aux device
$T2 = moretablet	Calls **moretablet submenu to tablet area 2

How To Do It

The menus themselves are easy to construct. Use any text editor to create an ASCII file; this can be done, for example, with WordStar in nondocument mode. In a pinch, EDLIN will suffice, but is rather primitive. A fairly rapid approach consists of using SideKick's notepad, which can be called up without leaving AutoCAD. (Be careful, though, to invoke SideKick from the text screen. Calling up SideKick from the graphics screen is believed to be hazardous to your monitor.)

One hint: After editing a menu in SideKick, (without leaving AutoCAD) you must reload it. The new version of the menu is only on disk, not loaded, when you save it from SideKick. To speed this up, every menu under development should have a macro called "Reload" somewhere on the first page: [Reload]MENU;nameofmenu;. When you have completely debugged the menu, delete the Reload macro. (For later versions, a macro "MENU;;" takes the default of the current menu, without having to include the name of the menu in the macro as above.)

The following is a pair of menus designed to let you and a co-worker play chess on your display. You will need to draw and block a chess board (just OOPS it back after blocking), and one of each of the six types of chess pieces in white. Your board should have a single snap point in the middle of each square. Make a copy of the six pieces and CHANGE these six to red. Block each piece individually, calling them redpawn, redking, whitepawn, whiterook, and so forth. (It helps if each block has a point dead center, at the base point, to serve as a handle for object selection.)

Put the pieces on the board using the promote.mnu, then switch to the chess.mnu. SAVE the drawing of the filled board as the starting point for future games. To move a piece, put the cursor on top of it, hit the 8 button, then place the cursor where you want to move to and hit the 0 button. To capture a piece, put the cursor on it and hit the 7 button, then move the capturing piece to that square.

Promote pieces by hitting the piece on the eighth rank with the 9 button, then using the promote.mnu (automatically called) to put down a queen, or whatever. Select the color of the piece desired first, then hit the type of piece. Usually, this piece will be a queen. The other pieces appear in the promote.mnu to make it easy to complete the starting board, and will probably not be used again, unless you use this system to solve chess problems. (That's another subject to save for a future volume!)

Chess.mnu: a 12-button puck menu
[8 MOVE]MOVE;\;0,0;
[7REMOVE]ERASE;\;
[9PROMOTE]ERASE;\;MENU;promote
Promote.mnu:
[1 Red]INSERT;red0^H
[2 White]INSERT;white0^H
[3 Pawn]pawn;\1 1 0;

[4 Knight]knight;\ 1 1 0;
[5 Bishop]bishop;\ 1 1 0;
[6 Queen]queen;\ 1 1 0;
[7 King]king;\ 1 1 0;
[8 MOVEMENU]MENU;chess;

A similar menu may be created for playing go. Why don't you try to make a go menu, along with a go board and stone blocks?

Here are some additional sample macros for you to use or modify for your own menus:

[BIG APER]APERTURE;10	Sets OSNAP aperture to 20 pixels.
[SML APER]APERTURE;5	Resets OSNAP aperture to 10 pixels.
[3 PT ARC]ARC;\ \	Makes an arc using 3 cursor points.
[ARC CONT]ARC;;\	Continues the last line or arc with another arc to the point spec'd.
[AREA]AREA;	Starts the AREA command.
[QUADRRAY]ARRAY;L;;R;2;2;@0,0;\	
	Makes a 2 × 2 array of the last block inserted.
[CLOKRRAY]ARRAY;L;;P;\ 12;360;Y	
	Makes a 12-copy circular array of the last item entered, with rotation.
[ATDSP ON]ATTDISP;on	Turns on attribute display.
[ATDSPOFF]ATTDISP;off	Turns off attribute display.
[ATDSPNML]ATTDISP;N	Sets attribute display to normal.
[ATTEDIT]ATTEDIT;	Starts attribute editing.
[EXTR DB2]ATTEXT;S;bom;list	Extracts attributes to list.txt, a dBASE II file based on a template file called bom.txt
[EXTR 123]ATTEXT;C;bill;items	
	Extracts attributes to items.txt, a Lotus file based on a template file called bill.txt
[AXIS ON]AXIS;on;	Turns axis on.
[AXIS OFF]AXIS;off;	Turns axis off.
[BASE]BASE;\	Establishes base point in drawing.
[Blip On]BLIPMODE;on	Turns blipmode on.
[Blip Off]BLIPMODE;off	Turns blipmode off.
[DoshBlok]BLOCK;doshes;y;@0,0;w;@-1,-1;@2,2;;	
	Redefines a block called doshes using the last item drawn.
[BREAK]BREAK;\ \	Breaks a line.
[CHAMFER]CHAMFER;\ \	Chamfers two lines.
[Chgto 69]CHANGE;w;\ \ ;LA;69;	
	Changes everything windowed to layer 69. (Layer 69 must already exist.)
[2pCIRCLE]CIRCLE;2P;\ \	Draws a circle through two points.
[3pCIRCLE]CIRCLE;3P;\ \ \	Draws a circle through 3 points.
[Yellow]COLOR;yellow	Sets the current color to yellow.
[CopyLast]COPY;L;;M;@0,0;\	Makes multiple copies of last object entered. Requires puck input.
[DBLIST]DBLIST	Lists drawing database.
[HorizDim]DIM1;HORIZONTAL;;\ \ ;	
	Dimensions one horizontal line, arc, or circle.
[Vert Dim]DIM1;VERTICAL;;\ \ ;	
	Dimensions one vertical line, arc, or circle.
[DIST]DIST;\ \	Gives the distance between 2 points.
[Divide12]DIVIDE;\ 12	Divides object into 12 equal segments.
[¼DONUT]DONUT;0;.25;\ ;	Makes quarter-inch solid circle.

Menu Macro	Description
[DRGMO ON]DRAGMODE;on	Turns dragmode on.
[DRGMOOFF]DRAGMODE;off	Turns dragmode off.
[AUTODRAG]DRAGMODE;A	Automatic dragmode.
[DTEXT]DTEXT;\.2;0;\	Dynamic text .2 inches high.
[DXFIN]DXFIN;standard	Imports a DXF file called "standard"
[DXFOUT]DXFOUT;;	Exports a DXF file with same name as drawing.
[Elev 1.0]ELEV;1.0;;	Reset thickness of 3-D entities to
[Elev 1.5]ELEV;1.5;;	values shown. Elevation of bottom
[Elev 2.0]ELEV;2.0;;	plane is not changed.
[45 Elips]ELLIPSE;\ \R;45	Does 45 degree ellipse within points entered.
[END]END;	Saves the drawing and exits.
[Erase L]ERASE;L;;	Erases last item added.
[EXPLODE]EXPLODE;\	Explodes a single block.
[Extnd217]LINE;17,0;17,11;;EXTEND;L;;\	
	Extends selected objects to a line 17 inches from left edge of drawing,
[MnuFiles]FILES;2;*.mnu	Lists all menus in directory.
[DwgFiles]FILES;2;*.dwg	Lists all drawings in directory.
[ScrFiles]FILES;2;*.scr	Lists all scripts in directory.
[FILL ON]FILL;on;	Turns fill on.
[FILL OFF]FILL;off;	Turns fill off.
[FILLET]FILLET;\ \	Fillets two intersecting lines.
[GRID ON]GRID;on;	Turns GRID on.
[GRID OFF]GRID;off;	Turns GRID off.
[1in GRID]GRID;1;	Sets grid to 1 inch intervals.
[½ GRID]GRID;.5;	Sets grid to ½ inch intervals.
[HtchEsch]HATCH;escher,O;.5;;\	
	Escher hatches one closed item.
[ArcHelp]HELP;ARC	Shows help screen for arcs.
[HIDE]HIDE	Removes 3-D hidden lines.
[ID]ID;\	Identifies a single locus.
[IGESIN]IGESIN;\	Imports an IGES file.
[IGESOUT]IGESOUT;krellman	Exports an IGES file named krellman.
[InsDoshs]INSERT;DOSHES;\.5;.5;0;	
	Inserts a ½-size doshes block.
[L ISOPLN]ISOPLANE;L	Sets to left isoplane.
[R ISOPLN]ISOPLANE;R	Sets to right isoplane.
[T ISOPLN]ISOPLANE;T	Sets to top isoplane.
[LayrSwap]LAYER;ON;2;OFF;1;S;2;;	
	Turns off layer 1, turns on layer 2 and makes it the current layer.
[B LIMITS]LIMITS;0,0;17,11;	Sets drawing limits to B-size paper.
[LINE]LINE;\ \;	Draws a single line.
[DashLTYP]LINETYPE;S;dashed;;	
	Sets dashed linetype.
[CntrLTYP]LINETYPE;S;center;;	
	Sets center linetype.
[ListThis]LIST;\;	Lists data for one entity.
[LtSca .5]LTSCALE;0.5	Sets linetype scale to .5
[LtSca 1]LTSCALE;1.0	Sets linetype scale back to 1.0
[MeasMark]MEASURE;\B;marker;y;1	
	Puts the block, "marker" along the object selected every inch, rotated if needed.
[GudyMenu]MENU;GOODIES;	Selects "goodies" menu.

[MInsPawn]MINSERT;pawn;\1;;0;1;8;1;	
	Puts 8 pawns in a row, 1 inch apart.
[MirrLast]MIRROR;L;;@0,0;@1,0;n;	
	Mirrors last object about itself.
[MoveL1Rt]MOVE;L;;@0,0;@1,0	
	Moves last object one inch to right.
[MSLIDE]MSLIDE;;	Makes slide with drawing name.
[OFFSET]OFFSET;T;\ \;	Creates a second polyline through point specified.
[OOPS]OOPS;	Restores last item erased.
[ORTHO on]ORTHO;on;	Puts ORTHO mode on.
[Snap I/S]OSNAP;int	Items will snap to intersections.
[PAN 5 Rt]PAN;5,5;@-5,0	Pans 5 inches to right.
[PAN 5 Lf]PAN;5,5;@+5,0	Pans 5 inches to left.
[PAN 5 Dn]PAN;5,5;@0,+5	Pans 5 inches down.
[PAN 5 Up]PAN;5,5;@0,-5	Pans 5 inches up.
[ClsPline]PEDIT;\C;X;	Closes a polyline and exits PEDIT.
[PLINE]PLINE;	Starts polyline.
[POINT]POINT;\;	Places single point.
[HEXAGON]POLYGON;6;\I;.5	Makes 1-inch diameter inscribed hexagon.
[OCTAGON]POLYGON;8;\C;1	Makes 2-inch diameter circumscribed octagon.
[12-A-GON]POLYGON;12;\I;.5	Makes 1-inch diameter inscribed dodecagon.
[PurgeAll]PURGE;A;	Begins purge process for all unused items. **Must be first command given.**
[QTEXT ON]QTEXT;on;	Turns on quick text.
[QTXT OFF]QTEXT;off;	Turns off quick text.
[QUIT]QUIT;	Kills editing changes.
[REDO]REDO;	Puts back an UNDO.
[REDRAW]REDRAW;	Redraws display.
[REGEN]REGEN;	Performs a regeneration.
[REGENOFF]REGENAUTO;off;	Turns off automatic REGEN.
[Widg=Giz]RENAME;B;widget;gizmo;	
	Renames block "widget" as "gizmo"
[Rot10Deg]ROTATE;L;;@0,0;10	Rotates last object 10 degrees.
[SAVEtemp]SAVE;temp	Saves drawing in file called "temp.dwg"
[.5 SCALE]SCALE;w;0,0;34,22;;0,0;0.5;ZOOM;A;	
	Rescales entire D-size drawing to fit B-size paper
[SelectLL]SELECT;w;0,0;4,4;;	
[PrpMidSn]SETVAR;OSMODE;130	Sets perpendicular & midpoint object snaps.
[HrGlsShp]SHAPE;hourglas;\1;0	
	Inserts shape "hourglas."
[SKETCH]SKETCH	Starts sketch mode.
[SNAP .25]SNAP;0.25	Sets ¼-inch snap.
[SNAP Iso]SNAP;S;I;0.25	Calls isometric grid, ¼-inch snap.
[SqrSOLID]SOLID;\@.1,0;@-.1,-.1;@.1,0;;	
	Makes 0.1 inch solid square.
[STATUS]STATUS	Displays drawing status.
[STRETCH]STRETCH;C;\ \;\ \	Stretches objects crossing window from base point to new locus.
[SpSTYLE]STYLE;special;simplex;1;.9;10;n;n;n	
	Creates a text style called special, slightly squeezed, 10 deg oblique.
[CFG TABL]TABLET;CFG;1;y;\ \ \20;4	
	Configures tablet for a single menu with 4 rows and 20 columns.
[1/8C TXT]TEXT;C;\.125;0;\	Does centered text ⅛ high.

[TIME]TIME;;TEXTSCR;	Displays drawing time.
[TRACE07]TRACE;.07;	Starts the TRACE command.
[TRIM ONE]LINE;@0,2;@0,-4;;TRIM;L;;\;	
	For trimming an *inserted block in two vertically
[UNDO]U	UNDOes the last operation
[UNITSET]UNITS;2;4;1;1;;;GRAPHSCR;	
	Set decimal units, 4 decimal places
[UR VW SV]VIEW;W;uprt;17,11;34,22	
	Creates upper right view
[UR VIEW]VIEW;R;uprt;	Displays upper right view
[LR VW SV]VIEW;W;lort;17,0;34,11	
	Creates lower right view
[LR VIEW]VIEW;R;lort;	Displays lower right view
[UL VW SV]VIEW;W;uplf;0,11;17,22	
	Creates upper left view
[UL VIEW]VIEW;R;uplf;	Displays upper left view
[LL VW SV]VIEW;W;lolf;0,0;17,11	
	Creates lower left view
[LL VIEW]VIEW;R;lolf;	Displays lower left view
[FASTZOOM]VIEWRES;Y;50	Enables fast zoom mode
[R 3D VEW]VPOINT;1,0,0	Right side viewpoint (3D)
[L 3D VEW]VPOINT;-1,0,0	Left side viewpoint (3D)
[F 3D VEW]VPOINT;0,-1,0	Front viewpoint (3D)
[B 3D VEW]VPOINT;0,1,0	Back viewpoint (3D)
[T 3D VEW]VPOINT;0,0,1	Top viewpoint (3D)
[U 3D VEW]VPOINT;0,0,-1	Underneath viewpoint (3D)
[VU FRONT]VSLIDE;fruntvu	Shows a slide called "fruntvu."
[WBL LEFT]WBLOCK;leftside;;0,0;w;0,0;18,24;;	
	Exports the left half of a D-sized drawing to a file called "leftside."
[ZOOM A]ZOOM;A	Zooms display to drawing limits.
[ZOOM P]ZOOM;P	Zooms display to previous zoom.
*[ZOOM W]ZOOM;W;\ *	Zooms display to window specified.
[ZOOM C]ZOOM;C;5.5,4.25;6	Zooms display to center point and height specified.
[ZOOM E]ZOOM;E	Zooms display to drawing extents.
[ZOOM LL]ZOOM;W;0,0;11,8.5	Zooms display to letter size lower corner.

6

Scripts

Scripts are pre-recorded sequences of commands stored in EDLIN, similar to menus. They are run by the SCRIPT command, or by invoking them along with AutoCAD from DOS. For more general information on scripts, see SCRIPT Command in the AutoCAD Glossary Section.

In addition to doing slide shows for presentations and instruction, scripts can be used to speed up editing of certain drawing features in multiple drawings.

Suppose you wish to change an arrowhead (block name: "arrowhead") in four drawings from a SOLID to a plain triangle. (Four drawings is just used here for an example. Several hundred could be involved in a major revision.) You could call up each drawing, draw a hollow arrow, BLOCK it under arrowhead, and regenerate the drawing before ENDing it. This will take quite a bit of time.

There is a slightly better way to do this task. Draw the new arrowhead in a separate drawing, called, "newarrow.dwg". You can then call up each drawing and INSERT the newarrow.dwg. When prompted for the Block name to insert, enter "arrowhead=newarrow." The drawing newarrow.dwg will be inserted into the current drawing, and the arrowhead block will be redefined according to the figure contained in newarrow.dwg.

You would have to do this four times, once for each drawing. You could, of course, create a little menu to take care of the repetitive commands and load it into each drawing before editing.

There is a much better way to correct the four drawings, using a script. Go ahead and create the newarrow drawing, first. Then get into WordStar (non-document mode) or other ASCII text editor and make the following script:

Script item:	What it does:
2	Selects "new drawing" from Main Menu
Laurel1	Calls up the first drawing
INSERT	Starts INSERT command
ARROWHEAD = NEWARROW	Redefines arrowhead block
0,0 1 1 0	Completes the insertion
ERASE L	Erases the added graphics
	Blank line exits ERASE
END	Ends the drawing.

36

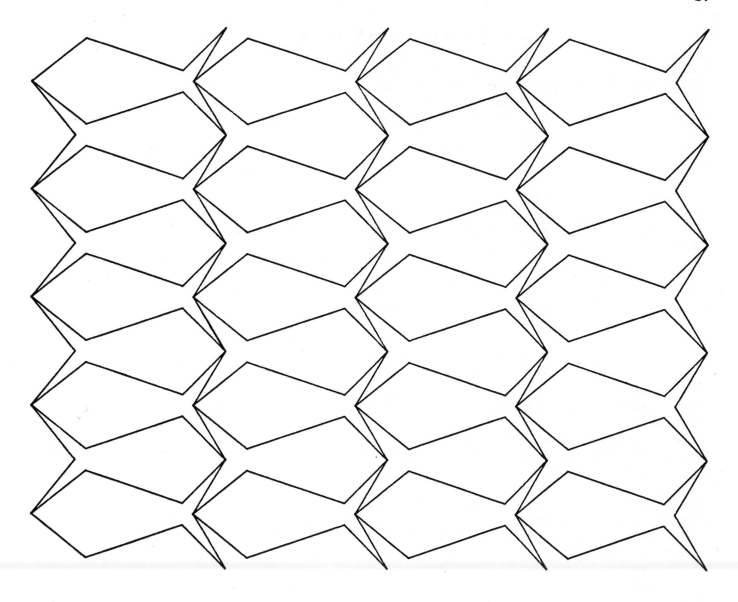

A school of fish created with MIRROR and ARRAY

2	Selects ''new drawing'' from Main Menu
Laurel2	Calls up the second drawing
INSERT	Starts INSERT command
ARROWHEAD = NEWARROW	Redefines arrowhead block
0,0 1 1 0	Completes the insertion
ERASE L	Erases the added graphics
	Blank line exits ERASE
END	Ends the drawing.
2	Selects ''new drawing'' from Main Menu
Hardy1	Calls up the third drawing
INSERT	Starts INSERT command
ARROWHEAD = NEWARROW	Redefines arrowhead block
0,0 1 1 0	Completes the insertion
ERASE L	Erases the added graphics
	Blank line exits ERASE
END	Ends the drawing.

38

Script item	What it does
2	Selects "new drawing" from Main Menu
Hardy2	Calls up the fourth drawing
INSERT	Starts INSERT command
ARROWHEAD = NEWARROW	Redefines arrowhead block
0,0 1 1 0	Completes the insertion
ERASE L	Erases the added graphics
	Blank line exits ERASE
END	Ends the drawing.
0	Exits AutoCAD

Much of the script is repetitive and can be blocked and copied, with minor editing. Save it in your AutoCAD working directory under the name OLIVER.SCR. Notice that, unlike menus, no semicolons are used—they don't work as a [Return]. Also, the 'What it does' column above will not appear in the actual script file.

Start the redefinition process by calling up AutoCAD and the first file and the script from DOS. The form of the command to do this is: ACAD Laurel1 OLIVER. (See ACAD in the AutoCAD Glossary Section.) Of course, you've got a backup of all your drawing files, just in case! The command will call up AutoCAD, make Laurel1 the default drawing, and invoke your script, "OLIVER".

The script will then start editing Laurel1 from the Main Menu, INSERT newarrow drawing, redefine the arrowhead block, END the drawing, and then repeat the process on the other three drawings before exiting AutoCAD. This could take several hours to do, if you had a hundred or so drawings to process. But because you have created a script to handle it, you can start the job rolling and go to the beach . . . or go do some more work.

Scripts can also be invoked with the SCRIPT command for editing drawings from within AutoCAD, while you are drawing. You can set up a different script to do each task, or you can put many tasks within a single script.

Another task which can be accomplished with scripts includes preparing a new drawing. You can set the limits, lay in a title block and border, INSERT a drawing containing standard blocks, start new layers and text styles, and so forth.

Here is a script for setting up a new drawing. It is designed to be invoked from within the drawing editor:

Script item:	What it does:
LIMITS 0,0 34,22	Sets the drawing limits
ZOOM A	ZOOMs to the new limits
LAYER N 1,2,3,4	Starts four new layers
(blank line)	Exits the LAYER command
LINE 1,1 33,1 33,21 1,21 C	Draws a border
INSERT equipmnt	Puts in standard blocks
0,0 1 1 0	Finishes insertion
SNAP .25	Quarter-inch snap
GRID 1.0	One-inch grid
LAYER S 2	Sets working layer to 2
(blank line)	Exits the LAYER command
QTEXT ON	Turns on Quick Text
STYLE J SIMPLEX 1 1 5 N N N	Sets text style

DELAYs in script files used for drawing and editing allow the operator to read prompts or messages on the text screen. If you intend to watch the batch process, a DELAY at certain spots will give you a chance to stop the script if you see something odd.

To stop a script during execution, enter [CTRL] C or a backspace. This will halt the script at the end of whatever command is in progress. To restart the script, enter

RESUME. If the script halted because of an error in the script, enter 'RESUME. (See Transparent Commands in the AutoCAD Glossary Section).

Two special commands are used within scripts to toggle between the text screen and the graphics screen: TEXTSCR and GRAPHSCR, respectively. Each of those commands may be run ''transparently'' under Version 2.6: while another command is in progress, 'TEXTSCR or 'GRAPHSCR (note the apostrophes) may be used to flip the screen to text or graphics, respectively.

Scripts run somewhat faster if the UNDO feature is turned off. See the UNDO Command in the AutoCAD Glossary Section for information on how to do so.

7

Third-Party Software

AutoCAD's success has resulted in a proliferation of third-party software designed to support, add to, and generally enhance the program. Additionally, other software products have the ability to do output in AutoCAD format.

It's not feasible to present a complete survey here. The software market is too volatile to allow up-to-date coverage of everything available even in this narrow area.

From time to time Autodesk publishes a catalog of AutoCAD Applications. They point out that the descriptions they publish are provided by the people who sell the software. They apparently do little or no reviewing themselves. Notwithstanding, the current issue of AutoCAD's Applications Catalog is a good place to start.

Your dealer may have copies of the catalog available or you can write Autodesk directly for information at this address: Autodesk, Inc., 2320 Marinship Way, Sausalito, CA 94965, Attn. Applications Marketing.

CADalyst, Cadence and *Final Draft,* the three most popular magazines devoted to AutoCAD, regularly review third-party applications packages. They also carry extensive applications package advertising. The combination of editorial content and advertising makes for an excellent and relatively current reference.

Users' Groups can also be a source of information about third-party software. Sometimes you'll find that such groups also develop and exchange their own utility programs.

Your AutoCAD dealer should know many of the applications packages that suit your needs. Try out the product before you commit to purchase—even AutoCAD dealers can occasionally be misled by manufacturers' claims.

When considering the purchase of an applications package, make sure the seller understands your needs. If you can test the program or talk with someone who has actually used it, you may be able to determine in advance if the program really does what you want it to.

Here is a list of some of the kinds of software packages that support AutoCAD.

ARCHITECTURAL PACKAGES

Symbol libraries for everything from floor plans through windows, and landscape details, are available from a variety of sources. Some are for architecture in general while others are designed for more specific applications.

Architectural tablet menu packages can also be purchased. Typically these help the user by providing predefined blocks, layers, door insertion macros, etc.

AUTOLISP COMMANDS

AutoLISP is a programming language developed for AutoCAD by Autodesk. It's based on the high level language, LISP. Although it's not necessary to learn and use AutoLISP to make efficient use of AutoCAD, if you like to program, you can make AutoCAD truly your own through customization.

As you might expect, third-party software developers have created various programs to make AutoLISP easier to use. There are tutorials, pre-written program routines that can be edited to your specifications, and utilities. If you get proficient at AutoLISP, you might even want to market your own applications.

AUTOWORD PLUS

AutoWord Plus allows you to convert text files into AutoCAD drawing files. Any word processor, text editor, or other program that can create ASCII files can be used with AutoWord.

AutoWord Plus also has the ability to translate database files, Lotus 1-2-3 spreadsheets, and other data files into AutoCAD drawing files.

AutoWord Plus is handy for generating such things as drawing notes and schedules, bill of materials, and so forth, using an inexpensive typist instead of a designer. Most designers can't type nearly as fast as a secretary, and get paid substantially more.

The AutoWord manual is a good one, and so is the telephone support. Your dealer might have AutoWord Plus, or you can obtain more information from Technical Software, Inc., 28790 Chagrin Blvd., Suite 300, Cleveland, OH 44122.

BILL OF MATERIALS/DATA BASE PROGRAMS

Bill of Materials and Data Base Programs can aid in extracting information from drawings for further manipulation resulting in bills of materials, estimating, costing, etc. Some of these programs are sophisticated enough to factor in escalation warnings, union rates, overtime, flex time, etc., while others provide a bare-bones approach. Many are designed to work specifically with dBASE II or dBASE III; others will operate with a variety of database managers and spreadsheet programs, so be sure the package you purchase is compatible with your existing software.

CIVIL ENGINEERING PACKAGES

Civil engineering packages include symbol libraries, three dimensional geography, earthwork computation, cross-section plotting and contour digitizing. Standard COGO functions are featured in many of these packages. Some are designed to accept data input from the field; others use data typically generated by municipalities.

ELECTRICAL PACKAGES

In addition to electrical engineering symbol libraries, there are packages which do electrical distribution mapping, design motor controls, and program logic controllers, etc. Some packages are general in nature, while others are structured to work with a specific manufacturer's standards.

FACILITIES MANAGEMENT PACKAGES

There are packages which approach facilities design and management from a generic point of view and others that are tied to specific suppliers of office furniture. Still other packages exist which are aimed at a particular category of facility design and/or management, such as restaurants and other food service operations.

LOTUS AND LOTUS-LIKE PROGRAMS

As wonderful as AutoCAD is, there are some applications better done on Lotus or Lotus-like spreadsheets. A spreadsheet is already set up to use columns and place the information in the proper place. Formulas are handled easily by spreadsheet programs. If your application is suitable for Lotus and you want the look of an AutoCAD drawing, use a program like AutoWORD to translate your spreadsheet into a drawing.

PLOTTING UTILITIES

Plotting utilities are programs designed to help you get your drawings from computer to plotter. There are utilities to assist with slides, that make AutoCAD think your printer is actually a plotter, or queue up your drawings in a spool for batch plotting, etc.

TEXT FONTS

AutoCAD provides 5 text fonts. Samples appear elsewhere in this book. The program also allows you to create additional fonts, also described elsewhere in this book. Third-party software developers have created even more text styles, should you want them.

SHAPE MAKERS

Shape maker programs enhance AutoCAD by reducing the time it takes to create custom shapes and text fonts. If you have lots of repetitive work with special shapes, or want to make special lettering, you might need such a package.

TABLET MENUS

Tablet menus speed up your work by providing additional commands and/or symbols that can be accessed with a digitizing tablet. AutoCAD allows you to create your own tablet menus and third-party software developers have published these types of menus for various industries. For example, there are special tablet menus for architecture, engineering, plumbing, HVAC, etc.

TRANSLATORS

Autodesk set the computer aided design standard for micro computers. But before and after AutoCAD there were other CAD programs. And now there are a variety of programs designed to either translate AutoCAD drawings, so they can be used by other CAD programs, or take the output from other programs to be used by AutoCAD. It can take some searching to find the one that fits your particular combination, but it's often worth the effort.

PRIMAVISION

Primavera is a program designed (among other things) to create project schedules using the critical path method (CPM). PrimaVision is an add-on package for Primavera which plots schedule charts. PrimaCAD is another add-on package to do schedule output in a form compatible with AutoCAD. AutoCAD's layering is utilized so you can suppress parts of your schedule drawing, such as borders and vertical weekly guidelines.

The greatest benefit of PrimaCAD is that it allows you to preview a schedule drawing in AutoCAD *before* you have plotted it. If you see a major error, or if you see that you could easily have squeezed the schedule onto fewer pages, you can change PrimaVision settings and redo the schedule in compressed format. You can also do minor (repeat, *minor*) editing changes on a Primavera schedule in AutoCAD, and then plot it. If you have to make *any* logic changes, you have to repeat the process from scratch. Ugh. The process works like this:

(1) Make your project data changes in Primavera.
(2) Recalculate the project.

(3) Run PrimaVision, with output to a file.
(4) Run the file through PrimaCAD to make DXF file(s).
(5) In AutoCAD, do DXF import(s) to make drawing(s).
(6) Preview the drawing.
(7) Do the final plotting from AutoCAD.

You can also use the AutoCAD compatibility of Primavera to shrink a schedule onto fewer pages using AutoCAD. You save plotting time, media, space, and resources, at a price, of course.

CAESAR II

Caesar II is a piping stress analysis program which can do output isometrics in AutoCAD format. These drawings serve mainly to assist in documenting the calculations for record purposes.

UTILITIES

Utilities programs have been described as software that "doesn't really do anything except make it easier to run other software which *does* do something." Included are such programs as those that unerase a file, unlock a read-only file, provide shells for file management, rearrange directories, etc. If there's something you want to do, chances are someone has developed a utility to do it. Magazines and users' groups are probably your best source of information about such utilities. You can find tons of public domain and shareware programs for these chores.

VOICE RECOGNITION

There are voice recognition packages that will teach your computer system to respond to your voice and you can use AutoCAD with them. Keep in mind, that you will have to calibrate the voice recognition package to your voice, meaning no one else will be able to talk to your computer.

TEACHING AUTOCAD

Some people learn from reading books, others learn better by having somebody show them how.

For example, you are applying for a job; the employer asks if you know AutoCAD. You think this is a kind of car and say "yes." They hire you to start in two weeks as an AutoCAD operator. You are going to go to a school, period. On the other hand, suppose you are working for a company and told to buy another AutoCAD package and get a second operator up to speed in two weeks. What do you do?

Plan A: Put an ad in the paper for an experienced operator. This is chancy. You may get little or no response to the ad. People who answer the ad may be totally unqualified. You will spend too much time interviewing to do anything else. And you could end up hiring somebody who doesn't work out. This is always a disaster for all concerned.

Plan B: Take a good employee and send him or her to school. This is usually better than hiring somebody from outside your business. You are dealing with a known quantity. The problems are: Who will do the work the employee was doing? Do you have the budget to send the employee to school? Should you send more than one person out to get training? Who will take over if your only trained operator gets sick?

The schools are typically very expensive. They are of greatest value when someone absolutely *must* learn CAD in a limited amount of time. There are a number of schools where you can obtain hands-on training in AutoCAD. AutoCAD maintains a list of approved schools.

Plan C: Go to a reliable agency and hire a temporary contract operator. If the temp works out, at the end of the contract period, hire him or her direct. This is not a bad approach, but even the best agencies will sometimes send you a real weirdo. You can easily get the agency to send a replacement, but by that time, you have used up valuable time. Proprietary applications menus are also a problem. If the temps have access to the menus, you could lose copies to your competitors. If you don't let the temps use your best menus, their output will suffer.

Plan D: Train several of your own people in-house. This is safer and usually less expensive than using a school. The more people you want to train, the greater the savings.

Another advantage of doing your own training is that you have full control of what is taught, when and where it's taught, and in what order. If you have developed proprietary applications menus, you can safely include them in your training sessions. Perhaps you can do the instruction after 5 P.M. or early in the morning, or on Saturdays.

In-house training also allows you to monitor the progress of your students. If someone is not catching on, you can drop that individual from the course, or take other corrective action. At the end of the course you will be fully familiar with the strengths and weaknesses of each student and can take that into account when you staff your station or stations.

If you do decide to do your own training, you will need some facilities:

§ You should have a place to teach the course, along with enough fully equipped workstations for your students. It is best if you have one PC with digitizer tablet for every student. An absolute minimum is two people per station, beyond that, they won't get enough hands-on experience.

§ You should prepare a written handout for each session. A command summary (see Appendix H) is useful for future reference. Sample drawings are also beneficial as a motivator; the fancier and more interesting the sample, the better.

§ You should provide each student with two floppy disks for use during the course. Encourage them to make double backups of *everything*. This is probably the most important single thing they will learn in the course: Back up everything.

§ A copy of this manual for each student.

§ There are also tutorials available to assist you in teaching AutoCAD. "The Instructor" comes with a special tablet menu and a series of inserts to place under a Lexan overlay. The inserts start out with a very few commands and gradually add new ones for each session. New commands are on a yellow background, making it easy to concentrate on them. (This also makes it easier to stay one lesson ahead of your students, if you aren't fully up to speed in AutoCAD yourself.) The software that comes with "The Instructor" includes system variable access, an on-screen calculator and other features.

The Instructor is available from Palisades Research, (213-459-7528) 869 Via de la Paz, Pacific Palisades, CA 90272.

8

Resources

You are not alone! There are a variety of resources for the AutoCAD user in addition to this book. Take a look at all of them and decide which suits you best.

USER GROUPS

Computer user groups, also known as Special Interest Groups or SIGS, developed right along with microcomputers. A user group is a club or organization that meets regularly to share ideas, problems, and solutions about a particular type of hardware or software.

An AutoCAD user group can be a real blessing to the new user. Finding user groups can be as simple as asking the dealer who sold you your package or as complicated as setting one up yourself. CADalyst magazine prints a list of AutoCAD user groups bimonthly, or whenever they get around to publishing. Unfortunately, the AutoCAD user groups are spread a little thinly in much of the United States and Canada. If you are not in an area covered by a user group, you may have to settle for a generic IBM PC/clone group. These groups often have one or more members who are AutoCAD users. The local computer newspapers found in most large cities often list generic user groups; if they don't, they may be able to help you find one. Don't hesitate to give them a call and ask.

Some Bulletin Board Systems (BBS) also have SIGS devoted to AutoCAD. Most well established BBS's carry listings of other local boards. AutoCAD has a BBS user forum on CompuServe.

If there isn't an AutoCAD user group in your area, your dealer may be willing to help you start one. Many user groups are dealer sponsored and meet at his facility or nearby. Such sponsored groups slightly inhibit user input regarding alternate sources of hardware and software, at least when the dealer is physically present.

It isn't particularly difficult to start an independent user group. It's usually just a matter of picking a time and place and letting other AutoCAD owners know. Putting a notice on an active, local BBS can generate members; so can a brief advertisement in computer newspapers. Sometimes a dealer who is too busy to sponsor a group will send out notices of your meetings to his clients for a month or two, to help you get started. Word-of-mouth can also get people to show up at meetings—just tell everyone you know who uses AutoCAD about your group.

MAGAZINES AND NEWSLETTERS

Magazines and newsletters are an excellent source of information. Articles are usually written by AutoCAD users and are based on practical experience. Magazines also offer late- breaking news. Even the advertisements are helpful.

CADalyst: The Journal for AutoCAD Users. *CADalyst* could be called a print version of an AutoCAD user group. Published six times a year, the slick magazine offers in-depth articles about specific AutoCAD projects, reviews of hardware and third-party software, and a wide selection of regular departments.

Many of the departments are based on AutoCAD user's problems and solutions that can provide invaluable information.

The advertisements in CADalyst are fascinating and useful, both for finding third-party software and for generating ideas.

One of the best features of CADalyst is that it's completely independent of Autodesk, AutoCAD's developer. This means you get an objective view of the product. Editor/Publisher Lionel Johnston has been known to print articles Autodesk wouldn't approve of, even if they got the chance, which they don't.

Your AutoCAD dealer might have sample issues of CADalyst available, but it's worth subscribing to on a regular basis. Subscription information can be had by writing CADalyst, 282-810 W. Broadway, Vancouver, B.C. Canada V5Z 4C9.

CADENCE: Using AutoCAD in the Professional Environment. *CADENCE* is published monthly in a slick format. It's more formal in presentation than *CADALYST* and is aimed specifically at professionals rather than all AutoCAD users. Each issue has a primary focus or theme, like space management or CAD/CAM. In addition to the monthly theme, there are columns devoted to productivity and efficiency. News about AutoCAD, and products to use with AutoCAD, are included each month, as are book reviews and software reviews.

If you're using AutoLISP, *CADENCE* is almost a must because it includes a monthly AutoLISP tutorial.

Like *CADALYST, CADENCE* is totally independent of Autodesk which means you get an objective view of AutoCAD. It also carries advertising. This alone might make the price of a subscription worthwhile.

CADENCE costs $34.95 per year in the United States and $44.95 outside the U.S. Their circulation department is P.O. Box 203550, Austin, TX 78758.

FINAL DRAFT: A Quarterly Newsletter for AutoCAD Users. *Final Draft* is Autodesk's answer to other AutoCAD publications. It comes to you automatically when you register your AutoCAD software and contains a variety of useful information. It does provide information about what Autodesk is doing, but it is a captive publication. It also carries CAD-oriented advertising, which can prove helpful.

Final Draft is worth looking at when it arrives, and since it's sent to registered owners, it could be worth advertising in if you have an AutoCAD product.

You can communicate with *Final Draft* at the Autodesk address, 2320 Marinship Way, Sausalito, CA 94965. Their phone number is 415-332-2344.

9

Plotting a Drawing

Plotting can be done from the opening menu or from within AutoCAD, using the PLOT command.

To plot from the opening menu, choose option 3. For a dot matrix printer plot, choose option 4. You will be asked to enter the name of the drawing you wish to plot. If you are still in a drawing, enter "PLOT." The following sequence of commands will appear:

Specify the part of the drawing to be plotted by
entering:Display, Extents, Limits, View, or Window <L>:

Plot will not be written to a selected file
Sizes are in Inches
Plot origin is at (0.00,0.00)
Plotting area is 12.000 wide by 9.000
Plot is not rotated 90 degrees
Pen width is 0.010
Area fill will not be adjusted for pen width
Hidden lines will NOT be removed
Plot will be scaled to fit the available area
Do you want to change anything? <N>:

Effective plotting Area:
Position paper in plotter.
Press RETURN to continue or S to Stop for hardware setup.
Processing vector:

Plot complete.
Press [Return] to continue:
(Main menu displayed.)

The above sequence will now be examined in detail, one prompt at a time:

Specify the part of the drawing to be plotted by entering:
Display, Extents, Limits, View, or Window <L>:

48

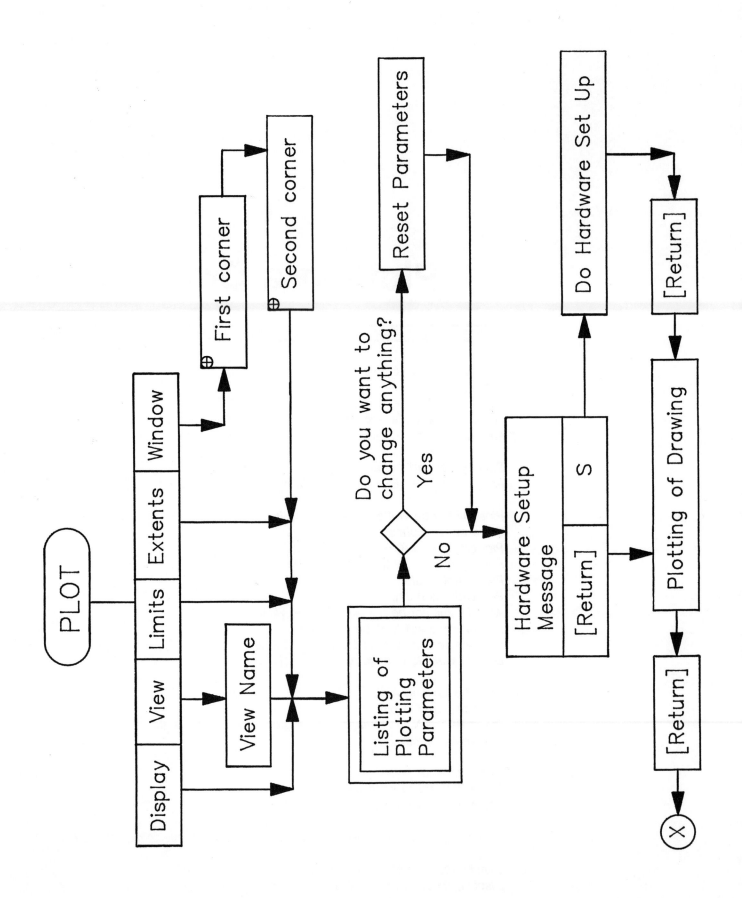

AutoCAD is looking for the area to be plotted. The plot can be of the entire drawing or it can be limited to a selected area or even a view. The Display option will plot the last area shown on the screen or the area shown at the time the drawing was ended, if you are plotting from the main menu. Extents acts like the Extents subcommand for ZOOM: only enough area to contain the objects drawn will be plotted. Choosing Limits will plot the area defined by the drawing limits. View will let you plot any particular view that was generated and saved during an editing session. If View is selected, AutoCAD will prompt for the View Name. With the Window option, AutoCAD will plot only the area defined by the coordinates of the window.

The next prompt you receive tells you what the current settings are for plotting:

Plot will Not be written to a selected file.
Sizes are in inches (millimeters).
Plot origin is at (X.XXX,Y.YYY).
Plotting area is XX.XXX wide by Y.YYY
Plot is not rotated 90 degrees.
Pen width is 0.010.
Area fill will not be adjusted for pen width.
Hidden lines will NOT be removed.
Plot will be scaled to fit the available area.

Do you want to change anything? <N>:

If any changes need to be made, enter Y at this point. The changes in plotting parameters may then be made in the following order:

Color, pen number, line type, pen speed changes

When you set colors in AutoCAD, you are also setting the pen number, the line type, and the pen speed. These values can be changed in this section of the program and, if desired, stored for future plots. The menu will appear as follows:

Entity Color	Pen No.	Line Type	Pen Speed	Entity Color	Pen No.	Line Type	Pen Speed
1 (red)	1	0	20	9	1	0	20
2 (yellow)	2	0	20	10	1	0	20
3 (green)	3	0	20	11	1	0	20
4 (cyan)	4	0	20	12	1	0	20
5 (blue)	5	0	20	13	1	0	20
6 (magenta)	6	0	20	14	1	0	20
7 (white)	7	0	20	15	1	0	20
8	8	0	20				

Line types	
	0 = continuous line
	1 = ...
	2 = ...
	3 = ———————-
	4 = - - - - - - - -
	5 = __ __ __ __ __
	6 = ___ ___ ___ ___
	7 = __ __ __ __ __
	8 = ___-___-___-___

Do you wish to change any of these parameters?<N>

AutoCAD allows the assignment of color numbers up to 255. Any colors higher than 15, however, will plot the same as color 1. These colors will not appear in the table above.

For multiple pen plots with a single pen plotter, the assignment of a different pen for the different layers will cause the plotter to stop for a pen change.

Some plotters support multiple line types. These will be shown in a line type table as above. These plotter-generated line types are for drawing entities which have AutoCAD's CONTINUOUS line type. If the drawing contains entities drawn with other types of line, use the plotter's continuous line.

Pen speed is either in inches per second or centimeters per second. If certain pens require slower speeds for uniform ink flow, the pen speed can be selectively slowed down for just those pens. This prevents having to reset the plotter settings and plot an entire drawing at a slower speed.

If you wish to change any of the settings for color, pen number, line type or pen speed, the program will step through each color option, showing each setting, and giving you the choice to change or accept the old value. To accept the old (current) value, hit [Return].

The plotting parameter setting routine will automatically loop back to color 1 and continue. Enter an X at any point to exit. (For later versions of AutoCAD, you may also respond with S to show the current table of parameter settings before continuing. Entering a C, followed by a number, will cause the routine to jump to the pen with that number. If you precede any value with an asterisk (*), that value will be used for all of the subsequent colors in the table, up to 15. Any earlier settings will not be affected.)

Write the plot to a file? <N>

AutoCAD allows the file generated for a plot to be written and saved as a .plt file. Third-party utility programs can be used to spool these plots for batch plotting to roll plotters or to plot a drawing from a .plt file while you continue to generate another drawing.

Size units(Inches or Millimeters)<default>:

The size units option in AutoCAD allows the user to specify the plot size in either English units (inches) or metric units (millimeters). To set this parameter, enter an I for inches or an M for millimeters.

Plot origin in Inches<default X,Y>:

The plot origin prompt allows the relocation of the start point of the plot. When using a plotter, the plot origin is located in the lower left corner of the paper. For a printer plotter, the upper left corner is used for the plot origin. The plot origin is normally taken as 0,0, but this can be altered to shove the drawing in any positive direction, as for example, where you wish to avoid overwriting a title block or border.

The previous Size units prompt determines the units to be used in any plot origin displacements. Suppose the units are in inches and that 2,2 is entered for the new plot origin. This would set the new plot origin two inches in the positive X-direction and two inches in the positive-Y direction.

Standard values for plotting size

Size	Width	Height
A	10.50	8.00
B	16.00	10.00
C	21.00	16.00
D	33.00	21.00
E	43.00	33.00
MAX	48.80	36.80
USER	12.00	18.00

Enter the Size or Width, Height (in Inches):

The plotting size option tells AutoCAD how large of a piece of paper it is to plot on. When you select a plotter during configuration of your system, AutoCAD remembers what paper sizes your plotter can handle. These sizes will be listed as choices. In addition, the maximum allowable paper size and any user defined sizes will be listed.

Rotate 2D plots 90 degrees clockwise?<N>

The plot rotation option allows turning the plot 90 degrees in the clockwise direction. This is very handy for multiple plots on a single sheet of paper and for drawings and sketches that are taller than they are wide (e.g., posters, calendars, and banners). The drawing origin will be moved from the lower left corner to the upper left corner of the paper.

Pen width <default>:

In order to completely and efficiently fill a SOLID or a TRACE or wide polyline, AutoCAD needs to know how wide a pen it is using. AutoCAD will then use the pen width to lay multiple lines next to each other with no gaps and a minimum of overlap. You may sometimes find it useful to specify a pen width greater than the actual pen being used; specifying a pen smaller than the one actually used will just waste ink.

Adjust area fill boundaries for pen width?<N>

The area fill adjustment option allows precise filling of SOLIDs, TRACEs and polylines. If you enter N here, the center of the pen will lie on the boundary line. If you enter Y, the pen will be moved over one half of the pen width and the resulting edge drawn will be exactly on the border line. Such precise plotting is not normally needed, but is offered for those with special requirements.

Remove hidden lines? <N>   (ADE-3)

In the creation of a three dimensional drawing, hidden lines can be generated. It is the user's option whether or not these lines will be shown in a plot. Note that removing these hidden lines slows down plotting significantly.

Specify scale by entering:
Plotted units = Drawing units or Fit or ? <default>:

Drawings created often have a scale associated with them. The plot scale prompt requests the scale to be plotted with respect to the drawing units. To do this first give the plotted units and then the drawing units, separated by an equal sign. If the Fit option is chosen, AutoCAD will give the largest plot for the available paper area. If you are not sure of the prompt, entering a ? will bring up a help screen.

Examples:

Units	Plotted units	Drawing units	Scale entry
Engineering	Half	Full	1 = 2
Engineering	Quarter	Quarter	1 = 1
Engineering	Full	Eighth	1 = 8
Architectural*	Quarter	Full	¼″ = 1′
Architectural	Quarter	Full	.25 = 1

Metric	Half	Full	1=2
Metric	Quarter	Quarter	1=1
Metric	Full	Eighth	1=8

Once the changes in settings have been made, AutoCAD gives a final check on the status of the area to be plotted and whether the plotter is ready.

Effective plotting Area: m wide by n high
Position paper in plotter.
Press RETURN to continue or S to Stop for hardware setup.

Once a [Return] is entered, the processing of the vectors can be viewed and the plot will begin.

Processing vector: nnn

When the plot is complete, AutoCAD signals that it is ready to return to other duties with the following message:

Plot complete.
Press RETURN to continue:

The following is a check list for plotting:

Plotting check list:

Item	Status
Drawing	
SAVEd	_____
ZOOM position correct for display option	_____
Within drawing limits	_____
Correct layers ON and OFF	_____
Computer	
On a dedicated surge protector	_____
Plotter	
Plugged into a surge protector	_____
Turned ON	_____
Power circuit has no motors or other surge sources	_____
Plotter cable	
Connected to plotter	_____
Connected to computer	_____
Not a tripping hazard	_____
Plotter selector switch set to correct computer	_____
Plotter paper	
Correct size	_____
Correct type	_____
Loaded into plotter	_____
Free to travel	_____
Plotter pen(s)	
Clean	_____
Full of ink	_____
Correct color ink	_____
Correct size	_____
Ink flows correctly	_____
Loaded in plotter	_____

10

Attributes (ADE-2)

An attribute is a piece of information contained in a drawing, describing a particular occurrence of an inserted block. For example, suppose you put two checkers into a drawing. One of them might have the attribute "black" and the other "red." These attributes or descriptors can be visible or invisible, constant or variable, verified or unverified.

Visible Attributes. These attributes show on the screen and are plotted. That is, each checker would have text near it telling what it is. Invisible attributes are not displayed, but are still there, waiting for someone to collect them from the drawing into a data list.

Constant Attributes. These attributes are identical for every insertion of the block containing them. Variable attributes can be altered when the block is inserted. For example, you might have a block with the constant attribute "checkerboard, $1.25." Every time you put that block into your drawing, that same data text would accompany it. On the other hand, when you INSERT a checker block, you would have the option of setting its color attribute to "red" or "black." That would be an example of a variable attribute.

Verified Attributes. If you want a chance to check the accuracy of a variable attribute when you insert its block, you can make it a Verified type. This is particularly important where the attribute is to be invisible. For example, you might want to verify another attribute telling that the checker is an ordinary "man" and set it to a "king" when needed.

Attributes allow you to take a drawing with many different items and extract the pertinent information about those items into a list. These lists can be used for inventory control, purchase orders, facilities management, bills of materials, etc., and also as checklists to ensure that you have the right number of each item in a drawing.

To prepare for the extraction of attributes, it is first necessary to (1) create symbols or drawing figures, assign the attributes, and then BLOCK each figure and enough area near it to include the attribute text. (2) The blocks are then INSERTed as needed into a drawing, filling out the variable attributes as you go. (3) A template or pattern file must be created.

A template file consists of a pattern file used to set the format for the extracted data. See the section on constructing template files, below Example of imported data.

Attributes only have meaning if they are associated with a block. If a block is constructed without attributes, the commands below will not work. Existing blocks can have attributes added, but any attributes associated with the original block can no longer be addressed.

Attributes can be in several levels in nested blocks. Nesting of attributes, however, forces the inner attributes to become constant.

Attribute location is not restricted to being inside of or even near a figure. As long as the area of blocking includes any attributes outside of the figure, those attributes will be included as a part of that block.

The commands used for creating and handling attributes are:

ATTDEF
ATTDISP
ATTEDIT
ATTEXT

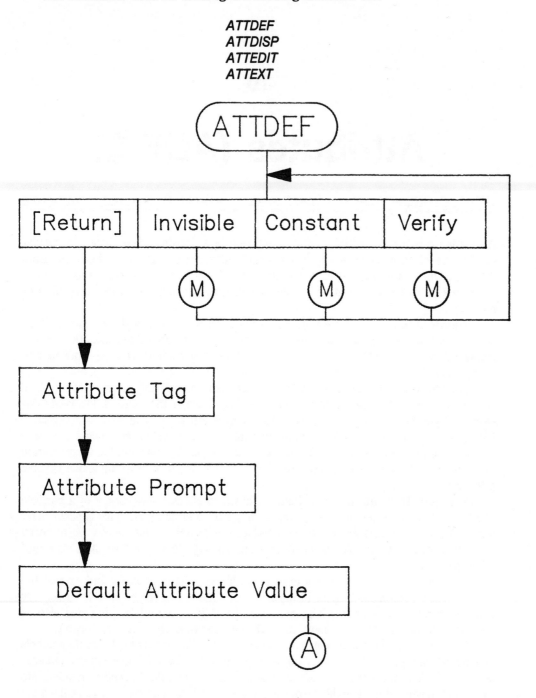

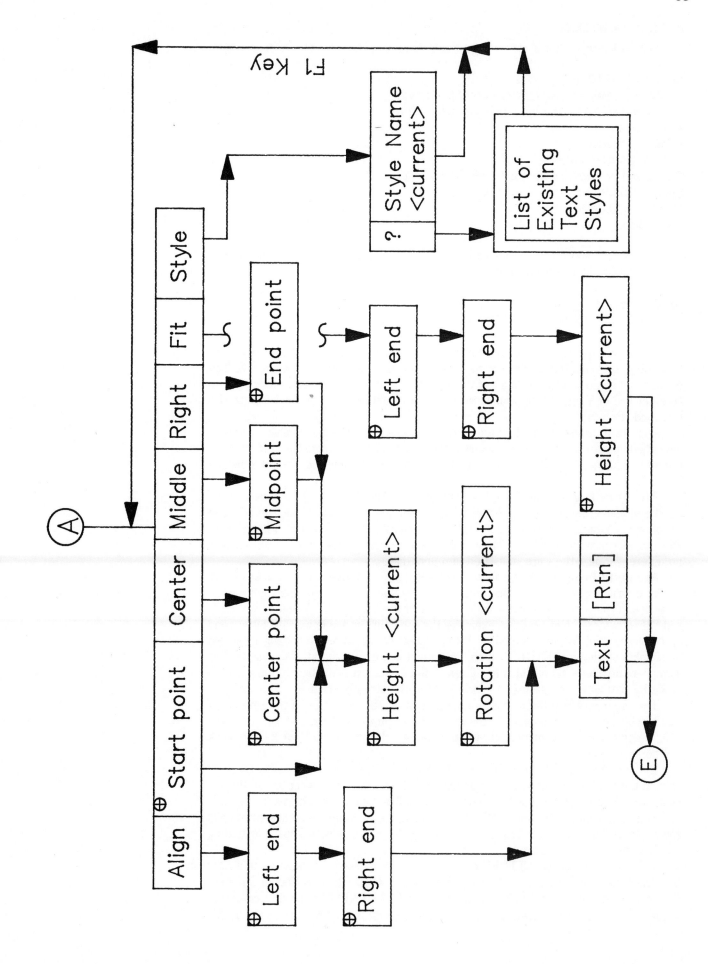

ATTDEF COMMAND

The ATTDEF command stands for attribute definition. The command sequence goes:

Command:ATTDEF
Attribute modes—Invisible:N Constant:N Verify:N
 Enter (I,C,V) to change, RETURN when done:
Attribute tag:
Attribute prompt:
Default attribute value:
Start point or Align/Center/Fit/Middle/Right/Style:
Height <0.200>:
Rotation <0.00>:
Command:

The options and prompts above will now be looked at one at a time, starting with the Attribute modes subcommand:

Attribute modes— Invisible:N Constant:N Verify:N
Enter (I,C,V) to change, RETURN when done:

This allows the user to set any combination of visibility, variability, and verification. Just enter the initial letter(s) of the mode(s) you wish to change: I, C and/or V. The N after any mode will toggle to a Y if that option is invoked. To reset a mode back to N, enter I, C or V again. The prompt will be repeated until you accept the settings with a second [Return].

The most frequent combination of these modes is probably visible, variable, unverified, and occurs in menu insertions. If the attribute is to be a constant, the attribute cannot be changed once it is blocked. It is necessary to redefine the block if a change is required.

Attribute Tag. The attribute tag is the name of the attribute. In the case of the checkers, above, there are two attribute tags: Color and Rank. The name can be made up of any characters except blank spaces. Examples of names are: Phone_no., Dewey_decimal, Price/dollars. The use of capital letters and lowercase letters makes no difference; all letters are translated into uppercase.

Attribute Prompt. The attribute prompt is a message that asks the user for the attribute value and can be anything sufficient to jog your memory for the right kind of response. Typical phrases could include: "Enter phone number", "Volume identifier" and "How much?". Note in these examples the use of upper and lowercase letters and spaces is accepted. What is entered is what will appear on the screen. If nothing is entered by simply entering a [RETURN], then the prompt defaults to the attribute name. For a constant attribute, no prompts are given. You can start the attribute prompt with a space by putting a backslash (\) at the front of the string you enter.

The order in which the attribute prompts appear on the screen is the reverse of that in which they were assigned to the block. For example, if you assign the attributes in a descending order of importance, the prompting order when you INSERT the block will be ascending.

Default Attribute Value. The default attribute value will appear in pointy brackets next to the attribute prompt. When you INSERT the block, if you want to use the default value, just hit [Return] and the default value will be taken. Examples are "None", "Vacant", Standard","Later", and "Not assigned". Upper and lowercase letters and spaces are permissible here. You can also start the default value with a space by putting a backslash (\) at the front of your entry.

The remainder of the ATTDEF options require responses the same as those for the TEXT command. (See the TEXT entry in the AutoCAD Glossary Section.) If a series of attributes are to be added to an object, a [RETURN] after the first command sequence will start adding the next attribute below the first, similar to the way the TEXT command does. Caution must be exercised when doing this because the ATTDEF modes (I,C,V) set in the previous ATTDEF will be the default values. Be sure to adjust these if necessary before continuing the next attribute definition.

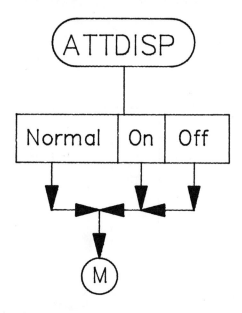

ATTDISP COMMAND

The ATTDISP command (''attribute display'') controls the viewing of attributes. All of the attributes of inserted blocks in a drawing can be made visible or invisible. The command sequence is as follows:

Command: ATTDISP
Normal/On/Off <current setting>:

The normal option displays the attributes as they were originally defined, visible or invisible. The On option allows viewing of all attributes. The Off option makes all attributes invisible.

ATTEDIT COMMAND

The ATTEDIT command allows the editing of attributes. This can be done on an individual basis or globally. All except the constant attributes can be edited. All or any portion of the attribute can be edited. The full string of characters can be replaced or just a portion of them can be modified. The ATTEDIT command proceeds as follows:

Command:ATTEDIT
Edit Attributes one by one? <Y>:
Block name specification <>:*
Attribute tag specification <>:*
Attribute value specification <>:*

The three specification lines allow you to screen out just certain blocks, tags, or values for editing. The input for these specifications can include the usual wild-card characters: * and ?. The * stands for *all* in a name, the ? is a space holder for any character. Thus if you use a block name specification of, say, ''AC*'', then all blocks beginning with AC would be selected for editing.

Note that the default for the three specification prompts above is an asterisk and will select all blocks, tags, and values, if you hit [Return] with no entry. One special technique: if you want to edit only blank (null) attribute values, enter a backslash (\ ) for the value specification. This will pick out only attributes that have no value.

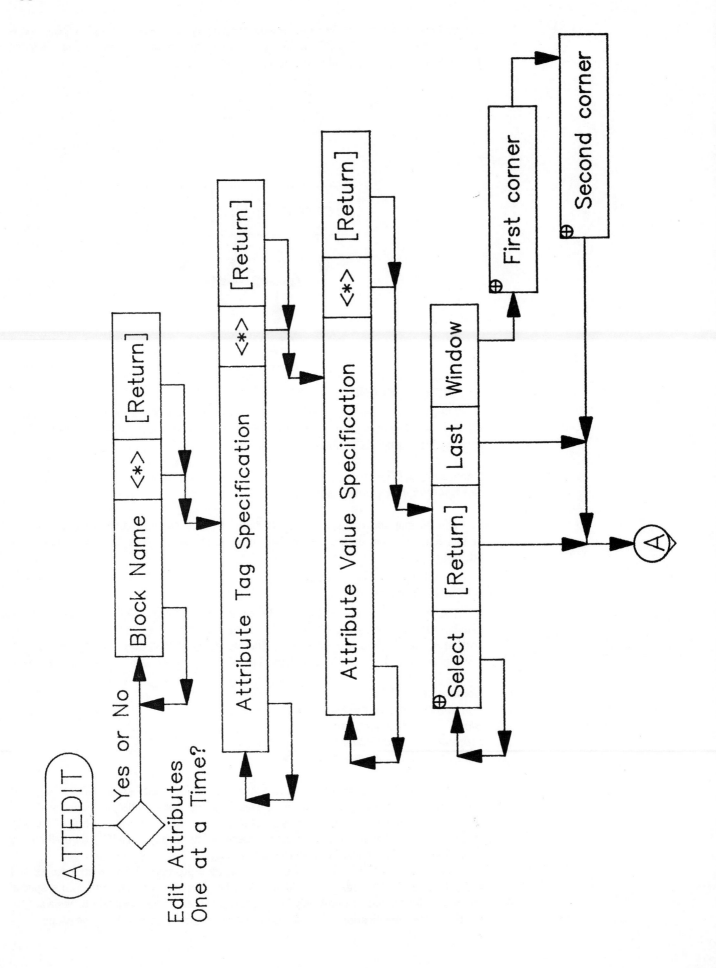

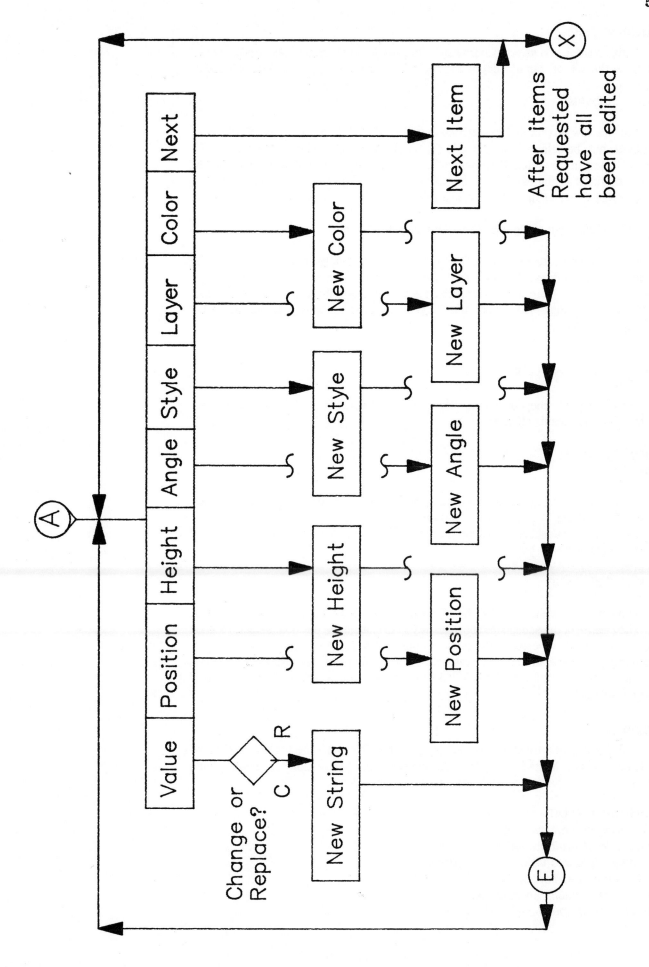

Individual Editing

At this point, if you selected individual editing at the initial prompt, only the attributes visible on the screen can be edited, and the following prompting sequence will occur:

Select Attributes:

You can now further limit the attributes to be edited within those specified above. Attributes may be selected for editing in the usual manner of selecting objects. See Selecting Objects in the AutoCAD Glossary Section for more information. As you window or pick individual attributes, they will be marked with an X. (If you don't like the selection set, [CTRL] C out of the command and restart it.) The next prompt will be:

Value/Position/Height/Angle/Style/Layer/Color/Next <N>:

Enter the first letter of one of the choices above to change that parameter in the attribute you are editing. When you are done with an attribute, select Next to move on to the next one. Note that if the attribute text was originally Aligned or Fitted type, there will be no Angle subsuboption in the prompt above. Aligned text will also have no Height prompt.

If you select the Value suboption, you will be prompted:

Change or Replace? <R>:

The Change subsuboption (C) will allow you to modify part of an attribute. The prompt for the Change subsuboption is:

String to change:
New string:

If you want to change the attribute value from "500 rupees" to "850 rupees", enter 500 for "String to change" and 850 for "New string".

The Replace subsuboption (R or [Return]) will delete the old attribute value and AutoCAD will ask you for

New attribute value:

Type in the new string or just hit [Return] if you want a blank for the new value.

The balance of the suboptions above allow you to change the position, height, rotation angle, style, layer, or color of the attribute being edited. The prompts involved vary depending on how the attribute text was justified. Read the prompts and defaults carefully.

To escape the command, hit [CTRL] C or hit Next repeatedly until you run out of selected attributes.

Global Editing

Global editing of attributes allows editing of both visible and invisible attributes. However, the editing is limited to the attribute value and no other variables. If global editing is required, then the command prompting will be as follows:

Command:ATTEDIT
Edit Attributes one by one? <Y>:N
Global edit of Attribute values.
Edit only Attributes visible on the screen? <Y>:
Block name specification <>:*
Attribute tag specification <>:*
Attribute value specification <>:*

Select Attributes:
String to change:
New string:
Command:

The response to these prompts is the same as for editing of attributes on an individual basis.

If you selected No (N) in reply to "Edit only Attributes visible on the screen?", then you will not be asked to further limit or select attributes. You will be put into the text screen and go directly to the "String to change" prompt. Since you are in text mode and since all attributes are selected (including the invisible attributes), the X marking feature is not available. The drawing will REGEN when you are done with editing.

When dealing with the "String to change" prompt, the wild card symbols will be interpreted literally as asterisks and question marks, not as wild cards. These strings must be explicit.

The entering of a null in the "String to change" subcommand will result in the "New string" being attached to the front of all strings being changed.

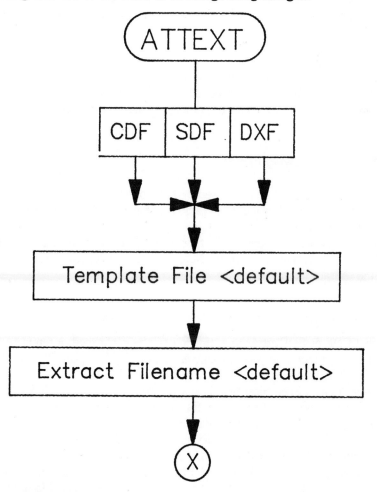

ATTEXT COMMAND

The ATTEXT or attribute extraction command creates files consisting of nothing but attributes. These files can later be imported into other programs for further processing. The type of program to be used for further processing determines what type of extract file should be created. Entering the command ATTEXT will give the following prompts:

CDF, SDF, or DXF attribute extract (or Entities) <C>:

Prior to the execution of the ATTEXT command, a template file must exist to execute a CDF or SDF attribute extraction.

The CDF or Comma Delimited Format option creates a file whose fields are separated (delimited) by commas. (This however can be modified by the template file.) These files can be read by dBASE II and other database files.

The SDF option has no delimiters, but uses fixed field widths. This file format is known as system data format (SDF). These files can also be read by dBASE II and other database files.

A DXF extract file will be like an ordinary Drawing Interchange File, except that only blocks, attributes, and end-of-sequence entities will be included. DXF file extractions are useful for editing drawing data files using a word processing program.

The Entities option gives you the ability to select only certain objects for inclusion in the extract file. Hit [Return] when you are through selecting objects and you will be returned to the CDF/SDF/DXF prompt.

If you have selected the CDF or SDF type of output file, the following prompt will appear:

Template filename <default>:

The template file is the pattern file used to set the format for the extracted data. The template file name can be any acceptable DOS filename. See the section below on constructing template files. DXF extract files don't need a template. Once a template file name is given, AutoCAD wants to know what file to write the information to:

Extract filename <drawing name>:

This is the file that will be processed by third party programs. The file name can be eight characters long. Do not use the same name as the template file or the template file will be over-written.

The extract file will be of the ".txt" type if a CDF or SDF extraction is performed. A DXF extraction will produce a .dxx file. Note that the default above will use the drawing name as the extract file name.

Template File Creation

Before a CDF or SDF attribute extraction can be performed, a template file must be constructed and stored in your working directory. The template file tells AutoCAD how information is to be arranged in the extract file.

The template file can be constructed using any text editor that produces ASCII files. WordStar™ can be used by creating the file in non-document mode. The file can also be created using database programs or Edlin. Be careful not to use tabs to line up columns when using a word processor; use ordinary spaces. The file name must conform to DOS conventions and must have an extension of .txt.

Each line in the template file defines a field. The type of field, its width, and the number of decimal places of the field (where applicable) are contained in each line. The field can be a character or a numeric type. The following list gives the different types of fields available for processing purposes:

Field name	Field data	Comments - (don't include template file)
BL:NAME	Cwww000	(block name)
BL:X	Nwwwddd	(X coordinate - block)
BL:Y	Nwwwddd	(Y coordinate - block)

BL:XSCALE	Nwwwddd	(X scale factor - block)
BL:YSCALE	Nwwwddd	(Y scale factor - block)
BL:LAYER	Cwww000	(layer block resides on)
BL:LEVEL	Nwwwddd	(block level - nested on)
BL:ORIENT	Nwwwddd	(rotation angle - block)
tag name	Cwww000	(attribute tag - character)
tag name	Nwwwddd	(attribute tag - numeric)

For the tag name(s), use the attribute tag name(s) assigned in the drawing. You need only include the attributes you want to extract, but you must have at least one tag name in the template file.

C	denotes a character field
N	denotes a numeric field
www	= field width - user defined
ddd	= decimal precision - user defined
000	= place holders that do not change

The template file may hold any or all of the first eight field names listed, in any order. Duplicates are not acceptable. The use of upper and lowercase letters in the template file does not make any difference. The characters are all treated as capital letters. The number of spaces between the field name and the field data string also has no effect. After the field name, AutoCAD is looking for the first nonblank character, this must be a ''C'' or an ''N''. The last line in the file must be followed by a [Return]. Example:

PERSON	*C015000*
TITLE	*C020000*
OFFICE	*N004000*
PHONE	*N005000*
BL:NAME	*C008000*
BL:X	*N007003*
BL:Y	*N007003*

This file calls for the attribute tag names PERSON, TITLE, OFFICE and PHONE, the block name and the X and Y coordinates of the block. The field data for the line beginning with PERSON shows that the field is a character type and is fifteen characters wide.

The line giving the X coordinate shows that the field is a numeric type with a field width of seven and a precision of three decimal places. If there is a chance that a text default from an attribute value might be entered into what would normally be a numeric field, then the field must be handled as a character field. An error message will occur if this is the case. The message will not clearly define the problem.

Lotus and dBASE III Attribute Importation

Lotus 1-2-3 can import and process attribute output files created by AutoCAD. The .txt attribute file created must be a double quote delimited file: the template file used must have as its first line: C:QUOTE ''.

After the extract file is created, it must be renamed into the spreadsheet program and use the Lotus command /FIB (File, Import, Both). Select the extracted file and it will be imported.The information between the double quotes will be placed in separate cells within the worksheet. The format will be left justified. No preparation of the width of the individual cells in the worksheet is necessary. If the imported data is wider than the cell width it is simply hidden from view. Opening the cell width will reveal the full contents of the cell.

For an example, suppose you are in charge of office space allocation for XYZ company. You are going to draw a plot plan showing the offices, the telephone number for the offices, who is assigned to each office, and their position.

Begin by creating a template file named "PHONE.TXT": Get into your favorite text editing program and input the following lines:

```
C:QUOTE              "
BL:NAME              C010000
office               c004000
person               c015000
position             c025000
phone                c004000
```

Enter a final [Return] after the last line. Do not add any spaces at the end of any of the above lines. Save this file in the same directory or subdirectory AutoCAD is in.

Exit the text editing program and call up the AutoCAD program. Select option 1, "Create a new drawing". Call this drawing "BOOKMKR".

Draw a rectangle eight units high by eight units wide. This is going to be an office cubicle. Now issue the command ATTDEF. Answer the prompting as follows:

Command:ATTDEF
Attribute modes—Invisible:N Constant:N Verify:N
Enter (I,C,V) to change, RETURN when done: I

Attribute modes—Invisible:Y Constant:N Verify:N
Enter (I,C,V) to change, RETURN when done: [Return]

Attribute tag:POSITION

Attribute prompt:Enter Person's Title

Default attribute value:None

Start point or Align/Center/Fit/Middle/Right/Style:
          Move the cross-hairs to a point inside of the rectangle
          and designate a point in the upper lefthand corner of
          the rectangle by entering a [Return].

Height <0.200>:[Return]

Rotation <0.00>:[Return]

Command:[Return]

Attribute modes—Invisible:Y Constant:N Verify:N
Enter (I,C,V) to change, RETURN when done: I

Attribute modes—Invisible:N Constant:N Verify:N
Enter (I,C,V) to change, RETURN when done:[Return]

Attribute tag:PERSON

Attribute prompt:Enter Person's Name

Default attribute value:None

Start point or Align/Center/Fit/Middle/Right/Style: [Return].

Height <0.200>:[Return]

Rotation <0.00>:[Return]

Command:[Return]

Attribute modes—Invisible:N Constant:N Verify:N
Enter (I,C,V) to change, RETURN when done:[Return]

Attribute tag:EXTENSION

Attribute prompt:Enter Phone No.

Default attribute value:None

Start point or Align/Center/Fit/Middle/Right/Style: [Return].

Height <0.200>:[Return]

Rotation <0.00>:[Return]

Command:[Return]

Attribute modes - Invisible:N Constant:N Verify:N
Enter (I,C,V) to change, RETURN when done:[Return]

Attribute tag:OFFICE

Attribute prompt:Enter Office No.

Default attribute value:None

Start point or Align/Center/Fit/Middle/Right/Style: [Return].

Height <0.200>:[Return]

Rotation <0.00>:[Return]

Command:BLOCK

BLOCK Block name or (?):CUBICLE

Insertion base point:
> *Move the cross-hairs to the intersection*
> *of the lines at the lower left hand corner*
> *of the rectangle and designate that point*
> *by entering a [Return].*

Select objects:W
> *Window the rectangle by first choosing a point*
> *to the left and below the rectangle. Choose the*
> *other point to the right and above rectangle*
> *(outside of it).*

Select objects:[Return]

What has been created to this point is a block called "cubicle". Within this block are four attribute tags called "office", "extension", "person", and "position". Three of these attributes are visible, "position" is invisible.

The block "cubicle" can now be inserted into a drawing like this:

Command:INSERT
Block name (or ?):cubicle
Insertion point:(Reader's choice)
X scale factor <1>:[Return]
Y scale factor <default=X>:[Return]
Rotation angle <0>:[Return]
Enter Attribute Values
Enter Office No.<None>:101
Enter Phone No.<None>:312
Enter Person's Name<None>:Milverton
Enter Person's Title<None>:Finance Manager

Command:[Return]
Block name (or ?):cubicle
Insertion point:(Reader's choice)
X scale factor <1>:[Return]
Y scale factor <default=X>:[Return]
Rotation angle <0>:[Return]
Enter Attribute Values
Enter Office No.<None>:103
Enter Phone No.<None>:316
Enter Person's Name<None>:Sholto
Enter Person's Title<None>:Project Manager

Command:[Return]
Block name (or ?):cubicle
Insertion point:(Reader's choice)
X scale factor <1>:[Return]
Y scale factor <default=X>:[Return]
Rotation angle <0>:[Return]
Enter Attribute Values
Enter Office No.<None>:105
Enter Phone No.<None>:320
Enter Person's Name<None>:Moran
Enter Person's Title<None>:Expediter

Command:[Return]
Block name (or ?):cubicle
Insertion point:(Reader's choice)
X scale factor <1>:[Return]
Y scale factor <default=X>:[Return]
Rotation angle <0>:[Return]
Enter Attribute Values
Enter Office No.<None>:107
Enter Phone No.<None>:325
Enter Person's Name<None>:Roylott
Enter Person's Title<None>:Architect

Command:SAVE

At this point it is necessary to decide which database or other third-party program the data are to be imported into. If the importation is to be into Lotus 1-2-3, execute the "ATTEXT" command directly below. For an importation into dBASE III, move down to the next "ATTEXT" command sequence.

For Lotus 1-2-3

Command:ATTEXT
CDF, SDF, or DXF attribute extract <C>:CDF
Template filename <PHONE>:PHONE
Extract filename <drawing name>:TELLY

Command:END

What has been created to this point is a template file called "PHONE.TXT" that was used to create a CDF type attribute extract file called "TELLY.TXT" from the drawing called "BOOKMKR.DWG". Exit AutoCAD.

For importation into Lotus 1-2-3

The extract attribute file called "TELLY.TXT" must be renamed or (safer) copied with a rename to "TELLY.PRN". Lotus 1-2-3 requires the ".PRN" file extension for importing purposes. Once this is done, move the file into the Lotus 1-2-3 directory or subdirectory. Call up the worksheet program. Import the extract file by using the following command sequence.

Keystroke	Command
/	Backslash
F	File
I	Import
B	Both
Telly	filename

An imported file will look something like this, depending on the exact contents of the file:

	Person	Office	Ext.	Position
CUBICLE	HOLMES	221	300	SAILOR
CUBICLE	WATSON	221	301	AUTHOR
CUBICLE	MILVERTON	101	312	FINANCIER
CUBICLE	MORAN	105	320	EXPEDITER
CUBICLE	ROYLOTT	107	325	ARCHITECT
CUBICLE	SHOLTO	103	316	MANAGER

dBASE III importation.

To prepare the extract file for importing into dBASE III, it is necessary to create an SDF type file format. To do this, follow the sequence below.

Command:ATTEXT
CDF, SDF, or DXF attribute extract <C>:SDF
Template filename <PHONE>:PHONE
Extract filename <drawing name>:FONE

Command:END

What has been created to this point is a template file called "PHONE.TXT" that was used to create an SDF attribute extract file called "FONE.TXT" from a drawing called "BOOKMKR".

Exit AutoCAD.

Transfer the file "FONE.TXT" to the database directory or subdirectory. Do not change the ".TXT" extension.

Before you can import into dBASE III, you have to create a database file. To do this, use the "CREATE" command in dBASE to create the database file called "MOBLIST".

.CREATE MOBLIST [Return]

Enter the following table for the records shown below.

Record No.	Field Name	Type	Width	Dec
1	BL__Name	Char/text	10	0
2	Office	Char/text	4	0
3	Person	Char/text	15	0
4	Position	Char/text	25	0
5	Phone	Char/text	4	0

Save the file.

To import into dBASE III, enter the following sequence of commands:

.USE MOBLIST
.APPEND FROM FONE SDF
.BROWSE

Once the appropriate form of your extract file has been incorporated in a database file, you can further process the information: create phone directories, office assignment lists, and so forth. The examples above are rather simple; the power of the use of attributes is much greater in the more complicated applications that you will develop.

Section 2

(AutoCAD Glossary)

Advanced Techniques

The AutoCAD Advanced Techniques Section could be called a reference manual. Here you will find, in alphabetical order, all the commands with detailed instructions on how to use them. AutoCAD files are listed here, as are other tidbits of information. If you have a problem, or want to know how to do something, this is the place to look.

A

ACAD—(See also Main Menu) is the command that calls the AutoCAD program from DOS. ACAD must be entered from the system prompt, in the directory containing the AutoCAD program files. (See Path Names for exceptions to this.) If ACAD is followed by the name of a drawing, that drawing will become the default drawing. For example:

acad wombat—   Makes wombat the default drawing in the Drawing Editor.

If a view name is added to the drawing name, that view will be called up:

acad wombat,leftelev—   Puts the view called leftelev onto the screen first (after you select "2" from the Main Menu and [Return] to take the default drawing.)

Scripts called via the ACAD command will start automatically and loop continuously if they start with the appropriate responses to AutoCAD. For example:

acad wombat slidshow—   Will start the "slidshow.scr" script, operating in the default drawing "wombat.dwg." The first line of the .SCR file must be "2." The second line should be "wombat" or an empty line to take the default drawing.

Calling a script and a view at the same time doesn't work.

Acad Utility Files—AutoCAD comes equipped with or creates the files described below.

Name	Description
acad.bak—	The old version of the acad.cfg file. Automatically created when you configure AutoCAD from the Main Menu. AutoCAD renames the old configuration file "acad.bak" and the new one "acad.cfg." If problems develop in the .cfg file, delete it and rename the acad.bak file "acad.cfg" to reuse it.

acad.cfg— The file which stores the information on how AutoCAD is configured for your system.

acad.err— When AutoCAD gives you a "FATAL ERROR" or "INTERNAL ERROR" message, it also tries to write diagnostic data into an acad.err file. You probably won't be able to do anything with this data, but Autodesk will find a hard copy of the file useful when helping you with a problem.

acad.exe— The executable main AutoCAD file invoked by "acad" from DOS.

acad.hdx— This is the HELP index file. If it is missing or erased, AutoCAD will automatically restore it based on what is in the HELP file. If you edit the acad.hlp file, delete the .hdx file and let AutoCAD do the updated index for you automatically.

acad.hlp— Contains the messages displayed when you use the HELP command. This file can be customized if desired.

acad.lin— Contains the definitions of the standard line types.

acad.mnu— This is the uncompiled version of the AutoCAD standard menu.

acad.mnx— This is the compiled version of the AutoCAD standard menu.

acad.msg— Contains the starting message which appears when AutoCAD is called. The message may be edited or deleted altogether if you get tired of looking at it. If there is no acad.msg file in your AutoCAD directory, AutoCAD will go directly to the Main Menu.

acad.ovl— Overlay file(s) that AutoCAD accesses as needed to execute certain commands.

acad.pat— The crosshatching pattern file.

acad.pgp— An ASCII file holding program parameters for execution of other programs from within AutoCAD. See External Commands.

ADE-1,-2,-3—ADE-1,-2,-3 refers to the three (as of version 2.6) Advanced Drafting Extensions. These ADE's can be added to the basic, *unextended* AutoCAD in sequence, i.e., ADE-2 requires that you have ADE-1 and ADE-3 requires ADE-2.

If you are trying to use an AutoCAD command, and AutoCAD absolutely refuses to recognize it, check to see whether you have the ADE that contains the command. Check also to see if you have loaded all of the AutoCAD disks onto your hard drive.

The following chart shows what is included in each ADE package.

ADE-1	ADE-2	ADE-3
Auto. dimensioning	Object snap	3D level 1
Fillets	Variable grids	Polylines
Line break	Isometric grids	IGES output
Axes	Named views	AutoLISP
Length formats	Dragging	Explosion
Angle formats	Screen setup	External commands
Crosshatching	Mirroring	Offset lines
Sketch	Slides	Rotation

Status line	Attributes	Scaling
Assoc. dimensions		Stretching
		Ellipses
		Polygons
		Donuts
		Curve fitting
		Selection highlight
		Layer freeze, thaw
		Dividing marks
		Trimming
		3D level 2
		Filmroll

ALIGNED Subcommand—(See DIM Command)

Angles—(See also Coordinates and the UNITS Command.) Angle references in AutoCAD follow the usual convention, unless you tell it otherwise. If you can remember back to Geometry I, angles are defined relative to a fixed line extending from the *origin* (the intersection of the X and Y axes, or 0,0), out to the right. Positive angles are measured counterclockwise, negatively clockwise from that line. Ninety degrees is straight up along the Y-axis, 180 degrees is straight left, 270 degrees is straight down and 360 degrees is the same as zero degrees. See Fig. GL-1.

If you wish, you can use the UNITS command to shift the zero degree line in any direction and/or make clockwise the positive direction.

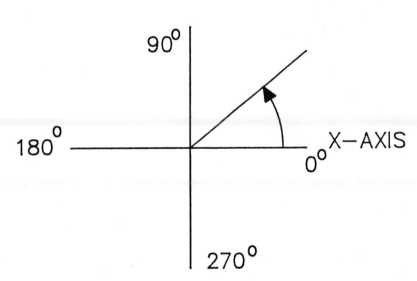

Note that arc and circle constructions and breaks preferentially move counterclockwise. This is part of the same convention.

Some countries measure angles in grads instead of degrees. The UNITS command can be used to allow you to work in grads. Other systems of angle measurement which are supported by AutoCAD are decimal degrees, radians, degrees/minutes/seconds, and "surveyor's units." If you feel some strange compulsion to work in one of these other angle formats, you probably are familiar enough with them to know how they work and what they mean without further explanation, except to show how they are displayed and entered:

System	Display	Input
Decimal Degrees	54.667	54.667
Degr./Min./Secs.	54d40'0.00"	54d40'

Grads	60.741g	60.741
Radians	0.9541r	0.9541
Surveyor's Units	N 35d20'0" E	N35d20'E

If you need to bypass some awkward system of angle notation and do input in good old Geometry I form, put "<<" in front of the desired actual angle. (This also applies to relative polar coordinate input.) Use this method of specifying angles in menus. A menu does not know what system of units has been set up in the working drawing when it is called. If you are working in surveyor's units and the menu is trying to work in grads, you are going to be less than thrilled by the result. If you have any reason to think your menus are going to be used with oddball UNITS settings, prefix all angle entries with << and use only conventional angle format.

ANGULAR Subcommand—(See DIM Command)

APERTURE Command—(See also OSNAP.) When you are using object snaps, point entry prompts will also cause a small target box to appear at the crosshairs. Only the items in or crossing this box will be accepted as objects to snap to. To adjust the size of this box, enter APERTURE, and then enter an aperture size of from one to fifty pixels. The box will remain at that new size until you reset it.

ARC Command—Arcs are incomplete circles. AutoCAD has eight different ways of constructing arcs.

Options under the ARC command are specified with the following letters:

A   (stands for included Angle)
C   (Center of the incomplete circle)
D   (starting Direction)
E   (End point)
L   (chord Length)
R   (Radius)

The lower case letter "p" will stand for the entry of a location via the tablet, other pointing device, or the keyboard. Keyboard specified numbers are shown with a "k." Other abbreviations are as listed above.

The eight arc methods are:

	Type	Entries				
(1)	Three points on the arc	p	p	p		
(2)	Start point, center, end point	p	C	p	p	
	* or	C	p	p	p	
(3)	Start point, center, included angle	p	C	p	k	
(4)	Start point, center, chord length	p	C	p	L	k
(5)	Start point, end point, radius	p	E	p	R	k
(6)	Start point, end point, included angle	p	E	p	A	k
(7)	Start point, end point, starting direction	p	E	p	D	p
	or	p	E	p	D	k
(8)	Continue previous arc or line	[Return]	p			

General Notes. An arc produced with snap off will usually be significantly different from one done with snap on.

ADE-2 provides the ability to drag the last parameter when specifying any type of arc. The first prompt after entering the ARC command is:

Center/< start point>

The various types of arc are discussed in more detail below:

(1) The Three Point Arc. This is identical to creation of a three point ("3p") circle, except that the first and third points are the start and finish points of the arc. The arc, if continued by a subsequent command, will continue from the third (finish) point.

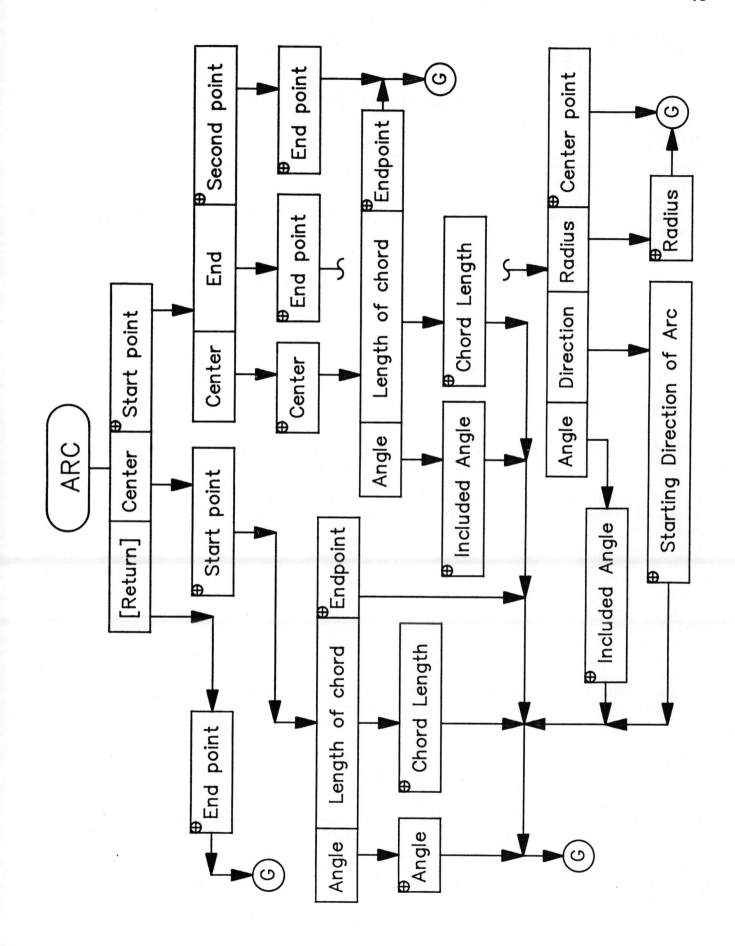

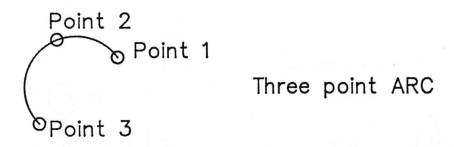

Three point ARC

---

(2) Start point, Center point, End point. Note that the start point and the center point are sufficient to determine the radius of the circle. The end point, therefore, only determines the length of the arc: an invisible line from the circle center through the end point truncates the arc.

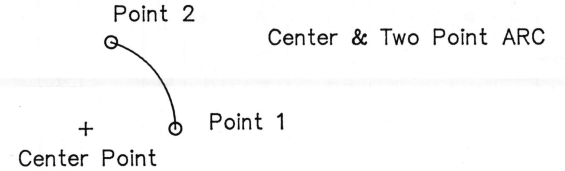

Center & Two Point ARC

(3) Start point, Center point, Included angle. The arc will be drawn from the start point, about the center, counterclockwise through the specified angle. Negative angles cause the arc to be drawn clockwise from the start point. (See the Figure on p 77.)

(4) Start point, Center point, Chord length. These three parameters, by themselves, are ambiguous: they determine any of four different arcs. The convention that arcs are drawn only counterclockwise from the start point eliminates two of them; the use of positive chord length to specify the minor arc (less than 180 degrees) and negative chord length for the major arc (greater than 180 degrees) eliminates the ambiguity.

(5) Start point, End point, Radius. This form of arc construction reduces ambiguity by using the counterclockwise convention and using negative radius values to call for the major arc.

(6) Start point, End point, Included angle. Using a negative value for the included angle will cause this command to draw the arc clockwise from the start point through the endpoint.

(7) Start point, End point, Starting direction. This is designed to construct arcs tangent to other entities. When a starting direction is called for by the prompt, enter an angle from the keyboard or enter a point whose location relative to the start point will determine the direction of the initial sweep of the arc.

(8) Continuation of a Line or Arc. Similar to number (7), above. To specify this kind of arc, use the null response ([Return]) to the first prompt. The arc will be generated from the end point of the last arc or line drawn, continuing initially in the final direction of that last entity, and then sweeping to the endpoint entered at the second prompt. **AREA Command**—This is the command that tells AutoCAD to calculate the area and perimeter of an enclosed space. The area is determined from any number of points you specify enclosing a space on a drawing. If you have not closed off the space by putting the last point on top of the first point, AutoCAD will assume the necessary closure. Once you enter the command, AREA, you are prompted for the first point, then the next point, the next and so on until you enter [Return].

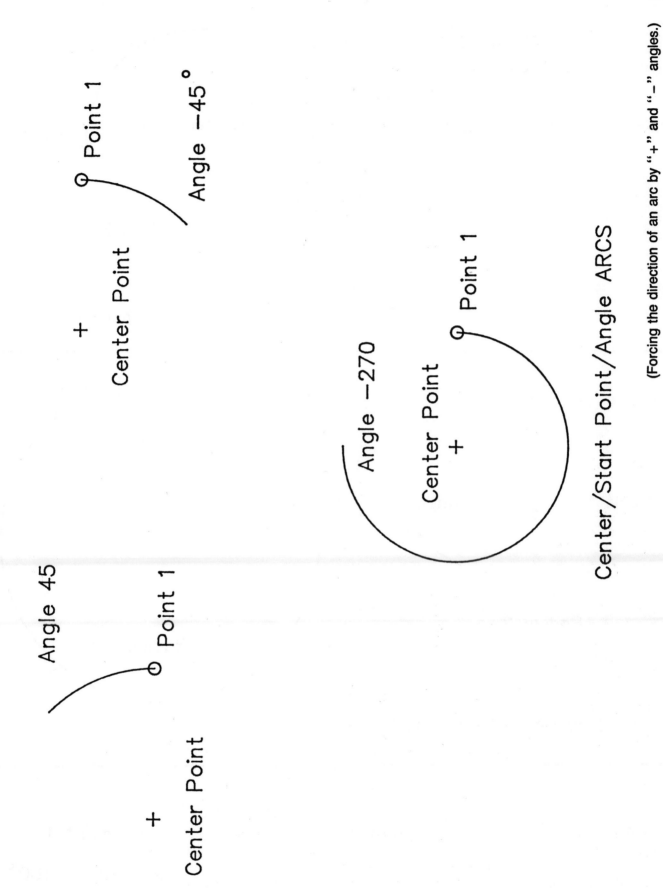

Point 1

Angle −45°

+ Center Point

Angle −270

Center Point +

Point 1

Angle 45

Point 1

+ Center Point

Center/Start Point/Angle ARCS

(Forcing the direction of an arc by "+" and "−" angles.)

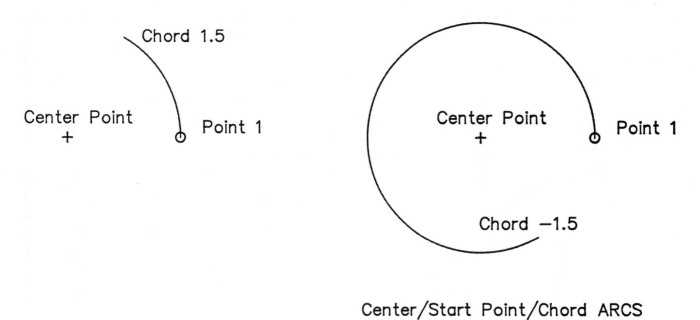

Center/Start Point/Chord ARCS

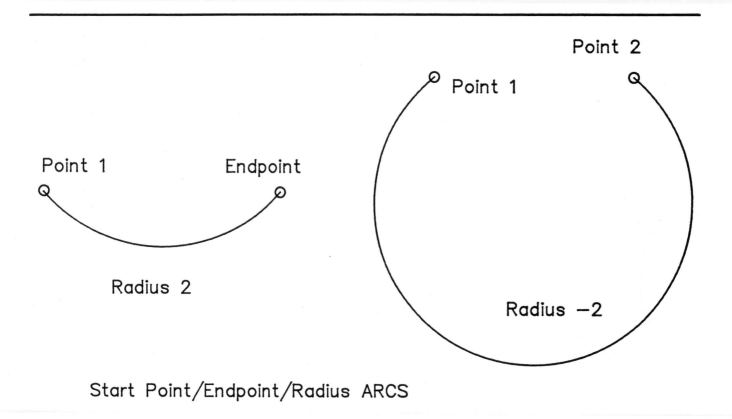

Start Point/Endpoint/Radius ARCS

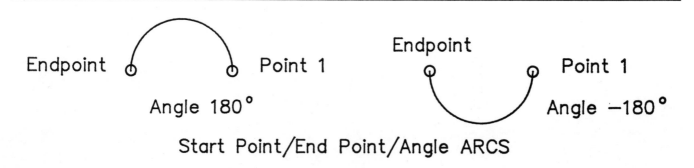

Start Point/End Point/Angle ARCS

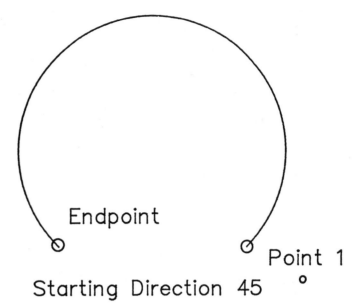

Endpoint

Point 1

Starting Direction 45°

Start Point/Endpoint/Start Direction ARC

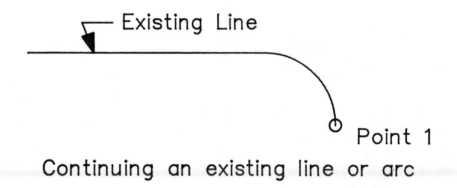

Existing Line

Point 1

Continuing an existing line or arc

The area and perimeter calculations are then stored as both AREA and PERIMETER system variables and may be accessed by SETVAR or AutoLISP.

AutoCAD Version 2.6 update notes: The initial prompt for the AREA command is now:

<First point>/Entity/Subtract:

Version 2.6 allows you to extract the area of a circle or polyline by just pointing at it. Select the Entity option to use this feature. This even works with open polylines; the area is assumed to be closed off with a straight line. Remember that fat polylines are defined by their centerline. The AREA command will give you the area up to the centerline for such polylines.

Under Version 2.6 you can also keep a running total of areas. When you start the AREA command, it is in "Add" mode with zero total area. It will give you the sum of all areas measured in Add mode. You can toggle it into Subtract mode from the initial prompt if it is already in Add mode, and vice versa. Areas computed in Subtract mode will be deducted from the running total.

To exit the AREA command, give it a [Return]. This will require changing any existing AREA macros created for older versions of AutoCAD.

Arithmetic Expressions—(See AutoLISP.) The latest versions of AutoCAD have been provided with the ability to use variables in doing input. See AutoLISP.

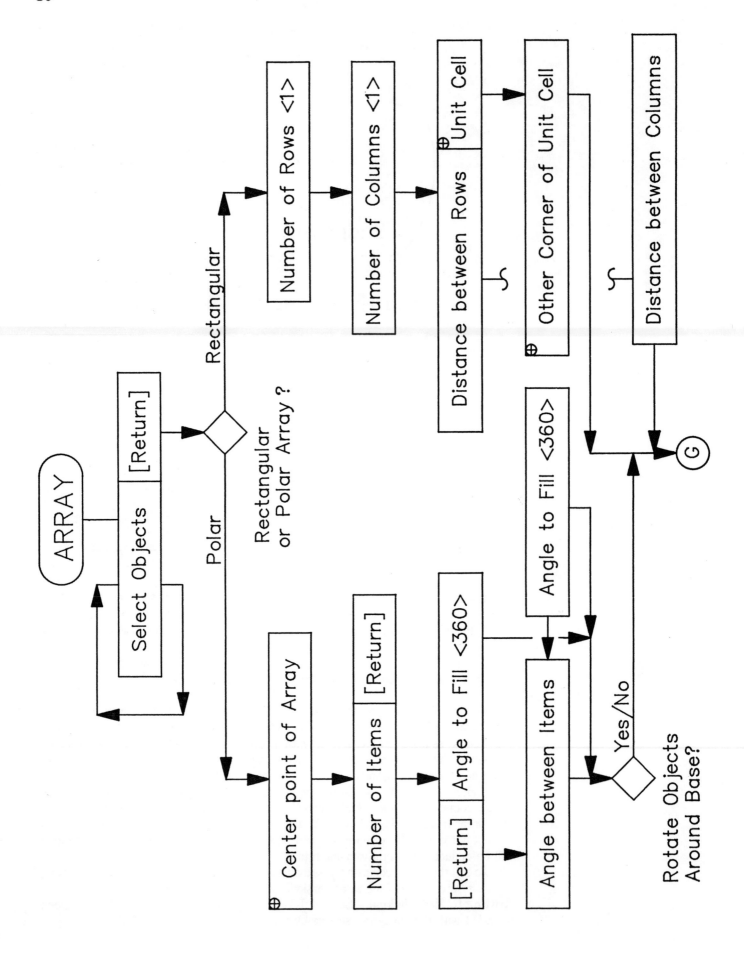

ARRAY Command—An object or group of objects in AutoCAD can be replicated in a regular, rectangular or round pattern to form what is called an *array*. Enter ARRAY, and then select objects (See ''Selecting Objects''). You will then be asked whether you want a rectangular *R* or polar *P* array.

As a general rule, note that whenever AutoCAD asks for a number of rows or columns or items, it is asking for the TOTAL count, including the original item.

After selecting R, for a rectangular array, you will be asked for the number of rows and columns. (Rows are horizontal, columns are vertical.) If you don't specify the number of rows or the number of columns, AutoCAD will assume a default value of one. The next prompt asks for

Unit cell or distance between rows:

The unit cell will define a rectangle whose width corresponds to the distance between columns and whose height is the distance between rows. Just enter a point where the first object is situated and then a second point in the direction you wish the array to be formed, displaced from the first point by exactly one column and one row. This is the surest way of specifying rectangular arrays; you are less likely to have the array built in a direction you are not expecting, which is usually a nasty surprise.

If you respond to the initial prompt by entering a number from the keyboard for the distance between rows (that is, vertically), you will then be asked to supply the distance between columns (that is, horizontally). If both the row and column distances are specified positive, the array will be built up and to the right of the first object. That is:

Row Distance	Column Distance	Resulting Array is Built
positive	positive	Up and to the right
positive	negative	Up and to the left
negative	positive	Down and to the right
negative	negative	Down and to the left.

Polar (round) arrays are a little trickier. The results can be quite different, depending on whether the objects being arrayed are blocks or separate entities.

After entering P for polar array, you will be asked to locate the center of the array. Next, you will be asked to enter the number of items in the array. (If you don't know the number but know the angular separation between items and how large an angle must be filled, hit [Return] and then supply those angles. AutoCAD will calculate the number of items for you.) After entering the number of items, provide either the angle to fill *or* the angle between items, but not both. To bypass the angle-to-fill, enter a zero and then provide the angular separation when prompted.

The array will be constructed counterclockwise from the first object about the center point, unless you specify otherwise by entering a negative angle for the angle-to-fill or the angle between objects.

For any polar array, the last prompt asks whether you wish the objects rotated as they are arrayed. If you answer ''no,'' you will usually find that it is best if the object(s) you are arraying have been blocked. Otherwise the relative arrangement of the individual pieces will probably be altered as the array progresses. This is because each object will have a different *handle* when AutoCAD determines the distance from it to the center of the array. Typical handles (or reference points) for various objects follow:

Arcs	Center point
Blocks	Insertion base point
Circles	Center point
Lines	One of the ends
Shapes	Insertion base point
Text	Starting point
Traces	One of the ends

To maintain the relative orientations of each entity, BLOCK the group and reINSERT it before creating the array.

Version 2.6 notes. When you use the ARRAY command on associative dimensioned entities to form a rotated polar array, the dimension set will adapt to suit, regenerated according to the latest settings of the dimensioning variables.

The ARRAY command can be used with 3D lines or faces, but will not change any Z coordinates. Only the X and Y coordinates will be manipulated.

ATTDEF Command—(See Chapter 10 on Attributes)

ATTDISP Command—(See Chapter 10 on Attributes)

ATTEDIT Command—(See Chapter 10 on Attributes)

ATTEXT Command—(See Chapter 10 on Attributes)

Attributes—(See Chapter 10 on Attributes)

AutoCAD can put information about a block into the drawing containing that block. Each insertion of the block can have its own separate set of data, or the data can be the same for all of that block's insertions. See the Attributes Chapter.

AutoLISP—The latest versions of AutoCAD allow you to enter a variable name when prompted for input. That is, instead of giving a number or a string of letters, you can provide a variable name which has been defined using AutoLISP functions. AutoCAD will process the information and execute the command using the correct value for the variable. This is only one of many AutoLISP features. There is insufficient room to include full coverage of AutoLISP here; a separate volume on the subject will be forthcoming.

For more information, see the AutoLISP Programmers Reference provided by Autodesk with copies of AutoCAD. AutoLISP allows you to create new AutoCAD commands to do specialized applications.

AXIS—(See also GRID)

AXIS Command—AutoCAD's ADE-1 uses the AXIS command to display a ruler line along the edges of the graphics area on the monitor. The spacing of the ticks along the ruler may be specified.

After entering AXIS, you will be prompted with several choices:

Tick spacing X X or ON/OFF/Snap/Aspect <current>:

You can set the spacing by entering a number, make the number a multiple of the Snap resolution by entering an X following a number, or change the status of the ruler line with either ON or OFF.

By specifying a spacing of zero, or by choosing the Snap option, you can lock the tick spacing to the current Snap resolution. If you do this, when you change the Snap resolution, the ruler lines will adjust automatically.

The Aspect option allows you to have different tick spacings on the horizontal and vertical ruler lines, unless you're using an Isometric Snap style.

ZOOMing out or a small tick spacing may create ticks too dense to see, in which case AutoCAD will display, "Axis ticks too close to display." Invoke the AXIS command and specify larger spacing if you want to display the ruler lines.

If you're using a feet-and-inches display format, some of the ticks may be double in size, indicating whole inches or whole feet. This will only occur if the specified spacing is an exact fraction of an inch or foot.

SETVAR and AutoLISP can also be used to control the axes.

B

Backup *.bak* Files—AutoCAD automatically makes a backup copy of your drawing every time the drawing in progress is SAVEd or ENDed. The old version of the file, (say, wombat.dwg) is renamed as the backup copy (wombat.bak). The newly saved version becomes the drawing file (wombat.dwg). In this way, if anything happens to the .dwg file, there is still a chance to recover the prior version. To process the .bak file, you should first make another copy on a floppy. Then rename the .bak file as .dwg and process it in AutoCAD.

Warning: This backup feature of AutoCAD is *not* a substitute for properly backing up your drawing files onto separate floppy disks every four to eight working hours. A file is not backed up unless it exists in at least two different places. If you do not have an extra copy on a separate floppy disk, and something happens to your working disk, you are up the proverbial creek. Hard drives *do* fail. Floppy disks can be lost, stolen, erased, formatted, or damaged, taking away your .dwg file *and* the .bak file in one fell swoop. Human nature being what it is, you will not pay any attention to this warning until you have lost at least one precious file and had to recreate it completely.

BASE Command—(See also BLOCK and INSERT.) Let's say you are doing a series of drawings of bicycles. You don't want to redraw the drive sprocket every time you start a new bicycle, so you make a separate drawing of the drive sprocket. The BASE command is used to give the sprocket drawing a *handle,* that is, a base insertion point, located right in the center of the sprocket. When you draw each new version of your bicycle, you can insert ''sprocket.dwg'' into it at the appropriate spot. The sprocket will be centered on whatever spot you insert it.

Enter BASE, and provide the new base point when prompted. If you don't use the BASE command, the base point will be 0,0.

Version 2.6 notes: BASE will now work with three dimensional points, either by entering the new base point from the keyboard or by snapping to the new base point with an object snap.

BASELINE Subcommand—(See DIM Command.)

BLIPMODE Command—When you enter points to select entities or locations on the screen, you will notice little crosses at those points. These are temporary marker blips that can be turned off, if desired, by entering BLIPMODE and then OFF.

To turn the blips on again, enter BLIPMODE and then ON. The initial BLIPMODE setting is determined by the original drawing and the setting can be changed at any time. In most cases, BLIPMODE will be on, the default for AutoCAD's standard drawing.

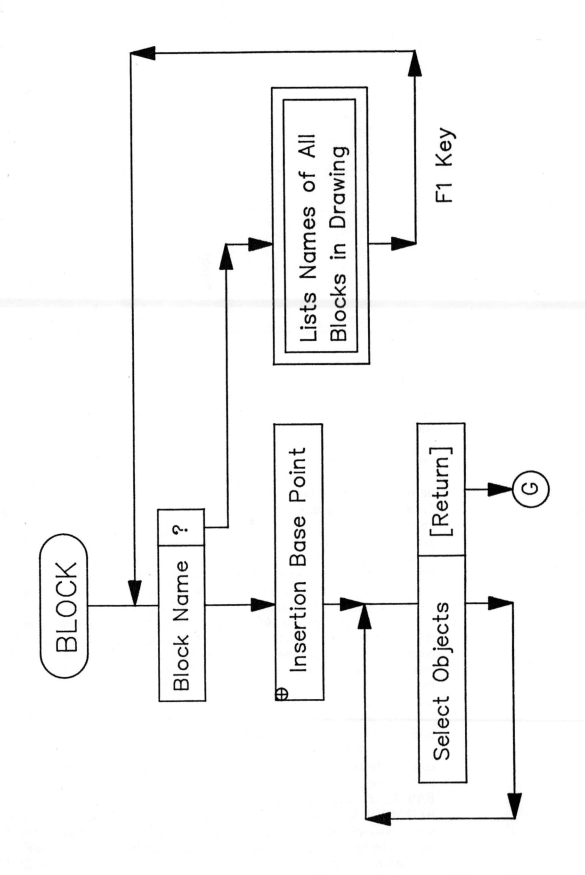

Temporary marker blips will be erased by any command that regenerates or redraws the drawing, i.e., REDRAW, REGEN, PAN, ZOOM, VIEW, etc.

BLOCK Command—(See also INSERT.) The BLOCK command is probably the most powerful feature of AutoCAD. With the use of the INSERT command, BLOCK permits rapid duplication of a group of items, with the ability to stretch the group in the X or Y direction and alter the angle of the group.

§ Enter BLOCK, then provide the block name of up to 31 characters as prompted. If you reply with a ? for block name, AutoCAD will respond with the names of all the blocks contained in the drawing.

§ If you provide a name which has already been used, you will be reminded that the block already exists, and asked if you want to redefine it. If you answer "yes," you can continue with the BLOCK command; when the block has been redefined, the drawing will regenerate and revise all insertions of the block with that name, except as noted below.

§ After providing a block name, you will be asked to provide an *insertion base point.* This is the handle that will be used to define where the block is inserted relative to the point where you insert it in the drawing; usually the handle will be dead center in symmetrical objects; sometimes the lower left or other corner is used as the base point. If the block is rotated during insertion, it will be rotated about the base point.

§ Select the objects that will comprise the block. (See Selecting Objects).

§ Objects that have been BLOCKed will disappear from the drawing. To restore them, enter OOPS.

Note the following about blocks:

§ Insertions of a block are a single entity and can't be partly erased, except as noted below.

§ Using blocks in a drawing reduces the file size considerably, because the entire description of the block is not repeated. Only the layer, location, orientation and any stretching of the block are recorded for each insertion. On a typical drawing, the file size might be reduced by a factor of two to four, or more. Not all CAD systems have this feature.

§ Blocks created on layer "0" will be placed on the current working layer when they are inserted. Blocks created on any other layer (or layers) will remain on that layer (or layers). The use of multiple layers and colors within a block is possible, though not always advisable.

§ For special handling of colors and linetypes in blocks, see the BYBLOCK and BYLAYER commands.

§ Redefinition of a block in a drawing will change all insertions of the block in that drawing into the new form. This *global* change is very useful where there has been a revision made to a component that occurs in many places in a drawing. Note that any other drawings containing the unrevised block must also be updated individually, either by editing, or by inserting a copy of the redefined block into them (See INSERT Command).

§ If necessary, blocks can contain other blocks. This should be avoided unless it will save significant drawing time; these *nested* blocks can create problems if it ever becomes necessary to translate to other CAD systems.

§ As explained under INSERT, a block inserted with an asterisk * ahead of the block name will be replicated in its entirety in the drawing database: every line, arc, trace, etc. These insertions of the block can be edited; they will *not* be globally updated by redefinition of the block used to create them.

BREAK Command—Part of a Line, Trace, Circle, Arc, or Polyline can be erased with the BREAK command. After entering BREAK, choose the object to be broken, and point to the desired break points. Selecting the object can be done with any selection method. If you point to an object, AutoCAD assumes the point is the place you want to begin the break. If it isn't, type *F*irst so you can choose the first point.

The second point can be anywhere near the object and AutoCAD will find the object's closest point to make the break. Repeating the same point for both the first and last points will result in splitting the object into two objects without erasing anything.

If you expect difficulty in hitting the exact same point twice, use a relative coordinate point from the keyboard when prompted for the second point: @0,0. (Just plain @[Return] will also work.)

When the two break points are not the same, BREAK will have the following effects:

A line will be split in two, if both points are within the ends of the line; the end of the line will be cut off if either point is at the end of the line, or if the second point is beyond either end.

Broken ends of a trace will be cut square.

Circles become arcs by counterclockwise erasing from the first to the second point.

Arcs, like lines, will be split in two if both points are within the ends of the arc; the end of the arc will be cut off if either point is at the end of the arc, or if the second point is beyond either end.

Polylines break in much the same way as lines and arcs. Be careful that the second point is not too far from the end you want to cut off. Ends will be cut square.

If you break a polyline to which a curve has been fit, the curve fit information will become permanent. You now can't decurve this polyline.

Closed polylines are broken as AutoCAD erases the portion between the specified points.

Breaks in closed polylines always result in an open polyline.

Button Menu—(See the section on Macros & Menus.) AutoCAD supports several digitizer tablets that have more than one button on the puck. Menus can be created to utilize these buttons to execute macros.

BYBLOCK Subcommand—(See also COLOR and LINETYPE Commands.) When setting colors or linetypes for subsequent entities, you can enter BYBLOCK instead of a specific color or linetype. This will cause new objects to be drawn in white (if setting color) or with continuous linetype (if setting linetype) until they are blocked, at this point they will revert to the color or linetype of the block insertion.

Note: As a rule, you should avoid having colors or linetypes set both for individual objects and by layer in the same drawing. Strange things can happen when using blocks made up of objects whose color and/or linetype are set by more than one method.

BYLAYER Subcommand—(See also COLOR and LINETYPE Commands.) When setting colors or linetypes for subsequent entities, you can enter BYLAYER instead of a specific color or linetype. This will cause new objects to be drawn in the color or linetype assigned to the layer that they are drawn on.

Note: As a rule, you should avoid having colors or linetypes set both for individual objects and by layer in the same drawing. Strange things can happen when using blocks made up of objects whose color and/or linetype are set by more than one method.

C

CENTER Subcommand—(See DIM Command.)

CHAMFER Command—(See also FILLET.) CHAMFER trims two intersecting lines, or two straight segments of a polyline, at a specified distance and generates a new line to connect the trimmed edges. When you enter CHAMFER, you will be prompted to point to the first line and then the second. The initial prompt is:

Polyline/Distance/<Select first line>:

You can also respond with distances, expressed in drawing units by entering *D*istance. You will then be prompted for the first and then the second distance values. These values will be stored and used for future CHAMFER commands until you make a change.

Figure GL-13 gives an example of CHAMFERing using the *D*istance option:

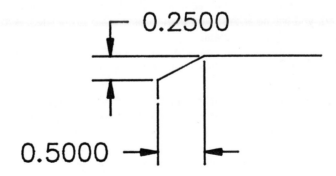

Unequal chamfer distances

An entire polyline can be chamfered at all vertices by responding with *P*olyline. You will be asked to select a single polyline. You will then be prompted for distance values and AutoCAD will tell you how many lines will be chamfered.

Figure GL-14 gives an example of chamfering an entire polyline:

87

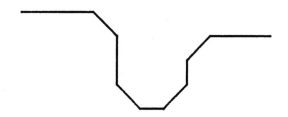

Polyline chamfer

CHANGE Command—If entities in a drawing need to be altered, it is usually faster to use the CHANGE command, rather than to erase and reinsert them. The CHANGE command works as follows:

(1) Enter *CHANGE*.

(2) Select the objects to change. (See Selecting Objects for instructions on how to do this.) Be careful not to pick too many objects: if you are going to give AutoCAD a change point, all line entities picked will be altered to pass through that point. Be careful also not to select too many different kinds of objects, to avoid confusion.

(3) The options next presented are: Properties/<change points>. The command will progress differently, depending on what you do at that point: see (3a) for Properties, (3b) if you choose a change point, or (3c) if you just hit [Return]. (Note that *DRAG* (ADE-2) can be entered at this time to permit dragging objects into place.)

(3a) If *P* is entered, you will be prompted to choose which properties are to be changed:

C to change color. Enter new color.
E to change elevation. Enter new (3D) elevation.
LA to change layer. Enter new layer. Requested layer must already exist.
LT to change linetype. Enter new linetype. Requested linetype must have been loaded.
T to change thickness. Enter a new thickness.

(4a) A null response to a prompt asking for the new value will leave that property unchanged.

(5a) After each option selection has been carried out, and the new value for that property entered, you will be asked if you wish to alter other properties. A null response will terminate the *CHANGE* command.

(3b) If you enter a point in response to the Properties/<change point> prompt, AutoCAD will alter object(s) according to the following rules:

Lines: The endpoint nearest the point entered will move to that point. If Ortho is on, an orthogonal line will result. If more than one line was selected, all of them will shift to pass through the new change point.

Circles: The circle will be redrawn about the same centerpoint to pass through the point entered. If more than one circle was selected, the change point will be discarded and you will be asked to supply a new radius for any circles.

Text: The text moves to the new location. You will then be prompted for a new text style, height, rotation angle, and text entry. A [Return] retains the old value. Note that text angle and height are entered in the same way as normal text: you either use numbers from the keyboard or use the cursor to show values relative to the text entry point. If more than one text entry was selected, the change point will be discarded and you will be asked to supply the appropriate new data.

Blocks: The block is picked up by its insertion base point and relocated to the new point. A new rotation angle can be entered, similar to an ordinary

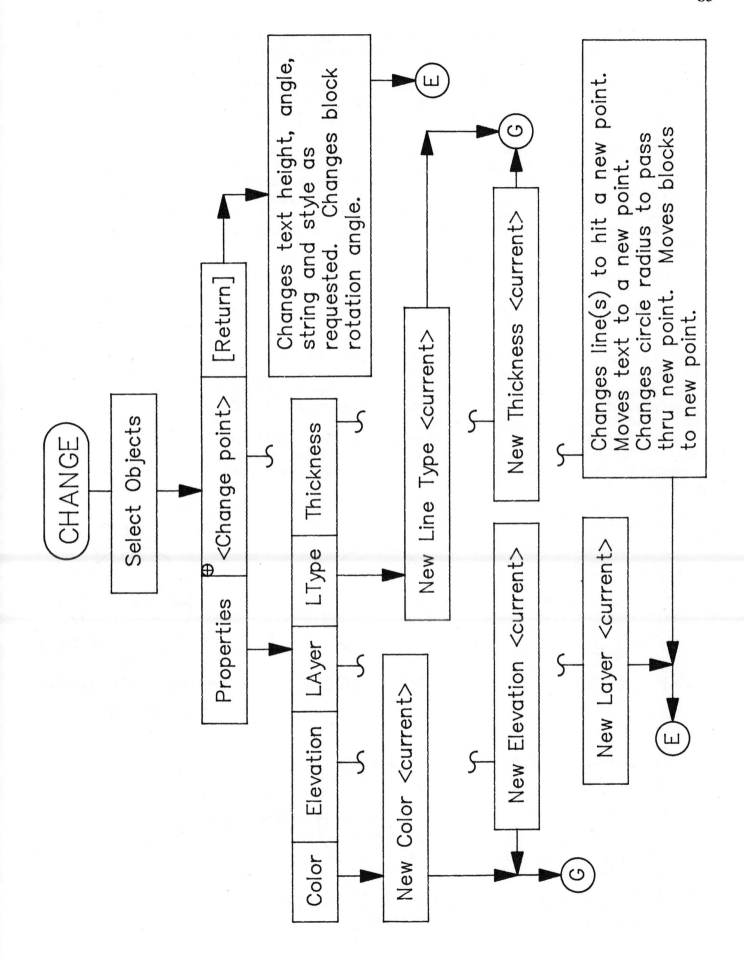

CHANGE

Select Objects

<Change point>

Properties [Return]

Changes text height, angle, string and style as requested. Changes block rotation angle.

Color | Elevation | LAyer | LType | Thickness

New Color <current>

New Elevation <current>

New Line Type <current>

New Thickness <current>

New Layer <current>

Changes line(s) to hit a new point. Moves text to a new point. Changes circle radius to pass thru new point. Moves blocks to new point.

E

G

G

E

INSERTion. If more than one block was selected, the change point will be ignored and you will be prompted for new insertion points and angles.

(3c) If you press [Return] in response to the Properties/<change point> prompt, a single selected text entry, block, or attribute definition will not be relocated but instead can then have its other properties altered, such as text style and string, height, or rotation angle.

Version 2.6 note: The *CHANGE* command can alter 3D lines. If you specify a new Z coordinate for one endpoint, that end will move to match the new Z value. No change will be made in the elevation of that point if only new X and Y values are entered.

CIRCLE—AutoCAD lets you use any of five geometric ways to define a circle: center and radius, center and diameter, two points at the ends of a diameter, tangent to two objects at a given radius, and three points. Each method is begun by entering CIRCLE. The initial prompt is:

3P/2P/TTR/<Center point>:

To draw a center-and-radius circle, enter a point where you want the circle's center, then enter a point where you want the circle's edge.

To draw a center-and-diameter circle, enter a point where you want the circle's center, then enter D. Enter the second point one diameter from the first point.

A two-point circle is begun by entering 2P at the initial prompt. Then enter the point where you want the circle's center, then enter the second point at the circle's diameter.

A three-point circle is begun by entering 3P. Next, enter three points and AutoCAD will construct a circle with all three points on the circumference.

A tangent-tangent-radius circle (ADE-2) is constructed by pointing to two lines or circles (or one of each) and then entering a radius. If these parameters are ambiguous (determine more than one possible circle), the circle nearest the tangent points will be constructed.

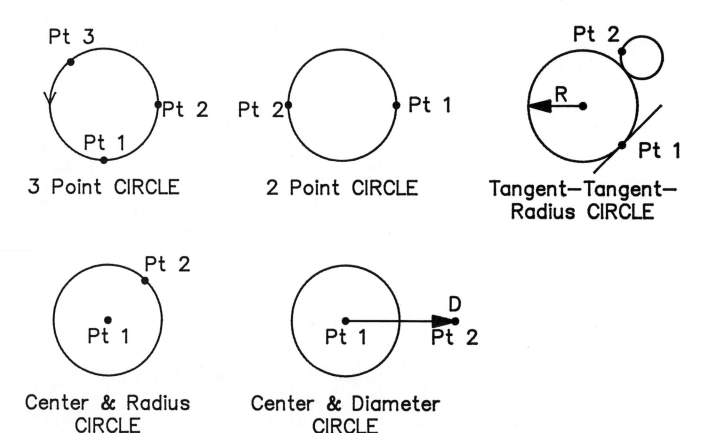

3 Point CIRCLE   2 Point CIRCLE   Tangent–Tangent–Radius CIRCLE

Center & Radius CIRCLE   Center & Diameter CIRCLE

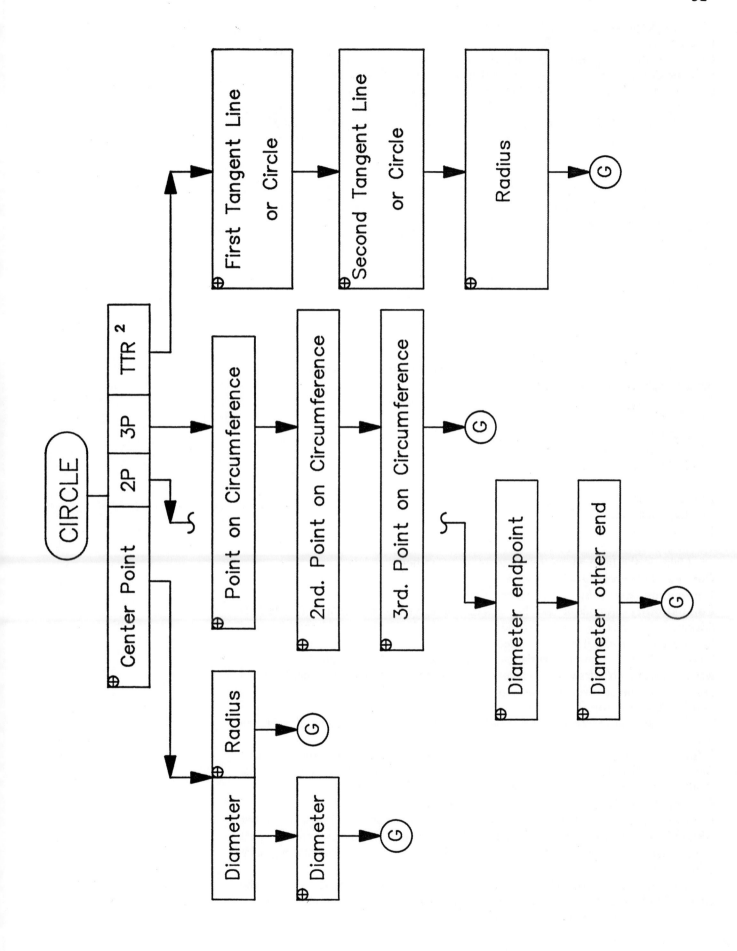

Circular Arrays—(See ARRAY Command.)

Circular Reference—(See Reference, Circular.)

Cleaning up the display—(See REDRAW Command.)

COLOR Command—You can set the working color for creation of new objects by using the COLOR command. Enter *COLOR* and provide a new color number (from 1 to 255) or standard color name, such as *green*. Everything drawn from then on will be in the new color. Instead of specifying a color at the prompt, you may use the *BYLAYER* or *BYBLOCK* subcommands as explained above. To change the color of existing objects, see *CHANGE*.

    Colors:

AutoCAD can recognize 255 different colors. The number of colors and how they are displayed depends on what type of display system you have. The first seven colors have been assigned standard names:

1 - Red
2 - Yellow
3 - Green
4 - Cyan
5 - Blue
6 - Magenta
7 - White

From here on the list varies quite a bit from manufacturer to manufacturer. Typically, the list might continue as follows:

 8 - Grey
 9 - Light red
10 - Light yellow
11 - Light green
12 - Light cyan
13 - Light blue
14 - Light magenta
15 - Light grey

Light, in the table above, refers to intensity, rather than hue.

Commands, entering—(See Entering Commands.)

Commands, External—(See External Commands.)

Compatibility—Autodesk Inc. has maintained upward compatibility of AutoCAD drawings since the early versions of the program. That is, if you have a drawing created by an earlier version, it can be worked on by the later version. The Main Menu has Task 8 available for upward translation, where necessary, as, for example, when you want to insert an old drawing into a new one. Note that once you have touched an old drawing with the new version, you can no longer use the old release of AutoCAD on it—it's a one way trip, even if all you did was plot the drawing.

There are third party programs available to do backwards translations, if you really need to do this.

Compiling—Main Menu Task 7 is used to *compile* shape files into the form that AutoCAD *LOADs* to do text. Shape files are created as ASCII files with a filename like "Gothic.shp". The compiled form will be renamed "Gothic.shx".

Configuring—(See Chapter 2, Configuring AutoCAD.)

Continuing Arcs and Lines—If you wish to continue an arc or a line with another ARC or LINE, enter the appropriate command and hit [Return] at the first prompt. That will establish the endpoint of the most recently drawn line or arc as the starting point of the new item.

Continuing an arc with a line forces the direction of the line to be the same as the ending direction for the arc; only a length of the first segment can be input.

CONTINUE Subcommand—(See DIM Command.)

Converting Old Drawings—(See Translation and Main Menu.)

Coordinates—(See also Polar Coordinates.) The coordinates of a point in AutoCAD follow the conventional notation from geometry. An X and Y value are given for each point, telling the distances of the point from an origin point, measured along the X and Y axes. The X and Y axes are perpendicular lines, crossing at the origin, X to the right, Y straight up.

The X and Y coordinates are written with the X value first, then the Y value, separated by a comma. The origin is 0,0, by definition. Drawings usually have the origin at the lower left corner. The upper right corner of a "D-size" drawing would be roughly 34,22. Negative X values are to the left of the origin; negative Y values are below the origin. If you don't understand all of this, see a text book on plane geometry or algebra.

The coordinates of the cursor location are displayed at the top of the screen. These can be toggled off or altered to polar form.

COPY—(See also MIRROR and MOVE.) Selected objects are copied at a specified displacement, leaving the original intact. Orientation and scale will be the same as the original, and each copy can be further manipulated and edited like any entity.

After entering COPY, select the object or objects, then tell AutoCAD the location where you want the copied object to appear by pointing to two locations or by entering an X,Y displacement pair that define the desired displacement. For example, if you enter a point on the object and then a point three inches up and two inches to the right, the copy will appear three inches higher and two inches farther to the right of the first object. If you enter a −2,−2 from the keyboard, the copy will appear two inches down and to the left of the original.

Multiple copies can be made by entering M at the Base point prompt, then responding with one of the new locations each time you're prompted for the Second point of displacement. To use the keyboard for locating copies, enter 0,0 for the Base point and then the X,Y displacements at each Second point prompt. Enter [Return] to end the multiple copy session.

Version 2.6 notes—The COPY command will, when used on 3D entities, change the Z coordinates as specified.

Copying Drawings—(See TABLET Command.)

Crosshatching—(See HATCH Command, plus the section on Custom Hatch Files.)

CRT—This stands for *cathode ray tube*. It means the display or monitor or TV screen on which you view graphics and text.

Cursor—The crosshairs that appear on the AutoCAD screen are called the cursor. The location of the cursor can be controlled by the keyboard or by a mouse or TouchPen™ or, better, by a digitizing tablet.

The cursor can be moved into the screen menu area by moving the puck or other pointing device to the right until part of the menu is highlighted. Move the cursor up or down to highlight the desired item. Pressing the *select button* on the pointing device will activate the highlighted command.

If you don't have a pointing device, you can control the cursor from the keyboard, using the cursor keys plus the following keys:

[Insert]	Places cursor in screen menu area
[Delete]	Aborts cursor
[Home]	Switches to tablet or mouse cursor
[Page Up]	Increases cursor movement produced with cursor keys
[Page Down]	Decreases cursor movement produced with cursor keys

The shape of the cursor changes when you are in Isometric mode, indicating which Isoplane you are working in. See SNAP and ISOPLANE Commands. When using object snaps, a small target box will appear at the intersection of the crosshairs. See OSNAP.

Curve fitting—(See Polylines.)

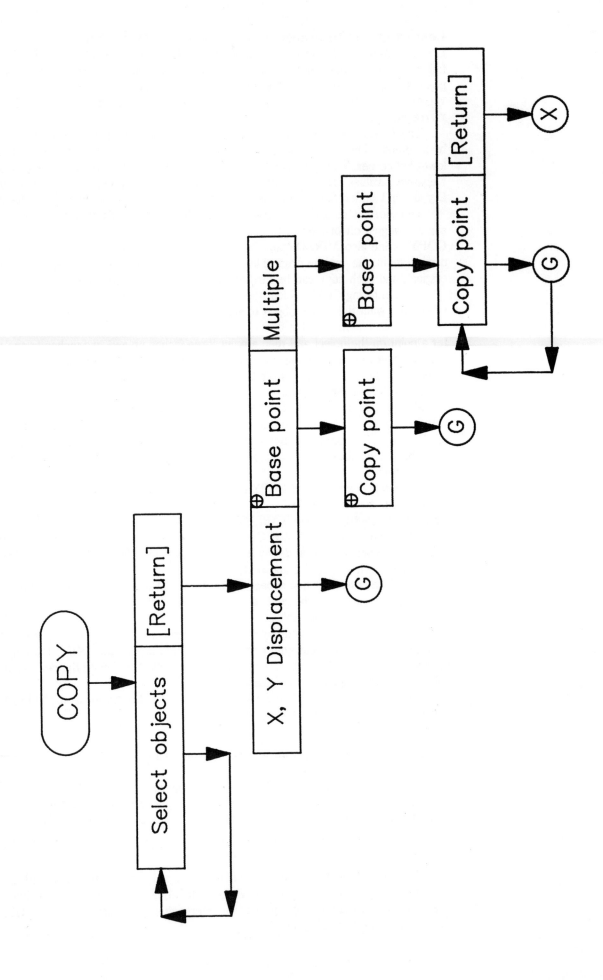

D

Date and Time—(See TIME Command.)

DBLIST Command—Lists information about every drawing entity. DBLIST is an excellent training and debugging tool. DBLIST can be interrupted with [CTRL] C. [CTRL] S will cause the listing to pause on the screen; any key can be used to restart the display. The list can be sent to a printer with [CTRL] Q. The output might take quite a long time to print or display, depending on the size of the drawing.

Default—This is the value or entry that AutoCAD will use if you don't specify a value. The default is shown in pointy brackets after the prompt. For example, if you are using the INSERT command, the initial prompt is: Block name (or ?) < *gezeets >:. If you press [Return] without entering anything, AutoCAD will repeat the last block inserted, in this case, it is a gezeets inserted with an asterisk. In this book, the default values are called out where significant. It is assumed that you will read the prompt and take advantage of the default values as much as possible.

DELAY Command—(See Scripts.) This command in a script file will pause the execution of the script in order for people to be able to see what is going on. Example: DELAY 1000 will halt the script for roughly 1000 milliseconds.

Deleting drawings—(See also Main Menu and *FILES* Command.) Obsolete drawings can be purged in DOS, through the Main Menu File Utilities option, or by use of the *FILES* command. See those categories for more information.

One suggestion: Don't use the DEL command in DOS. This is too close to the *DIR* command. Imagine your surprise when you look up at your CRT some day and see that you, speedy typist that you are, have just entered *"DEL *.dwg"* instead of *"DIR *.dwg"*! (Time to whip out your Norton.) Use the good old CPM form of the command: ERASE.

Deleting objects—(See *ERASE* and *PURGE*.)

Digitizer Tablet—(See Tablet Menus, *TABLET* Command.)

Digitizing—This refers to *tracing* an existing drawing using the puck on a digitizer tablet that has been calibrated using the TABLET command. See *TABLET*.

DIM Command—(ADE-1.) It is assumed that if you need to do dimensioning, you already know what extension lines, tolerances, leaders, center marks, and so forth, are. If not, a drafting text book will clarify terms for you, along with any of the following that is not clear in context.

Enter DIM to begin dimensioning. AutoCAD will replace the normal *Command:* prompt with *Dim:* to remind you that you are in dimensioning mode. The commands listed below create dimensioning. Only the first three letters of each need be entered.

While the Dim: prompt is up, you will find that normal AutoCAD commands do not work, except for the following:

REDRAW works just as in normal drawing.

STATUS will work, but the output is not the normal status screen, but a summary of all of the dimensioning toggles and variable settings.

STYLE allows you to change the style of dimension text.

UNDO steps you back through the dimensioning work you have just done, but will not *UNDO* drawing until you *EXIT*.

The toggles (function keys for *GRID* on/off, *SNAP* on/off, etc.,) will work as usual, as will object snap modes.

Some additional utility commands for dimensioning are:

CENTER draws center lines for a circle or arc.

LEADER draws a line, very much like the LINE command, except that an arrow is placed at the first (*leader start*) point. Start from the object to be dimensioned, and move toward where you want the dimension data placed. Hit [Return] without moving the cursor when you reach the point where you want to place the text.

EXIT will end dimensioning and put you back to draw mode, as will [CTRL] C.

AutoCAD's semi-automatic dimensioning will do four kinds of dimensioning: Linear, Angular, Diametrical, and Radial.

RADIUS calls up radial dimensioning. Select a circle or arc; AutoCAD will prompt with the measured radius. Hit [Return] to take the default value, or enter the desired value. If the text does not fit into the circle, AutoCAD will ask you where it is supposed to place the dimension. A center mark will be added if the dimensioning variable *"DIMCEN"* is toggled *ON*. (See below, under dimensioning variables.)

DIAMETER invokes diametrical dimensioning. Select an arc or circle. You will be prompted to supply dimension text; the default shown will be the measured diameter. Press [Return] or enter your own value. If the text doesn't fit, you will be asked where to put it.

ANGULAR starts angle dimensioning. Select two nonparallel lines, then supply a location for the arc. You will be prompted to enter the dimension text with the measured angle shown as the default. Next, provide a location for placement of the text; the default for the text location is in the middle of the arc. If the text will not fit, you will be asked for another location.

UPDATE will take selected existing dimension entities and revise them to match the current dimension variable settings. An UPDATED dimension becomes the Last dimension and can be accessed by *BASELINE, CONTINUE,* and *LEADER* commands.

HOMETEXT lets you move text from an existing dimension to its default location.

NEWTEXT is used to revise the text for existing dimension. If you just hit [Return] and don't enter any text, the existing text will be replaced with the actual computed dimension. See below under dimension text for using < > brackets with this command.

Linear dimensioning can be of several different types and each type is called by its own command:

HORIZONTAL creates a horizontal dimension line.

VERTICAL creates a vertical dimension line.

ALIGNED creates a dimension line parallel to the line determined by the extension line origin points specified.

ROTATED is similar to aligned, except that the user is asked to supply an angle for the rotation of the dimension line.

BASELINE creates a dimension starting from the baseline of the previous dimension, offset enough to miss the previous text.

CONTINUE continues the next dimension from the last extension line of the previous dimension.

The following general methods apply to all types of linear dimensioning:

Dimension text and arrows are normally automatically placed in the middle of the extension lines. If they won't fit, they will be placed outside the extension lines, near the second extension line.

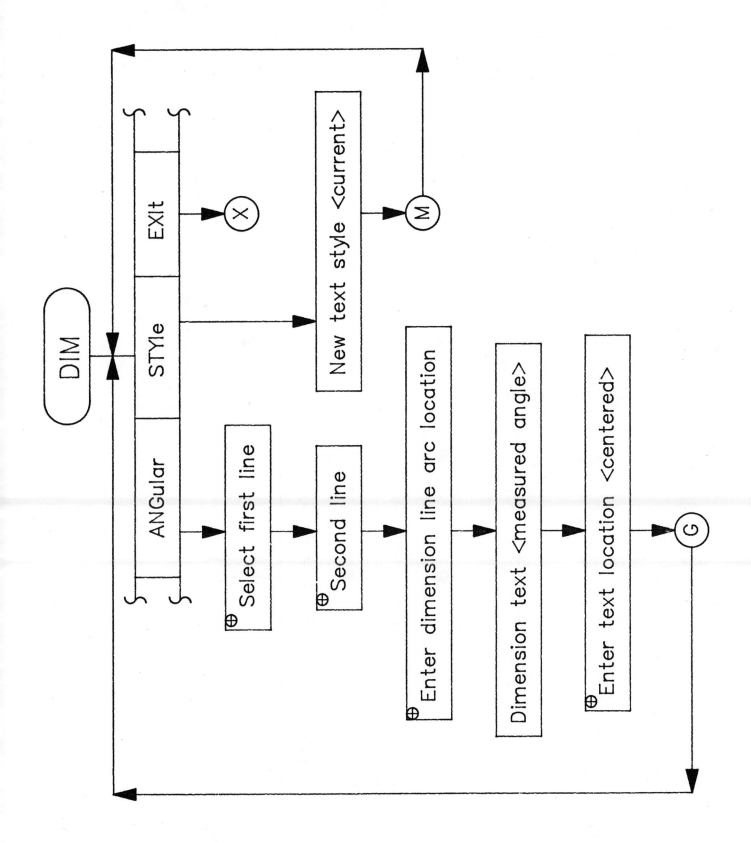

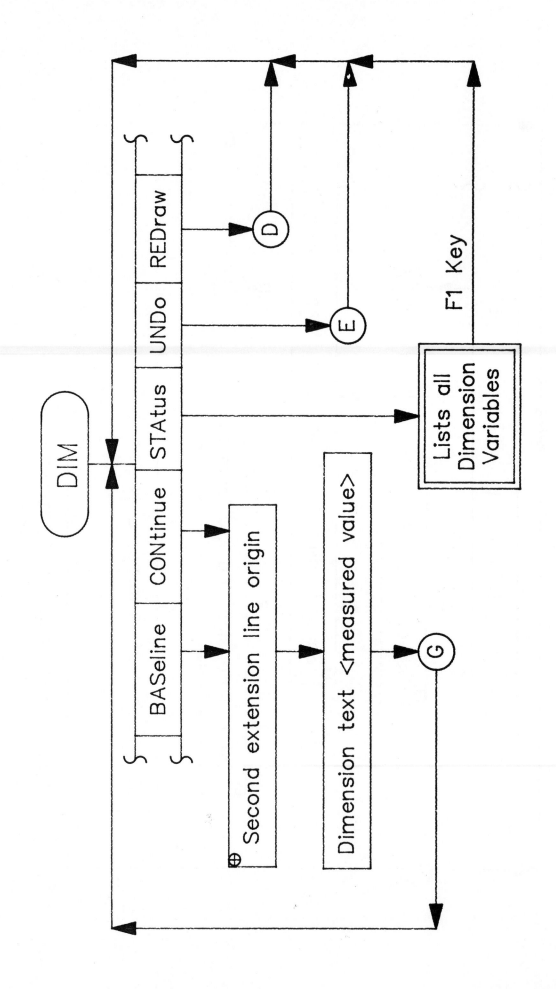

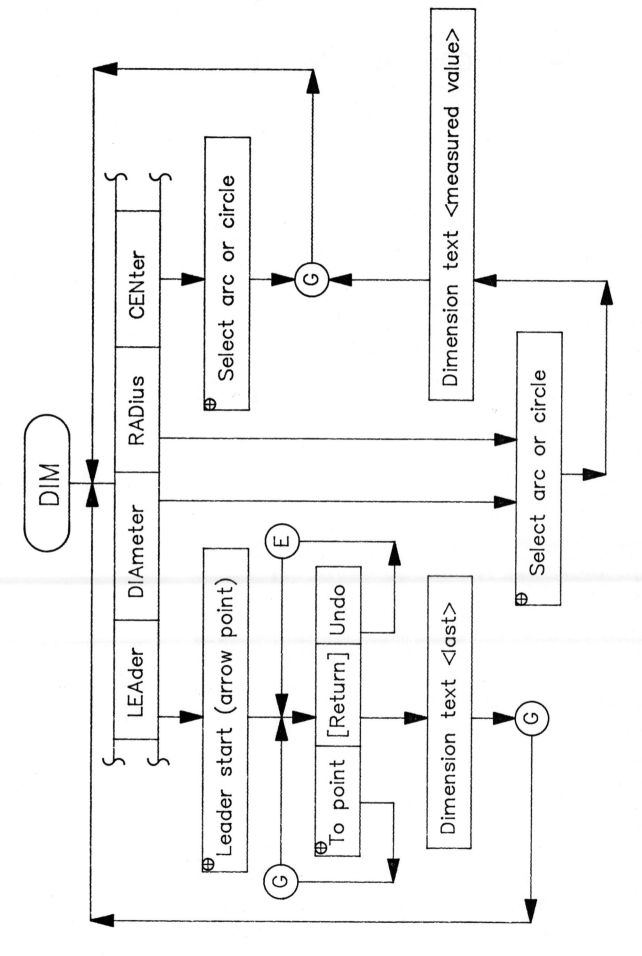

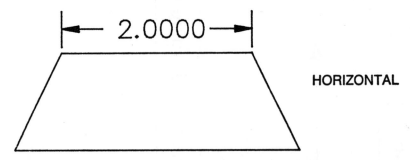

HORIZONTAL

The prompt: "First extension line origin or RETURN to select;" can be answered:

[Return] (or [space bar]) will allow you to select a circle or arc or line by pointing to it. Windowing won't work. Be careful when selecting a circle to dimension with the ALIGNED command: the selection point determines one end of the diameter whose endpoints will be the origins of the extension lines. Extension lines will then be provided automatically.

Responding with a point determines the start point for the first extension line. You will then be asked for: "Second extension line origin:"

Once the extension line origins have been specified, the prompt becomes: *"Dimension line location:"*. Select a point where you want the dimension line to lie. The extension lines will project to fit the parameter.

The next prompt calls for dimension text. The default figure in brackets is the value that AutoCAD has calculated. Hit [Return] to take the default, or enter the desired text from the keyboard. If you enter a space, no text will appear. If you use a pair of brackets < > somewhere in your text, anything before the < > will be added in front of the default text; anything after the < > will be appended to the default text. Example:

Prompt: Dimension text <12.632>:
Reply: About < >, more or less [Return]
Result: About 12.632, more or less

Associative Dimensioning—AutoCAD Version 2.6 has associative dimensioning. Any dimensioning created while the Dimension Variable called "DIMASO" (See below) is on will be associative. That is, if you stretch, scale, rotate, fold, spindle, or mutilate the object dimensioned, the dimensioning will change to match the new angle, size, or whatever. Associative dimensioning sets are each a single entity. To separate them into lines, arcs, arrows and text, use the *EXPLODE* command.

Associative dimensioning works with all of the linear dimensioning commands and with *ANGULAR, RADIUS,* and *DIAMETER. LEADER* and *CENTER* commands do not draw associative dimensioning.

Dimension entities will be modified to match the objects they measure if those objects are operated on by the following commands:

ARRAY (Polar type only)
EXTEND
MIRROR
ROTATE
SCALE
STRETCH
TRIM

Remember to include dimension entities in any selection set used for these commands. The *Crossing* type window is best for grabbing objects along with the dimensioning.

Definition Points—Dimensioning entities are laid out according to the positioning of points that define certain loci within the dimensioning. These points are drawn on a non-plotting layer called *"DEFPOINTS"*. The *DEFPOINTS* layer can be turned off for ease

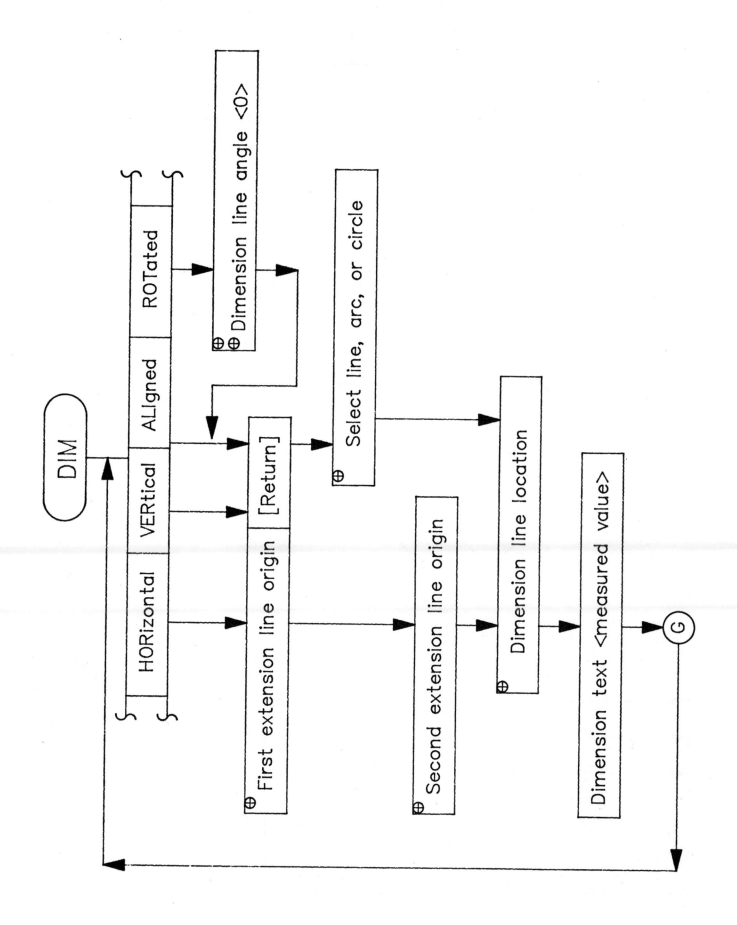

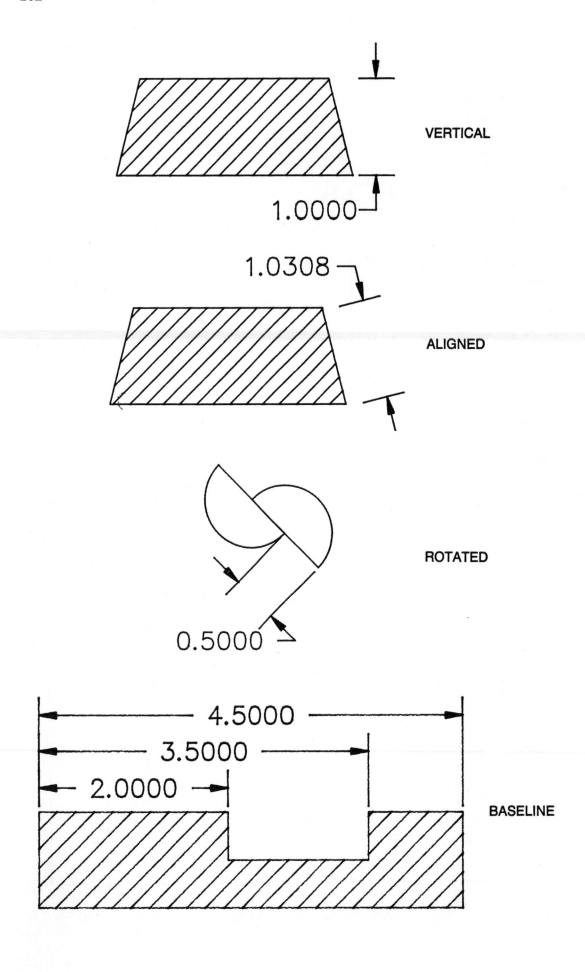

VERTICAL

1.0000

1.0308

ALIGNED

ROTATED

0.5000

4.5000

3.5000

2.0000

BASELINE

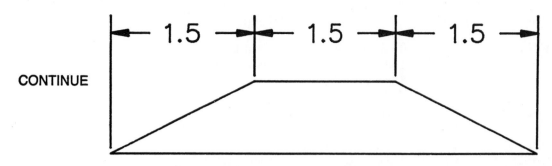

CONTINUE

of locking onto dimension entities (instead of hitting the definition points by mistake), but that layer must be turned on in order to *STRETCH, TRIM,* or *EXTEND* dimensioning.

Here are the locations of the definition points for dimension entities:

ANGULAR dimensioning—The dimension line arc location point, the endpoints of the lines selected to define the dimension required, and the text midpoint.

DIAMETER dimensioning—The selection point on the circle and the opposite end of the diameter line, and the text midpoint.

LINEAR dimensioning—The extension line specification points, the intersection of the dimension line and the first extension line, and the text midpoint.

RADIUS dimensioning—The arc or circle selection point, the center point, and the text midpoint.

Stretching Dimensions—To *STRETCH* dimensioning, make sure that the *DEFPOINTS* layer is on and that you include the necessary definition point(s) in the object selection set Crossing window. If the dimensioned object is affected by the *STRETCH,* the calculated dimension text will be updated automatically.

Extending or Trimming Dimensions—Dimensioning can be *EXTENDED* or *TRIMMED* along with the dimensioned object. If the extension line definition points are not arranged parallel to the dimensioned object, the results will be incorrect. *STRETCH* should be used for this case.

Dimensioning Variables—The format of dimensioning in AutoCAD is controlled by 25 variables stored in a file. They are listed below, along with their initial values. To change any of the settings, enter the name of the variable at the *"Dim:"* prompt. AutoCAD will show you the current value and ask for a new value. Enter a new setting or hit [Return] to leave the current value alone.

Name:	Normal:	Controls:
DIMSCALE	1	Overall scale factor for dim. variables
DIMASZ	0.18	Arrow size
DIMCEN	0.09	Center mark size
DIMEXO	0.0625	Extension line origin offset from entity
DIMDLI	0.38	Dimension line increment for CONTINUE
DIMEXE	0.18	Extension above dimension line
DIMTP	0.	Plus tolerance for DIMTOL OR DIMLIM
DIMTM	0.	Minus tolerance for DIMTOL OR DIMLIM
DIMTXT	0.18	Text height
DIMTSZ	0.	Tick size (arrows used if = zero)
DIMRND	0.	Round dims.to nearest x drawing units
DIMDLE	0.	Dim. line extension if ticks on (w. DIMTSZ)
DIMTOL	OFF	Show dim. tolerances (using DIMTP, DIMTM)
DIMLIM	OFF	Show dim. limits (using DIMTP, DIMTM)
DIMTIH	ON	Text inside extensions is horizontal
DIMTOH	ON	Text outside extensions is horizontal
DIMSE1	OFF	Suppress the first extension line
DIMSE2	OFF	Suppress the second extension line
DIMTAD	OFF	Place text above the dimension line

Name:	Normal:	Controls:
DIMZIN	0	0 = Omit 0 feet, 0 inches exactly
		1 = Include 0 feet, 0 inches exactly
		2 = Include 0 feet
		3 = Include exactly 0 inches
DIMALT	OFF	Alternate units selected (e.g., 12″[30.48])
DIMALTF	25.4	Alt. units scale factor (e.g., in. to mm.)
DIMALTD	2	Alternate units decimal places
DIMASO	ON	Makes associative dimension entities
DIMLFAC	1	Global scale factor for all dim. measurements
DIMBLK	(.)	Arrow block name (e.g., DOT)
DIMSHO	OFF	Enables dragging of dimension calculation
DIMPOST	none	Puts a suffix after the dimension
DIMAPOST	none	Puts a suffix after the alternate dimension

DIM1 Command—This form of the DIM command is used when you are going to do only one dimensioning operation and then go back to normal drawing.

Directories—Hard drives usually are divided into directories and subdirectories, rather than having all the files in the main (root) directory. Things slow down a lot after you have put about 100 files into a directory. It is also a little easier to clean up your disk drive if you put related items into their own directory.

For example, suppose you are doing some drawings for an architect. If you create all of these drawings in a directory by themselves, when the project is complete you can copy them out from that directory onto floppies by *"copy *.dwg a:,"* instead of having to copy them one at a time. You can also clean them off the hard drive, once they have been backed up, by ''erase *.dwg''. For more information, see ''Path Names.''

Display—This refers to the screen or CRT that allows you to view computer text and graphics.

DIST Command—The DIST Command measures the angle and distance between designated points and displays the distance in drawing units.

The calculated distance is stored as a *DISTANCE* system variable and can be accessed by *SETVAR* or AutoLISP.

Version 2.6 note: The *DIST* command now will work with 3D entities.

DIVIDE Command—(See also MEASURE.) Lines, arcs, circles, and polylines can be divided into a specified number of equal parts using *DIVIDE*. (This doesn't really split the object into pieces. To do that you must use the *BREAK* command.) Marker *POINTs*, or *BLOCKs* as described below, are placed at the dividing points created along the object.

After entering *DIVIDE*, select a single object by pointing. You can choose to divide the object into between 2 and 32,767 segments. When the number is entered, *POINT* entities will be placed along the object. These *POINTs* can be used for object snap points for subsequent constructions.

Responding to the initial prompt with *B*lock lets you enter the name of a currently defined *BLOCK* within the drawing. That *BLOCK* will be placed along the *DIVIDEd* object instead of marker points. You then can choose to have the *BLOCK* rotated around its insertion point to match the tangent line of the entity at each point by answering *Yes* at the prompt, or *No* for no rotation.

DONUT Command—The *DONUT* command lets you draw circles and rings that are filled. After entering the command, you will be prompted for an inside diameter and then an outside diameter. The diameters of the most recent *DONUT* are displayed as defaults that can be taken by hitting [Return] at the prompt. Designate two points to register each diameter or enter a numeric value. To draw a filled circle, enter zero for the inside diameter.

After you have specified the diameters, you will be prompted for the center points of the *DONUT*(s). *DONUT* center points can be dragged, allowing you to preview its

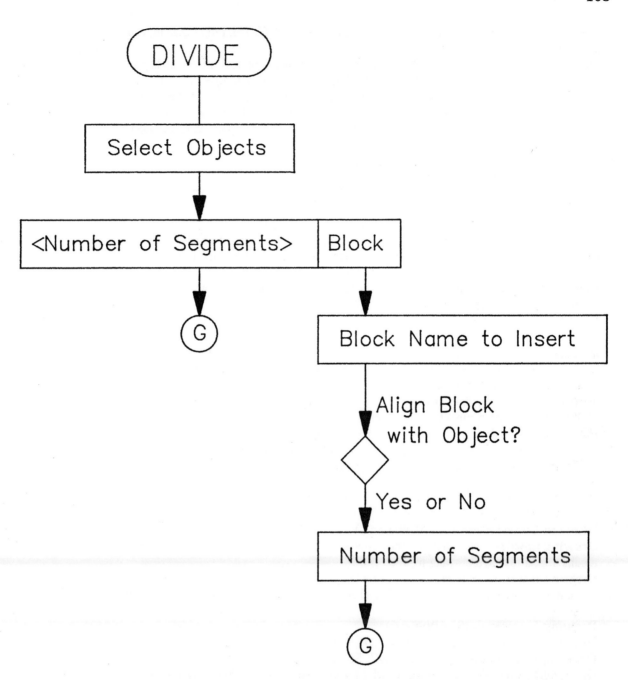

orientation relative to other objects. Hitting [Return] will cause a *DONUT* to be drawn at each point chosen. A null response to the prompt will end the command.

Since *DONUTs* are actually closed polylines, they can be edited with *PEDIT* and any other polyline edit command. *"FILL"* must be on for the *DONUT* to appear as a solid ring.

DOS File Names—The DOS file-naming convention under PC or MS-DOS consists of the following: each name can have from one to eight characters, followed by a period and from one to three suffix (*extension*) characters. Characters can be any letter or number, upper or lowercase (although DOS will convert the file name to uppercase.) Additional allowable characters are the hyphen (-), underline (__), and dollar sign ($).

DOUGHNUT Command—This version of the *DONUT* command is provided by AutoCAD for people who don't know how to spell *DONUT.*

Dragging—This refers to moving an entity around the screen with the cursor before final placement. In some cases, as in *MOVE,* the entire object will move; in other cases, the object can be ROTATEd about its insertion point, or *STRETCH*ed, rather than moved in its entirety. See *DRAGMODE*.

DRAGMODE Command—(ADE-2) This command toggles on and off the ability to *DRAG* objects. The initial prompt is: *ON/OFF/Auto < current setting >*. If you enter A for Automatic, every operation that supports dragging will automatically start dragging the object(s) affected. If you reply ON, you can initiate dragging by entering *DRAG* at the appropriate step when you are in a command that can be dragged. Replying OFF will stop all dragging.

Commands that can be dragged include:

Command	Can drag	Enter DRAG at prompt for:
ARC	Last parameter	Last parameter
CHANGE	New location	Change point for dragging all items
		New location for individual items
CIRCLE	Radius	(Automatic)
COPY	Displacement	Base point or displacement
DONUT	Center point	Center of Donut
ELLIPSE	Eccentricity	Other axis distance/Rotation
		Rotation around major axis
INSERT	Insertion point	Insertion point
	X/Y scale factors	X scale factor; Corner point
	Rotation angle	Rotation angle
MIRROR	Mirror line angle	Second point
MOVE	Displacement	Base point or displacement
POLYGON	Radius	(Automatic)
	Size	Second endpoint of edge
ROTATE	Rotation angle	Rotation angle/Reference
SCALE	Scale factor	Scale factor/Reference
STRETCH	New location point	New point

Drawing Conversion—(See Main Menu.)

Drawing Editor—This AutoCAD term refers to the part of the program that creates, modifies, and displays drawing files.

Drawing Extents—This refers to the rectangular space that will just barely enclose all the entities placed in the drawing so far. This can be larger or smaller than the Drawing Limits.

Drawing Insertion—(See *INSERT*.)

Drawing Insertion Point—(See *WBLOCK, BASE* Commands.)

Drawing Interchange File—(See *DXF* File.)

Drawing Limits—The space within which you intend to draw. See *LIMITS*.

Drawing Names—Drawing names must follow the DOS naming convention as described under DOS File Names, above. The file type, or suffix, is always .dwg. Note that once you are within AutoCAD, the .dwg extension is assumed automatically and should not be entered when you are prompted for a drawing name.

Drawing Regeneration—This is the recalculation of the drawing floating point database to produce integer pixel assignments needed for the display image. See also *REGEN*.

Drawing Units—(See *UNITS*.)

DTEXT Command—(See also *TEXT*.) This stands for Dynamic Text. Normal *TEXT* entry in AutoCAD involves typing in a line of text and hitting [Return] before the text is placed on the screen. When using the *DTEXT* form, each character is placed on the display as it is typed. It can be backspaced out, if needed. Regardless of the type of justification specified, all text will be displayed left-justified and will be rejustified after [Return] is pressed. The "Text:" prompt remains active after each line is entered, waiting for another line. Entering [Return] on an empty line will terminate the *DTEXT* command.

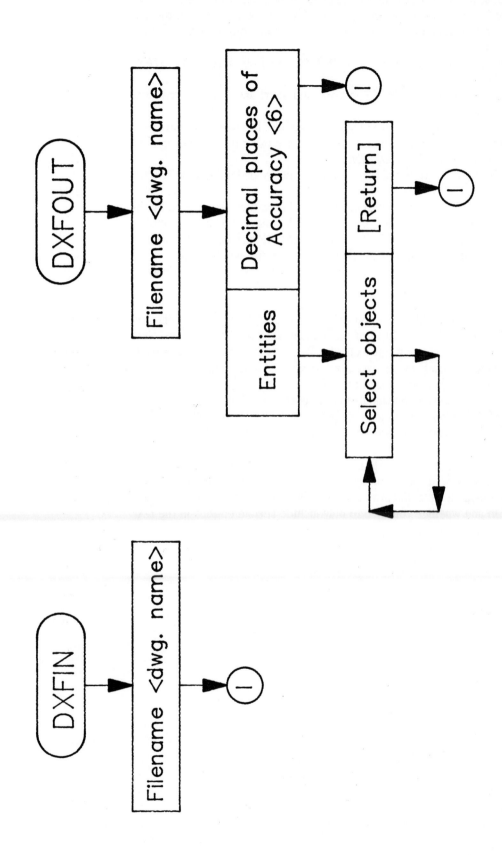

Aligned text will be forced to a uniform height per the first line, but will continue to align to the original baseline width. Interesting, but maybe not too useful.

If a cursor point is selected with the puck, the *DTEXT* cursor (a small box the size of the text being entered) will move to the new point specified. Any text pending will be entered at the old location.

Menus for entry of text will not work with *DTEXT*. In all other respects *DTEXT* works just like *TEXT*.

[CTRL] C will step out of the *DTEXT* command and abort any text entered since the command was initiated.

DXB Files—This stands for Binary Drawing Interchange File, in essence a binary form of a *DXF* file. This type of file is created by CAD/Camera and other digitizing programs. It can be loaded up into AutoCAD by *DXBIN.*

DXBIN Command—Enter *DXBIN* and then the file name to load a *DXB* file into the drawing editor.

DXF Files—This stands for Drawing Interchange File. These files are created by the *DXFOUT* command from AutoCAD. They are an ASCII data file containing a complete description of everything in the drawing. The basic format of DXF files is: Header Section, Tables Section, Blocks Section, Entities Section. The file suffix will be .dxf.

DXF files are created by a number of other third-party programs, such as Primavera Project Planner™, AutoWord™, etc.

Most AutoCAD users will not find DXF files of much interest. For those who do, it is suggested that they use the *DXFOUT* command to create *DXF* files of several different small drawings and compare the structure of the various sections listed above. Note that DXF files can be edited by using, for example, WordStar in non-document mode to make alterations in text entries, etc. Power users might find it advantageous to write programs to perform specialized operations on DXF files.

DXFIN Command—This is the command used to import a *DXF* file into an AutoCAD drawing. If the AutoCAD drawing in progress is brand new, the entire *DXF* file will be loaded. If the drawing has already been worked on, only the Entities Section of the *DXF* file will be loaded.

DXFOUT Command—Export a *DXF* file from your drawing by using the *DXFOUT* command. You must provide a name for the file. A suffix of .dxf will be provided automatically; do not include the suffix in your output file name. You will also be asked to specify a precision and whether you wish to only include certain entities in the *DXF* file. If you ask for entities only, the *DXF* file will not contain Table or Block Sections.

Dynamic Text—(See *DTEXT* Command.)

E

Editing Drawings—(See *Main Menu*.)

ELEV Command—(ADE-3) This 3-D command sets both the new elevation and the thickness of any extruded objects drawn. The elevation corresponds to the z-axis height of the base plane for objects. The thickness is the height of the top of objects from the base plane. Negative thickness indicates extrusion *BELOW* the base plane.

The command operates as follows: Enter *ELEV*. The initial prompt asks for the *"New current elevation:"* Enter the height above the X-Y plane. The second prompt asks for *"New current thickness:"* In each case, enter the desired value or the <current> default.

All entities drawn after the use of the *ELEV* command will assume the thickness and elevation to be set. Vertical lines are constructed by constructing a point extruded in the z-direction.

To view extruded objects, use the *VPOINT* command.

ELLIPSE Command—AutoCAD includes two ways to draw ellipses: Axis plus Eccentricity or Center and Two Axes. It will also construct *Isometric Circles,* that is, circles built in the current isometric drawing plane, if isometric *SNAP* is *ON*.

Actually, the ellipses drawn are polylines with sufficient segments to simulate an ellipse. Ellipses can be trimmed or broken to create elliptical arcs.

The command is initiated by entering *ELLIPSE*. The initial prompt is:

"<Axis endpoint 1>/Center/Isocircle:"

The Isocircle option is only provided if isometric SNAP is active.

Axis plus Eccentricity—Select the endpoints of one axis as prompted. The third prompt will ask for: *"<Other axis distance>/Rotation."* Rotation here does not mean turning the ellipse about its center. It refers to foreshortening a circle by tilting it about the first axis specified, into the z dimension. This will make the first axis the major axis. To take this option, enter *R* and then specify a tilt between 0 and 89.4 degrees.

If instead you enter a point at the third prompt, the distance from the midpoint of the first axis to the point will be used as the length of the second half-axis. This distance can be dragged. Alternatively, you can type in a length for the second half-axis.

Isocircles—To do isocircles, reply I to the initial prompt. The present isometric drawing plane determines the orientation and eccentricity of an isocircle. You need only

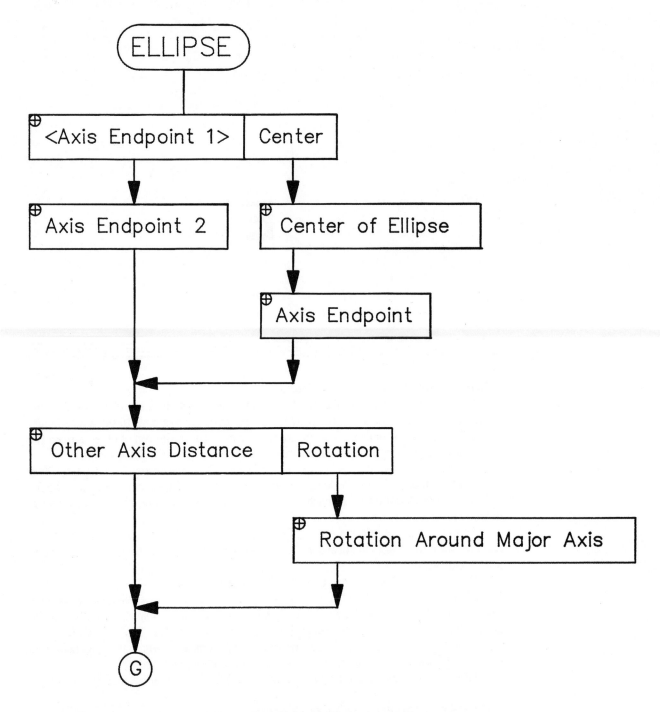

provide the center of the circle and the radius (or D, followed by a diameter), as prompted. The *ISOPLANE* command can be used to reset the iso drawing plane.

Center and Two Half-Axes—The other method for constructing ellipses is to reply *C* to the initial prompt. You will then be asked to locate the center of the ellipse, followed by an axis endpoint. This axis endpoint will determine the angle of orientation of the ellipse, so be careful where you put it. The next prompt will be *"<Other axis distance>/Rotation:"* Enter *R* to specify a tilt between 0 and 89.4 degrees. Alternatively, enter a point to show the length of the second half-axis. This can be dragged. Or you can type in a length for the second half-axis.

END Command—Update the drawing file and return to the Main Menu with the END command. The updated drawing will carry the .dwg type; the old drawing will be renamed as a .bak file and the old .bak will be deleted.

Entering Commands—AutoCAD commands can be entered by typing them in lowercase or uppercase, when the *"Command:"* prompt is present. Initiate the command by hitting [Return], [Enter], or the space bar. Commands can also be entered by the use of keyboard macros using SuperKey™ or by AutoCAD menus. (See Chapter 5, Macros & Menus).

When entering choices in response to AutoCAD prompts, any option in the prompt that has its first letter capitalized can be selected by entering only that letter.

If you make a mistake during the processing of a command, you can cancel it by hitting [CTRL] C.

If you make a mistake while typing in a line, you can either backspace to the mistake or hit [CTRL] X and wipe out the entire line.

If you discover a mistake after the command is completed and exited, you can back up one step, or more, via the *UNDO* command.

Entities—Entities refers to visible objects placed in a drawing. Including *ARCs, CIRCLEs, BLOCKs, SOLIDs, LINEs, TRACEs,* Poly*LINES,* SHAPEs, *TEXT, POINTs,* and Attributes. A count of the number of entities in your drawing is given by the use of the *STATUS* command.

Entity selection—(See Selecting Objects.)

ERASE Command—(See also *OOPS* and *UNDO.*) Delete objects from the drawing database with *ERASE.* After entering the command, specify the object(s) and press [Return].

ERASE *L*ast allows you to move back through the drawing by hitting L repeatedly, erasing the most recent entity each time.

AutoCAD remembers which objects were *ERASE*d last and allows you to restore them to the drawing with *OOPS.* See *OOPS.*

EXIT Subcommand—(See *DIM* Command.)

EXPLODE Command—(See also *BLOCK* and *INSERT.*) BLOCKs are *INSERT*ed in AutoCAD as a reference to the defined *BLOCK* contained elsewhere in the drawing database. That is, the entire *BLOCK* is not reproduced in detail, unless you have INSERTed it with an asterisk. In essence, each occurrence of a gizmo block says ''another one just like the one named 'gizmo', above''. If you change the definition of 'gizmo', each *INSERT*ion of the block will be changed, globally. That's the good news. The bad news is that you can't edit the *INSERT*ed *BLOCK*; when you try to *ERASE* one part of it, the whole thing disappears.

Sometimes there are some occurrences of a *BLOCK* that you don't want to be globally changed along with the others. Or maybe you want to change a few details in one or two *INSERT*ions and leave the others alone. For these cases, use the *EXPLODE* command. This command will replace an *INSERT*ion with the entire *BLOCK* definition; every line, arc, jot, and tittle will be added to the database at that location.

You won't see any change on the screen, so be careful what you *EXPLODE.* After *EXPLODE*ing, the block occurrence can be partially *ERASE*d and edited, or you can redefine the *BLOCK* without that occurrence being altered.

Note: You can only explode one level of a block at a time. If a block is *nested*, that is, contains other blocks, it will have to be *EXPLODE*d as many times as it has levels of nesting. Of course, if one *EXPLODE* command gets you to the level you want, you can stop at that point.

Version 2.6 note: *EXPLODE* has been modified to allow exploding a dimension entity into arcs, arrows, lines, and text. The initial prompt has been changed accordingly:

Select block reference, polyline, or dimension:

If you *EXPLODE* a 3D block insertion, the z values will also be adjusted according to the z scale factor and the height of the insertion relative to the original block.

EXTEND Command—This command is used to lengthen objects in a drawing. It resembles the *TRIM* command: First, limiting (boundary) edges must be selected, then objects to be lengthened. The AutoCAD prompts for this are not easy to follow, so try experimenting with this command before you commit to using it anywhere important.

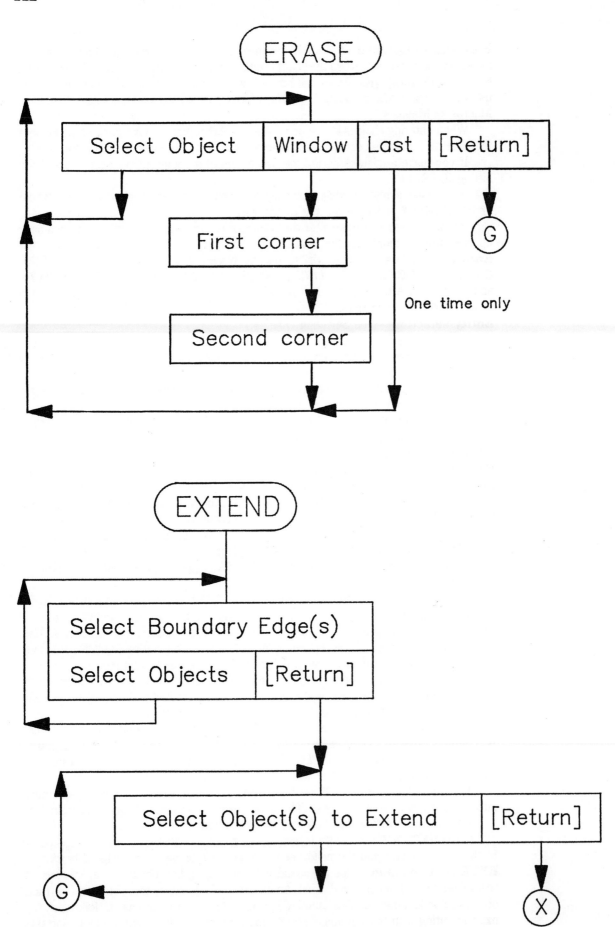

The point used to select objects for lengthening will determine which end of those objects will be extended. That end will be lengthened to meet the nearest boundary object. Further extension requires reselecting the lengthened object. Limiting edges can be arcs, circles, lines and polyline centerlines.

Entities to be lengthened can include arcs, lines, traces, and open polylines. Tapered polylines, when extended, will continue to widen or narrow. A narrowing polyline will not narrow past zero width: if extending a narrowing polyline would take it below zero width, the vertex will be pulled out to meet the boundary line, changing the taper angle as needed.

Version 2.6 note: EXTENDing associative dimension entities will result in a corrected dimension, regenerated according to the latest settings for the dimensioning variables.

Extended Memory—Memory beyond 640 kilobytes can be accessed by AutoCAD if the memory conforms to either the Lotus/Intel or IBM extended memory standards. This memory, where installed, will result in somewhat faster processing and fewer disk accesses.

Extents—(See Drawing Extents.)

External Commands—(ADE-3) (See also *SHELL* Command.) Other programs can be accessed from within the Drawing Editor: DOS, Text Editors, CAD/camera™, Modem software, Database managers, etc. To run these programs, you must first create

Extension line definition points parallel to object:

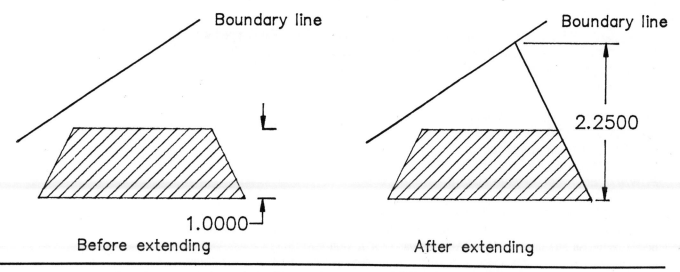

Before extending — After extending

Extension line definition points NOT parallel to object:

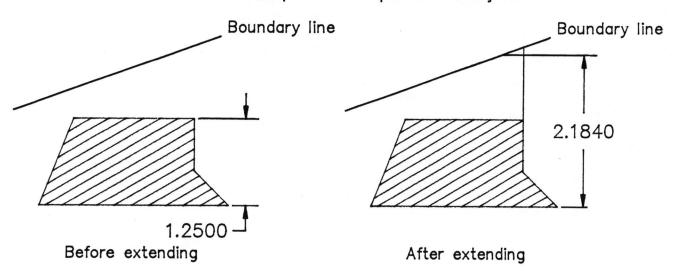

Before extending — After extending

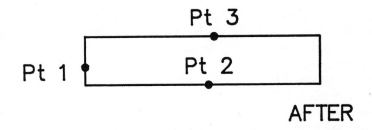

AFTER

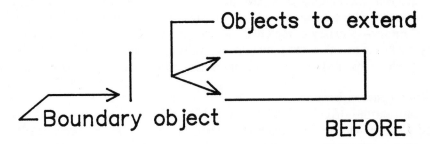

BEFORE

a *program parameters file*, acad.pgp, to provide AutoCAD with the information needed. To make this file, get into *EDLIN*, or SideKick™ or WordStar™ and create an ASCII file as follows:

Name the file acad.pgp. (If you wish, you can clone the acad.pgp file shipped with AutoCAD to serve as a starting point.) Each line in the file will consist of Command name, DOS command,required RAM,*prompt,return code

An example:

```
SHELL,,131000,*DOS Command: ,0
SH,,24000,*DOS Command: ,0
DIR,DIR,24000,File specification: ,0
EDIT,EDLIN,40000,File to edit: ,0
PCWRITE,ED,146000,File to edit: ,0
```

Each field is separated from the others by commas.

The first field in each line will be the name of the external command. It must not be the same as any internal AutoCAD command, or it won't work.

The second field contains any operating system command (like DIR) or command for execution by other software (e.g., *CAMERA*, for CAD/Camera™). If there is no command required, just put in a comma and continue with the third field.

The third field tells AutoCAD how much RAM to give up for running the other program. You should enter a large enough figure to cover the size of the program plus any RAM file space it will require plus an extra 4,000 bytes for the resident part of the DOS command.com file. In any case, don't make this memory reserve less than 24 kilobytes. If you are running under UNIX, just put a 1 in this field.

The fourth field is for a prompt for any additional user input to be appended to the command defined in the second field. If you don't put an asterisk in front of the prompt, either the space bar or [Return] will enter the response to the prompt. If the response must contain spaces, place an asterisk in front of the prompt.

Some external commands used in conjunction with CAD/Camera or other programs create block definitions. If this is the case, the prompt field is used for the block name and must be a kosher block name. See *BLOCK* for details on block naming.

The fifth field consists of zero or the sum of the following:

1: for loading a copy of the *DXB* file "$cmd.dxb" into the drawing and then erasing the *DXB* file.

2: for making a block of the *DXB* file loaded above.

4: for flipping the screen back to graphics at the end of the command.

Extraction of Attributes—(See *ATTEXT* Command.)

F

Fast Zoom Mode—(See *VIEWRES* Command)

File Extension—This refers to the characters after the decimal point in a file name. See below under File Names.

File Names—(See also DOS File Names.) File naming under AutoCAD follows these formats:

Type of file:	No. Chars.	Suffix ("extension")
AutoLISP program	8	.lsp
AutoSHADE file	8	.flm
Backup file	8	.bak
Block names	31	—
Compiled menu	8	.mnx
DXF file names	8	.dxf
DXB file names	8	.dxb
Drawing names	8	.dwg
Extract files (DXF)	8	.dxx
Extract files (CDF)	8	.txt
Extract files (SDF)	8	.dxx
Hatch patterns	8	.pat
IGES files	8	.igs
Layer names	31	—
Linetype library	8	.lin
Menu source file	8	.mnu
Plotter output file	8	.plt
PRPlot output file	8	.lst
Script files	8	.scr
Shapes, source file	8	.shp
Shapes, compiled	8	.shx
Slide names	8	.sld
View names	31	—

As a general rule, within AutoCAD, you should not enter the suffix for a file name. For example, when AutoCAD asks for a drawing name, you should only enter a 1 to

116

8 character name, without the .dwg suffix. AutoCAD will supply the suffix for you when needed.

File Size—(See also Temporary Files.) AutoCAD files can run anywhere from a few thousand bytes up into the megabyte range. If you want to store a drawing on a single floppy, you are limited to 360 kilobytes or 1.2 megabytes, depending on what kind of drive you have. If you want to store the drawing *and* work on it on a single floppy, you are limited to half of that amount, because AutoCAD will try to make a .bak file every time you call up the drawing to work on it. The *REGEN* time for *ZOOMing* and *PANning* gets larger for bigger files, but the net effect will vary depending on what hardware you have, which version of AutoCAD you are using, and how you use it.

AutoCAD inherently makes efficient files by the use of block references: instead of replicating all of the entities in an added block insertion, AutoCAD just places the name of the block, its location, orientation and size into the file.

FILES Command—You can copy, delete, list and rename files while using the Drawing Editor using the *FILES* command. When you enter *FILES*, AutoCAD will display the file utility menu—the same one used by the Main Menu:

0. Exit File Utility Menu
1. List Drawing files
2. List user specified files
3. Delete files
4. Rename files
5. Copy file

Enter selection (0 to 5) <0>

Simply enter the number of your choice. Hitting a [Return] will take the default, exiting the menu. You will be given the opportunity to name the drive containing the files you wish to work with. You can specify types of files to list using wildcards, such as: "*.mnu" or "INST??.DWG." Follow the prompts.

FILL Command— The *FILL* command is a toggle. When it's *ON*, the interiors of traces, solids, and wide polylines will be filled on the screen. When it's *OFF*, these objects will not be filled. You can change the toggle any time you want and existing entities won't be affected until you *REGENerate* or *REDRAW* the drawing.

FILL can also be accessed with *SETVAR* and AutoLISP through the *FILLMODE* system variable. Note that drawings *REGENerate* faster on the screen if *FILL* is *OFF*.

FILLET Command—*FILLET* connects two arcs, circles, lines, or nearby polyline segments with a smooth arc at a specified radius. When you enter *FILLET*, you will be prompted:

Polyline/Radius/<Select two objects>:

Taking the Radius option (enter an R) lets you reset the fillet radius by entering a value from the keyboard or by entering two points one radius apart. Setting the radius to zero is a useful option—it allows you to connect (without filleting) two lines that don't . intersect by using the *FILLET* command on them.

The Polyline option *(enter P)* is used to fillet an entire polyline. Every vertex will be *FILLETed* to the current radius. Existing fillet-like arcs between segments will be replaced with a *FILLET*. If the current radius is set at zero, segments with an arc between them will meet at a point. Divergent and very short segments will not be affected by the *FILLET* Polyline option.

Selecting two lines or polyline segments with the cursor will cause a fillet to be drawn between them. The lines need not meet, as mentioned above. They will be extended enough to reach the fillet arc. If one line already extends past the intersection point, its shortest end will be lopped off at the fillet. You can *FILLET* two intersecting segments of a polyline or two segments that are separated by only one other segment. The intervening segment, if any, will be eliminated.

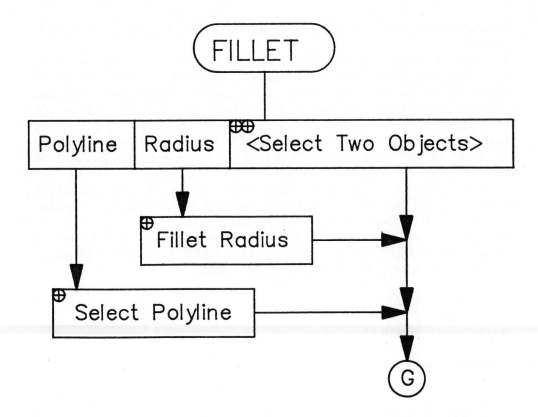

The fillet arc will be on the current working layer unless both segments are on one layer, in which case the arc will also be put on that layer. The same holds true for the fillet color and linetype: the arc color and linetype will follow the segment color and linetype if both segments are similar.

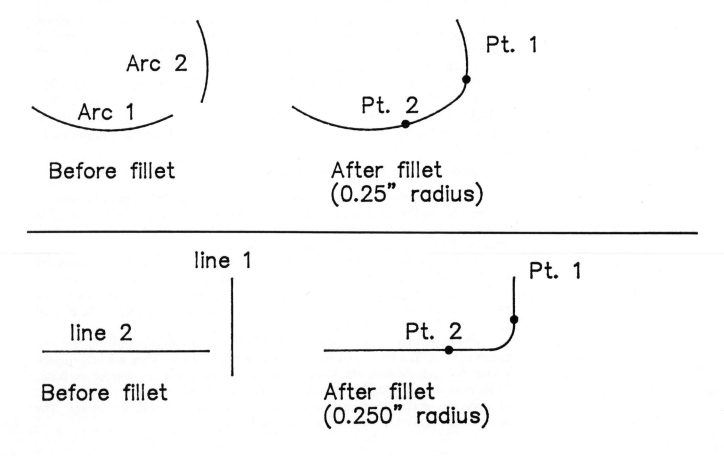

Arc 2

Arc 1

Before fillet

Pt. 1

Pt. 2

After fillet
(0.25" radius)

line 1

line 2

Before fillet

Pt. 1

Pt. 2

After fillet
(0.250" radius)

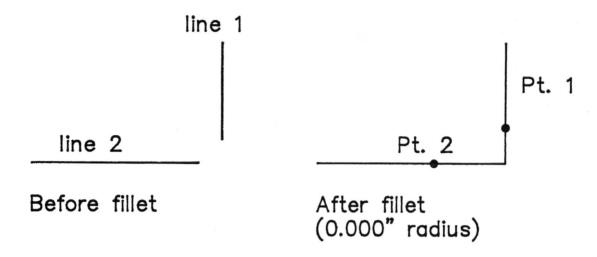

line 1

line 2

Pt. 1

Pt. 2

Before fillet

After fillet
(0.000" radius)

If there is any ambiguity in the *FILLET*ing, AutoCAD will select the fillet it thinks you mean by choosing the one whose endpoints are nearest to the two points you entered.

FILLET works with arcs and circles, except that circles are not trimmed at the fillet.

FILMROLL Command—(Version 2.6.) Under Version 2.6 of AutoCAD you can create a file for AutoSHADEing. The extension *".flm"* will be appended to the name you provide at the prompt. Details on AutoSHADE will be released later.

Flip Screen—In order to see what commands have been entered, along with any data that AutoCAD has put on the screen in the form of text, you can leave the graphics screen by hitting the F1 button. To return, hit F1 again. See Scripts for Flip Screen in scripts and menus.

Fonts—AutoCAD comes with four basic fonts: txt, simplex, complex, and italic. Txt is a very efficient font in that it *REGEN*s faster and *PLOT*s faster than the others. The O's in Txt are squared off completely, for example, and there are virtually no arcs in any of the letters or other characters. Simplex, on the other hand, has many smooth curves in its characters. Complex is even fancier, with double stroked lines and serifs. Italic also has serifs, but is tilted slightly and uses different letters than Complex.

Each font is supplied in two forms: a compiled .shx file that AutoCAD can read, load, and use directly, and a user-editable before use.

Txt font is very fast

Simplex font is slower

Complex font is very slow

Italic font is also slow

Creating your own fonts is possible, either by making a copy of the original .shp file and revising to suit, or by the use of third-party font makers. See the Appendix on Shapes for full directions on writing shape definition files. Custom fonts are also available from a number of sources to save you the time of making your own.

Freezing Layers—(See *LAYER*.) Freezing layers is a way to speed up drawing or plotting by suppressing recalculation of those layers during a *REGEN*. For more information, see the *LAYER* command.

Function Keys—(See also Toggle Settings.) These are the ten keys labelled F1 through F10 at the left edge or along the top of your keyboard. They can be programmed to do macros by the use of Prokey™, SuperKey™, or other keyboard macro definition programs. AutoCAD uses the following function keys:

F1: Flip screen
F6: Coords on/off
F7: Grid on/off
F8: Ortho on/off
F9: Snap on/off
F10: Tablet on/off

G

Grads—(See UNITS Command.)

GRAPHSCR Command—This command will toggle to the graphics screen if you are presently at the text screen. You can put this command in menus and scripts, and you may invoke it while in the middle of another command by placing an apostrophe in front of it: *'GRAPHSCR*. See also Transparent Commands.

GRID Command—GRID displays a reference grid of dots. The dots can have any spacing you desire. *GRID* can be toggled off and on at any time using the F7 key. The spacing is easily adjustable. Grids are never plotted, only displayed as a visual reference.

After entering *GRID*, the initial prompt is:

Grid spacing(X) or ON/OFF/Snap/Aspect <current>:

You can set the grid spacing in terms of drawing units. Using the same spacing for both *SNAP* and *GRID* can be helpful, but it's not mandatory. If you set the *GRID* to zero, the grid spacing automatically adjusts to the Snap resolution; entering S at the initial prompt accomplishes the same thing.

You can also set the grid spacing to a multiple of the snap spacing by entering an X after a number. For example, to set the grid spacing to 4 times the snap interval, enter "4x".

Entering A or Aspect lets you choose a grid with different X and Y spacing. You'll be prompted in the appropriate places. This option won't work if Snap is set for isometric.

If you set the grid spacing too small, it won't be displayed. AutoCAD will tell you the grid is too dense. Enter *GRID* again and make the spacing larger if you need to see the grid at the current *ZOOM* distance.

When you choose *ON*, you activate the previous grid spacing; *OFF* removes the grid from the screen.

The system variables *GRIDMODE* and *GRIDUNIT* can be controlled by the *SETVAR* command or AutoLISP.

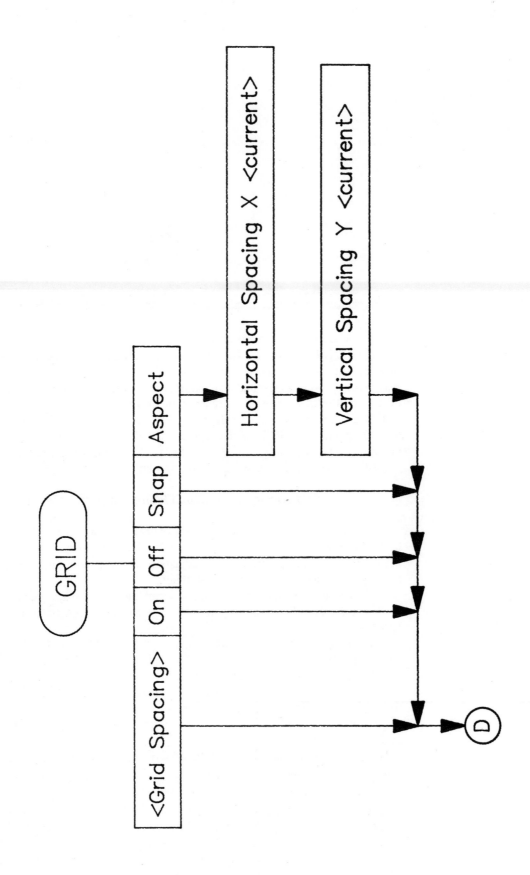

H

HATCH Command—AutoCAD has 41 different *PATTERNS* of crosshatching. Others can be defined by the user, if really necessary. AutoCAD also does three *STYLES* of hatching, more will follow about this.

You can crosshatch within closed boundaries defined by complete arcs, circles, lines, blocks, and polylines. If there is a gap or an overlap, strange things will happen.

Gaps, for example, will allow the crosshatching to leak out and fill up your entire drawing. No problem, though, if that happens. Just hit [CTRL] C to stop the hatching process, and then do an ERASE Last on it; the hatching is one big block and will disappear as one entity, (unless you have put an asterisk in front of the pattern name, in which case you have a jillion individual lines to clean up). Then go back and close off the gap(s).

Overlaps can be even more frustrating. Unless each entity chosen as a hatch boundary lies only on the boundary, you will very likely get no hatching, or hatching where you don't want it. You can get around this problem by breaking or erasing the boundary overhang and putting it back as a separate entity. Another method is to get onto a new layer, retrace the desired boundary exactly with another set of lines and arcs, turn off the original layer, perform the hatching on a third layer, and then turn the original layer back on. If you're worried about the extra set of lines, they can be eliminated or turned off.

To crosshatch an area, enter HATCH. The initial prompt is:

Pattern(? or name/U,style)<default>:

Enter the name of the hatch pattern you wish to use. If you can't remember the names, enter a question mark and AutoCAD will list them all for you. If you reply *"U"*, AutoCAD will let you specify a simple pattern by entering an angle and a spacing and whether you want to double hatch the area. Follow the prompts. Angle and spacing can be defined by providing two points to define those parameters. Entering *Y* at the latter prompt will cause another set of hatch lines to be drawn 90 degrees from the first.

Styles—Another important facet of hatching has to do with how AutoCAD lays in the hatch lines when the boundary line contains other entities that were also selected (as, for example, if you window selected the boundary): It starts at the outer border and moves inward until it hits a selected line. Then it turns off the hatching and continues inward until it reaches another selected line, turns hatching back on, and so forth.

If you have a group of five concentric circles, for example, and you select the outer circle for hatching by windowing it, you will end up with alternating zones hatched, as

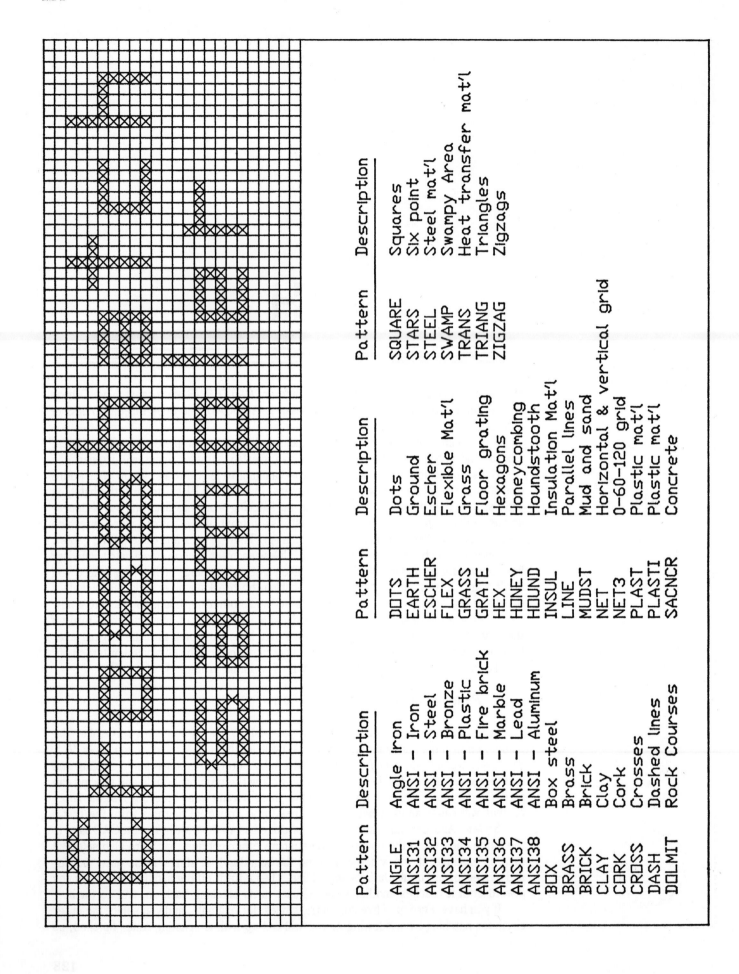

Pattern	Description
ANGLE	Angle Iron
ANSI31	ANSI – Iron
ANSI32	ANSI – Steel
ANSI33	ANSI – Bronze
ANSI34	ANSI – Plastic
ANSI35	ANSI – Fire brick
ANSI36	ANSI – Marble
ANSI37	ANSI – Lead
ANSI38	ANSI – Aluminum
BOX	Box steel
BRASS	Brass
BRICK	Brick
CLAY	Clay
CORK	Cork
CROSS	Crosses
DASH	Dashed lines
DOLMIT	Rock Courses

Pattern	Description
DOTS	Dots
EARTH	Ground
ESCHER	Escher
FLEX	Flexible Mat'l
GRASS	Grass
GRATE	Floor grating
HEX	Hexagons
HONEY	Honeycombing
HOUND	Houndstooth
INSUL	Insulation Mat'l
LINE	Parallel lines
MUDST	Mud and sand
NET	Horizontal & vertical grid
NET3	0-60-120 grid
PLAST	Plastic mat'l
PLASTI	Plastic mat'l
SACNCR	Concrete

Pattern	Description
SQUARE	Squares
STARS	Six point
STEEL	Steel mat'l
SWAMP	Swampy Area
TRANS	Heat transfer mat'l
TRIANG	Triangles
ZIGZAG	Zigzags

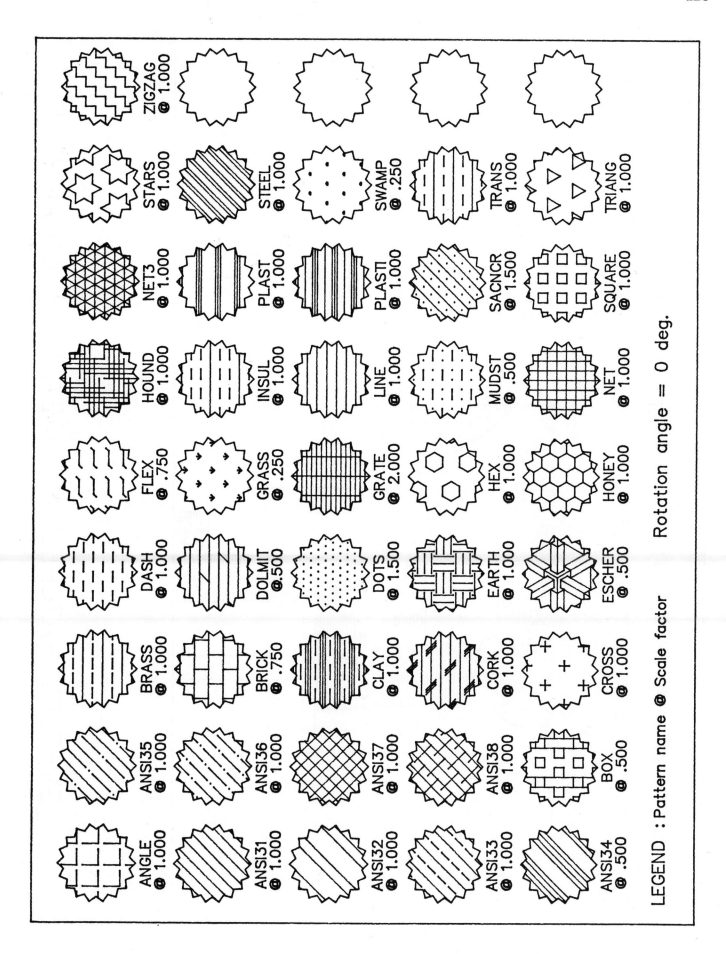

ZIGZAG @ 1.000

STARS @ 1.000
STEEL @ 1.000
SWAMP @ .250
TRANS @ 1.000
TRIANG @ 1.000

NET3 @ 1.000
PLAST @ 1.000
PLASTI @ 1.000
SACNCR @ 1.500
SQUARE @ 1.000

HOUND @ 1.000
INSUL @ 1.000
LINE @ 1.000
MUDST @ .500
NET @ 1.000

FLEX @ .750
GRASS @ .250
GRATE @ 2.000
HEX @ 1.000
HONEY @ 1.000

DASH @ 1.000
DOLMIT @ .500
DOTS @ 1.500
EARTH @ 1.000
ESCHER @ .500

BRASS @ 1.000
BRICK @ .750
CLAY @ 1.000
CORK @ 1.000
CROSS @ 1.000

ANSI35 @ 1.000
ANSI36 @ 1.000
ANSI37 @ 1.000
ANSI38 @ 1.000
BOX @ .500

ANGLE @ 1.000
ANSI31 @ 1.000
ANSI32 @ 1.000
ANSI33 @ 1.000
ANSI34 @ .500

LEGEND : Pattern name @ Scale factor   Rotation angle = 0 deg.

125

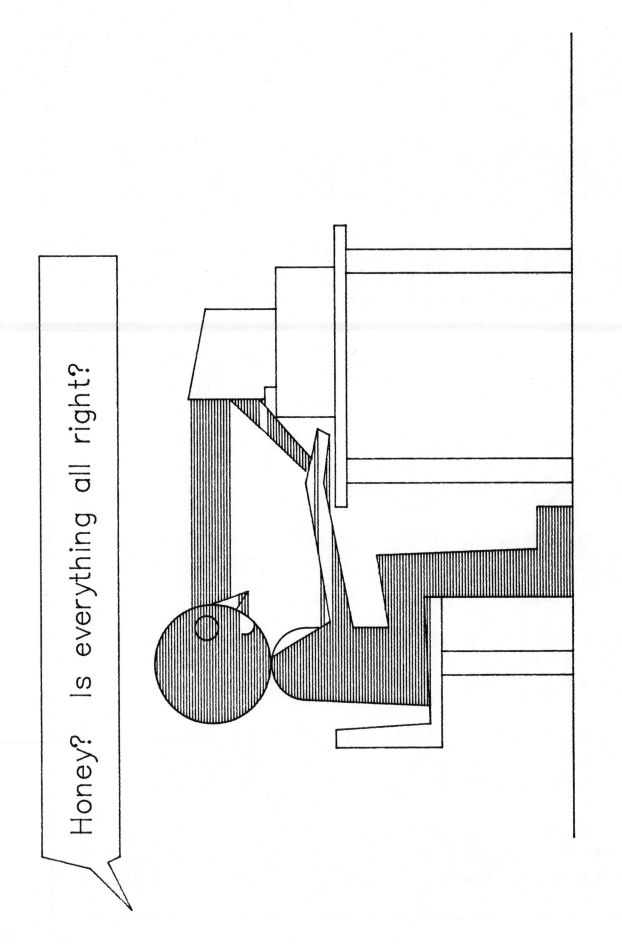

SMEDLEY HATCHES AN AREA WITH A GAP IN IT.

AutoCAD skips every other circle. This is called the "Normal" style of crosshatching. If you don't specify a style, AutoCAD will use the Normal style.

Alternatively, there is a second style of hatching: You can tell AutoCAD to "Ignore" internal selected stuff and hatch right through it. (It still won't hatch through text, though.)

A third style of hatching is "Outermost." This consists of turning off the hatching when it hits an interior selected item and not turning it back on. The result is that only the outermost part is hatched, with no hatching anywhere except in the outer zone.

To specify a style of hatching, add the first letter of the style to the pattern name, separated by a comma. For example, *"*U,N"* or *"Escher,I"* or *"*Line,O."* See above for the significance of the asterisk.

After you have supplied a pattern name, and style if desired, AutoCAD will ask you for a scale and angle for the pattern. Enter numbers or points to define those variables, or select the defaults.

Next, AutoCAD will prompt you to *"Select objects."* Hit each entity on the hatching boundary, as well as any objects within the boundary that you don't want hatched. Window selection is probably the best way to select objects for hatching.

All of the patterns are such that one vector will start at the *SNAP* origin (0,0). If you want to shift the pattern so it will look better where it intersects its boundary, you can use the *SNAP* command to shift the location of the *SNAP* origin.

Similar to the *TEXT* command, if you hit [Return] immediately after completing one *HATCH* command, AutoCAD will pop you back into *HATCH*ing without repeating the initial prompts. You will only be asked to select objects for hatching. The same pattern, style, angle, and spacing will be used as in the previous operation.

HELP Command—Entering *HELP* or *? [Return]* will allow you to access AutoCAD's on-screen help function. The initial prompt is:

Command name (RETURN for list):

If you hit [Return], a list of AutoCAD commands will be displayed on the screen. If you enter the name of a command before you hit [Return], information about that command will be displayed.

If you're in the middle of a command, you can get information by typing an apostrophe followed by either the word *HELP* or a question mark (?), provided the prompt is not asking for a text string. [CTRL] C will stop the *HELP* display. On single-display systems, *HELP* changes the screen to the text screen; the *FLIP SCREEN* key (F1) will return you to the drawing.

The text of *HELP* is stored on a disk file called "acad.hlp," and can be edited and revised with a word processor or text editor for customized applications.

Under the latest versions of AutoCAD, if you need help while you are in a command, you don't have to [CTRL] C out of the command. Just enter *'HELP* (note the apostrophe). AutoCAD will bring up the HELP screens for the command you are in.

Hidden Lines—(3-D) These are lines that would not be visible from the viewpoint of the observer because they are behind other objects or surfaces. The normal 3-D AutoCAD drawing is a *wire-frame* drawing: all lines show, as if the object were constructed from old coat hangers. To eliminate the hidden lines from the drawing, use the HIDE command.

HIDE Command—(ADE-3. See also Hidden Lines.) Enter *HIDE* and wait. The screen will blank out because AutoCAD is busy doing other things. Eventually you will see your 3-D drawing as it would look if the surfaces were opaque.

If you want to show the hidden lines in another color, instead of suppressing them, use the *LAYER* command to create a new set of layers. Give each new layer the same name as an existing layer, but put *"HIDDEN"* in front of the old names. The *HIDE* command when used will then punch all hidden lines on layer *VALLEY*, for example, to the new layer *HIDDENVALLEY*. You can set the color for the *HIDDEN* layers to contrast with the others for maximum visual effect. Or you can turn off the *HIDDEN* layers completely.

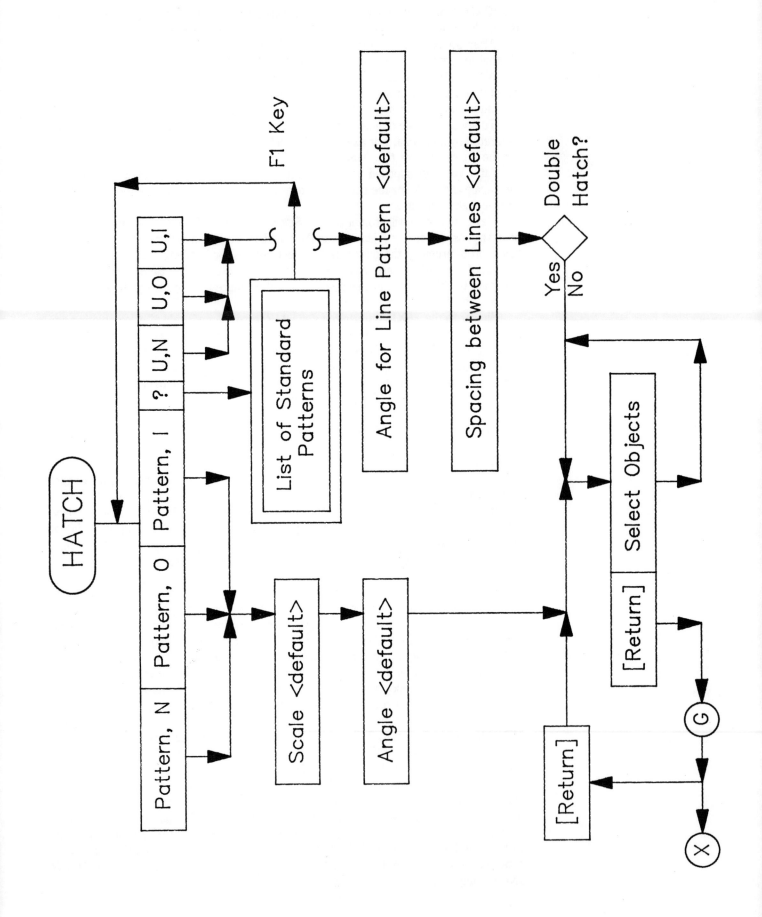

Version 2.6 notes: Under this version of AutoCAD, non-convex faces of 3-D objects will be drawn as wireframes when the *HIDE* command is invoked.

Highlighting—(See Selecting Objects.)

HORIZONTAL Subcommand—(See *DIM* Command.)

I

ID Command—This command is seldom used because of the coordinates that AutoCAD displays at the top of the screen. You pretty much know where you are at all times, as long as the *COORDS* are turned on.

To use this command, enter ID and then specify a location with the cursor. AutoCAD will display the X,Y drawing coordinates for that point. If you enter a pair of coordinates via the keyboard, the position on the drawing corresponding to those coordinates will be highlighted on the screen with a blip, unless BLIPMODE has been turned off. The next time the screen is redrawn, the blip will disappear.

Version 2.6 notes: If you have the 3D package, (ADE-3), the ID command will work with X, Y, and Z dimensions.

IGES Files—AutoCAD can read and write interchange files in the Initial Graphics Exchange Standard format. An *IGES* file is an intermediate graphics data file that is arranged in a standard format. This is useful if you have more than one type of CAD program running and need to make translations back and forth. The two commands for implementing this type of translation are *IGESOUT* and *IGESIN*.

To translate from AutoCAD to another CAD program that supports *IGES*, use *IGESOUT* to create the *IGES* file. Then get into the other program and use the appropriate commands to convert the *IGES* file to whatever type of drawing file is used by that program.

To translate from another program to AutoCAD, first create the intermediate *IGES* file from that program and then use the *IGESIN* command in AutoCAD to convert the *IGES* file to an AutoCAD drawing.

IGESIN Command—Initial Graphics Exchange Standard interchange files can be converted to AutoCAD drawings. Begin by choosing *"Create New Drawing"* from the Main Menu, then enter *IGESIN* and respond with the name of the *IGES* file and press [Return]. If the system stops because of errors, the partial drawing will be retained and you will receive an error message.

IGESOUT Command—AutoCAD drawings can be used to create an Initial Graphics Exchange Standard file with *IGESOUT*. Simply enter *IGESOUT*, the file name and press [Return]. Since the .igs identifier is assumed, it's not necessary to add it to the file name.

This command will write over a file with the same name, so be careful to specify a unique name.

Initials—Options in a prompt that are capitalized are selected by entering only the initial letter.

130

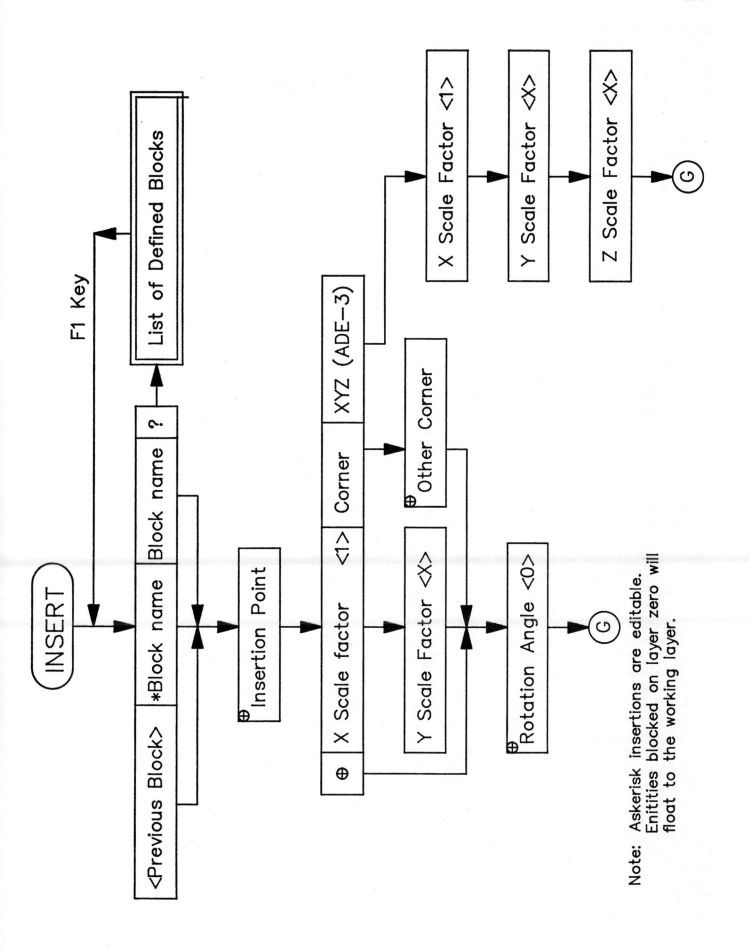

Inquiry Commands—This term refers to commands that ask AutoCAD for information about the drawing. The information will appear in the prompt area. If they overflow past the prompt area, the display will flip to the text screen. See these commands for more details: *LIST, DBLIST, STATUS, ID, DIST,* and *AREA*.

INSERT Command—(See also MINSERT Command.) This is the other half of the most powerful feature of AutoCAD. (See the *BLOCK* command.) You can insert copies of either blocks or drawings into your current drawing.

Inserting Blocks—Blocks to be *INSERT*ed must already be in your drawing: they must have been created (*defined*) in your drawing or contained in your drawing as part of another drawing previously *INSERT*ed. Note that they are not necessarily a visible part of your drawing, yet.

Enter *INSERT*. The initial prompt is: *Block name (or ?)<Lastused>*. The name of the last block INSERTed will be shown as the default. If you enter a question mark, you will be shown a list of all the blocks defined in that drawing so far. Blocks that have not yet been *INSERT*ed in your drawing will not be shown.

Enter the name of the desired item. If you put an asterisk in front of the block name, AutoCAD will replicate the entire block, every line, arc, and so forth, in the database, for that *INSERT*ion. This is inefficient, it makes the database a bit larger, but it will allow you to edit the *INSERT*ed entities: you can *ERASE* parts of the block and replace them, etc.

As you INSERT the block with an asterisk, you can rotate the block or make it larger or smaller, but you can't give it different X and Y scales or flip it backwards or upside down. Note that after an asterisk insertion, the default block will have an asterisk in front of it.

After you have entered a block name, you will be asked where you want to place it. You can enter coordinates from the keyboard or by using your pointing device. Next you will be prompted for an X scale factor:

X scale factor<1>/Corner/XYZ:

Replying *XYZ* to the initial prompt is possible with ADE-3. That will let you specify scale factors for all three dimensions when INSERTing a 3-D block.

The X scale factor can be indicated by entering a number, or by taking the default value of 1. Negative values for X cause the block to be INSERTed backwards.

Entering *C* for Corner allows you to set the X and Y scale factors together by selecting another point whose location relative to the insertion point gives an X and a Y distance. The block will be given X and Y scales equal to the X and Y distances.

Note that if your block was originally created to fill a one-inch by one-inch square, the Corner method will cause the block to just fit within the rectangle defined by the insertion point and the corner point. If you're going to use the corner method a lot, using 1 × 1 blocks is a good idea.

If you define just the X scale factor, you will be prompted for a Y scale factor, with a default value of X. Negative Y values will put the block in upside down.

The next prompt calls for a rotation angle. The default is zero degrees; a point can be entered to define a line from the insertion point, whose angle is used to rotate the block. If *ORTHO* is on, you can only use angles of 0, 90, 180, and 270 degrees.

Dragging of the following parameters is possible if ADE-2 is installed: Insertion point, rotation, X and Y scale factors. See *DRAGMODE*.

Remember that blocks created on layer 0 will move to the current working layer upon insertion.

Version 2.6 notes: INSERT has 3D capabilities under Version 2.6 of AutoCAD if ADE-3 is present. A Z-dimension coordinate and scale factor can be entered from the keyboard or a macro during insertions. If the Z coordinate is not specified, the current elevation will be used.

INSERTing Drawings—Drawings to be INSERTed need only be accessible to AutoCAD, on your disk somewhere, where AutoCAD can find them. If the drawing is on a floppy disk, you can tell AutoCAD where, by putting the disk letter in front of the drawing name. Example: b:reducer. If, on the other hand, the drawing is on your hard drive, you can give a path, if necessary: /piping/reducer.

An *INSERT*ed drawing becomes a defined block within your drawing. If you *INSERT* reducer.dwg, as above, you can draw additional ''reducer'' copies by using the *INSERT* command the way you would to *INSERT* a normal block. You no longer have to show a path. (If you don't want to call the block ''reducer'' you can rename it as you *INSERT* the drawing by calling for, say, swage=/piping/reducer. You now have a block in your drawing called ''swage''.)

Every block definition within the *INSERT*ed drawing is now a defined block within your drawing. If reducer.dwg contains other blocks besides the reducer, they will also be useable. Note they do not have to be visible when INSERTed; defined blocks are not always *OOPS*ed back into a drawing, or used after definition. You could have a blank drawing called pipestuf.dwg, containing one of every piping fitting as a defined block. You could *INSERT* that drawing every time you start a piping drawing and then use the blocks it contains. (When you finish the new drawing, you might want to END it and then call it back up and immediately PURGE it, to get rid of any unused blocks. See the *PURGE* command.)

If you wish to update a drawing containing a block (''mungo'') that has been revised elsewhere, when you *INSERT* the revised ''mungo.dwg'', reply to the Block name prompt with ''mungo=''. The equals sign will cause all mungos in your drawing to match the new version at the first regeneration.

If you want to redefine a block in your drawing, but don't want any more insertions of that block, when you *INSERT* the drawing that holds the latest version, use the *INSERT* command as above, but do a [CTRL] C when asked for an insertion point. This will update your drawing but will not add a picture of the *INSERT*ed drawing anywhere visible.

Asterisks work the same way as in blocks: the entire visible insertion will be editable. If you don't use an asterisk, and you try to erase any visible part of the *INSERT*ed drawing, you will find that the whole thing disappears. No problem, though. Either *OOPS* it back on-screen, or, better, do an *INSERT* with an asterisk in front of the drawing name and AutoCAD will put it back in, in editable form.

A handy trick for doing asterisk insertions when you don't know where the basepoint or handle is for the drawing: Insert the drawing without the asterisk; drag the graphics into position, hold the puck firmly at its current location, and do a [CTRL] C to cancel the insertion. Without moving the puck, repeat the *INSERT* command with an asterisk in front of the drawing name. The inserted drawing will be where you want it.

There are some other surprises possible when *INSERT*ing one drawing in another. Normally, any duplicated block definitions will be ignored. Early versions of AutoCAD have been known to lock up when there were large numbers of duplicate blocks, however.

Any layers, linetypes, or text styles in the *INSERT*ed drawing will be carried over to the current drawing. Named views are lost. If any layer, text style, or block names are duplicated, the ambiguity will be resolved in favor of the current drawing, rather than the *INSERT*ed drawing. Make sure that any shape files used in the *INSERT*ed drawings are in your working directory when you do further editing of the combined drawing.

Isometric Drawing—(ADE-2) An isometric drawing is a two-dimensional representation of a three-dimensional object. Isometric drawings are sometimes used for machine parts, piping, and structures. See below. By definition, there is no perspective shown in an isometric drawing.

Isometric Grid—(ADE-2) (See also *SNAP* and *ISOPLANE* Commands.) The isometric, three-axis drawing grid is accessed by the *SNAP* command. Enter *SNAP*, then enter *S* for ''Style'', and *I* for ''Isometric.''

This grid consists of a hexagonal array of snap points that make it easy to draw lines at 30, 90, 150, 210, 270, and 330 degrees. Each snap point is indicated by a superimposed grid of dots. The dots are only for reference and do not plot. The crosshairs will shift to match the grid and, initially, the Left Isoplane.

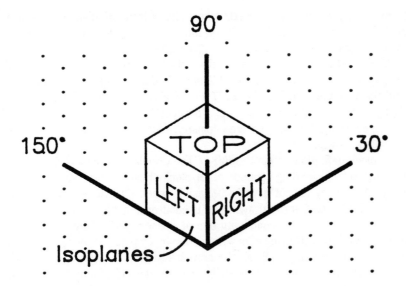

ISOPLANE Command—There are three axes or *directions* in an isometric drawing: (1) up/down, (2) 30 degrees/210 degrees, and (3) 150 degrees/270 degrees. Because the *ORTHO* mode and cursor control keys can only function in two of these three directions at a time, AutoCAD has assumed three imaginary planes. Only one of these planes is active at any time, and the cursor keys and ORTHO work only in that plane. Isocircles (see *ELLIPSE*) will be created in the active isoplane.

The three isoplanes are Left, Right, and Top. The Left isoplane works in directions (1) and (3), as listed above. The Right isoplane directions are (1) and (2); Top isoplane corresponds to axes (2) and (3).

To select a different isoplane, enter *ISOPLANE*. The initial prompt is:

Left/Top/Right/(Toggle):

Enter the appropriate initial or hit [Return] to toggle clockwise to the next isoplane.

Instead of using the *ISOPLANE* command, you can toggle around clockwise by using [CTRL] *E*.

If you turn *ORTHO* off and leave *SNAP* on, depending on the scale of your drawing you might find it is not necessary to reset the isoplane to draw. Isocircles (using the *ELLIPSE* command) do require being in the proper isoplane.

L

LAYER Command—AutoCAD lets you draw on different *layers,* just as if you were drawing on transparent overlays. Layers can be turned on and off, plotted separately, *frozen* to speed up *ZOOM*s and *PAN*s, set to be different colors or to plot with different pens. (Older versions of AutoCAD only permitted the use of 256 different layers, named 0 through 255.)

Enter *LAYER.* The initial prompt will be:

?/Make/Set/New/ON/OFF/Color/Ltype/Freeze/Thaw:

Each of these options is discussed below in detail, with the required response to the initial prompt shown in parentheses. Remember that wildcard characters can be used in entering names of existing layers.

Query (?)—Entering a question mark will result in a prompt: *"Layer name(s) for listing < * >:"* You can either enter layer names that you wish information about or you can just hit [Return] and AutoCAD will provide a complete list of all layers and their status, color, and linetype.

Make (M)—Entering an *M* will allow you next to create a new layer and make it the active (working) layer. You will be asked for a *"New current layer"* name; enter whatever name you wish, using the standard convention for AutoCAD names. If that layer already exists, it will be turned on and made the current layer. If it has been "frozen", it must first be "thawed" before it can be made the current layer.

Set (S)—This is used to set the current layer. Use this if the layer already exists.

New (N)—Create new layers with this option. You can enter more than one new layer name: separate the names with commas. The new layers will be in the ON state, and will initially be assigned color 7 and linetype *CONTINUOUS.* The current layer is not changed.

OFF (OFF)—You can eliminate existing layers from the display and from plotting by this option. (You can turn them back on later, if needed.) Provide the names of the layers you wish to turn off, separated with commas. If you accidentally turn off the present layer, you will not be able to see anything you draw. AutoCAD will warn you if you try to do this.

ON (ON)—Layers that have been turned off can be turned back on, unless they have been frozen. Enter *ON* in response to the initial prompt, then provide a list as above of the layers you wish to turn on.

135

136

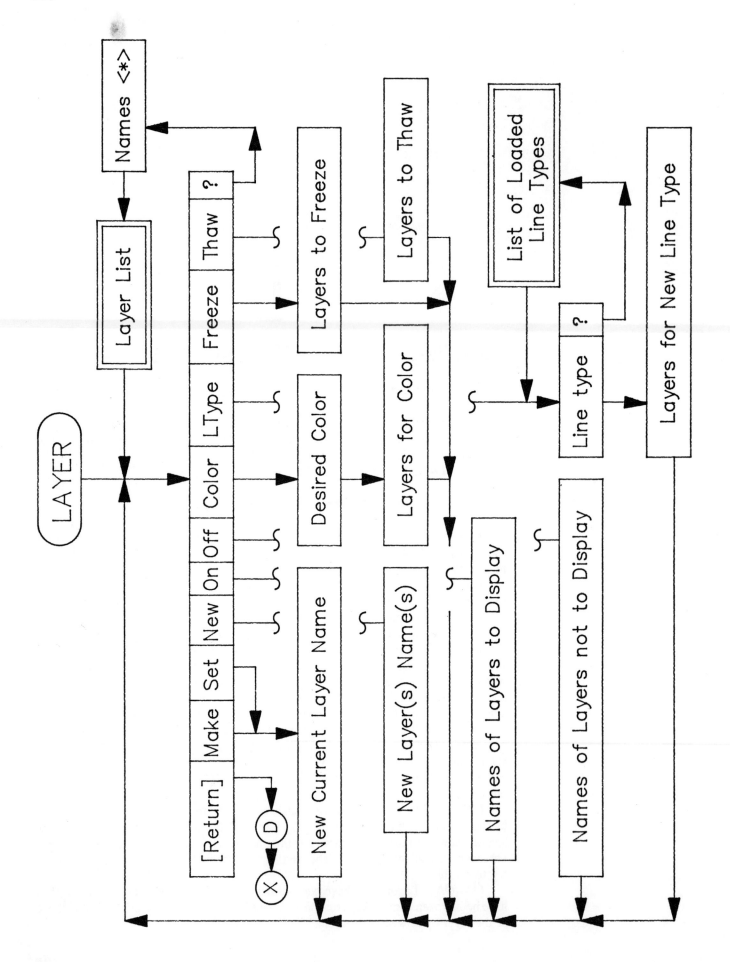

Layer name	State	Color	Linetype
O	On	7 (white)	CONTINUOUS
USC	On	7 (white)	CONTINUOUS
TROJANS	On	7 (white)	CONTINUOUS
JACK	On	1 (red)	CONTINUOUS
DOC	On	1 (red)	CONTINUOUS
REGGIE	On	5 (blue)	CONTINUOUS
CAROL	On	2 (yellow)	DOT
HAPPY	On	2 (yellow)	CONTINUOUS
BUZZ	On	7 (white)	DOT
KIT	On	7 (white)	DOT
ROBERTSON	On	1 (red)	CONTINUOUS
9	On	7 (white)	DOT
8	On	1 (red)	CONTINUOUS
7	Off	7 (white)	CONTINUOUS
4	On	1 (red)	DOT

-- Press RETURN for more --

Color (C)—Use this response to change the color assigned to a layer. You will be prompted for a color; enter a standard color name (like *RED*) or a number from 1 to 255. Then enter a list of which layers you want to have that color. The layers entered will turn on and show in the color assigned. If you prefix the color with a minus sign (−), those layers will be off instead of on.

Linetype (L)—Like colors, linetypes can be assigned to particular layers. Enter a linetype, and then a layer list. If you can't remember which linetypes have been loaded, enter a question mark (?) when prompted for linetype. If the linetype you enter has not been loaded yet, AutoCAD will load it from the acad.lin file.

Freeze (F)—Layer Freeze and Thaw are just like layer *ON* and *OFF*, except that frozen layers are not recalculated during *ZOOM*s and *PAN*s. This can save considerable time if there are a lot of entities on a layer or layers that are not going to be worked on again and that you don't need to see in order to draw on your present layer. You can't freeze the current layer.

Thaw (T)—This will turn frozen layers back on and *REGEN* the drawing.

LEADER Subcommand—(See *DIM* Command.)

LIMITS Command—LIMITS lets you choose the boundaries for the current drawing and turn on and off AutoCAD's checking whether input points are within limits. There are three *LIMITS* functions:

1. The range of coordinates you can use is specified when *LIMITS* is turned *ON*. This tells AutoCAD how big *the paper* is that you want to draw on.

2. The visible grid portion of a drawing is controlled by LIMITS.

3. *LIMITS* determines what part of a drawing is displayed with a *ZOOM* All command, subject to adjustment to fill your available screen space with the height or width of the drawing, whichever is the limiting dimension.

When you enter *LIMITS*, the initial prompt is:

ON/OFF/<Lower left corner> <current value>:

If you enter a point, that point will be used as the lower left corner of the drawing boundary. If, instead, you hit [Return], the current lower left corner will be reused. You will then, in either case, be asked for the upper right corner. The present value will be shown as the default for that corner.

The *ON* and *OFF* options toggle *limits checking*, the AutoCAD feature that prevents you from entering points outside the drawing limits.

You can change the drawing limits with the *LIMITS* command during drawing by entering *LIMITS* and responding to the prompts. Keep in mind that the lower left corner of a drawing can be any point, including negative coordinates, beyond the origin.

The *LIMCHECK, LIMMIN,* and *LIMMAX* system variables are affected by *LIMITS*.

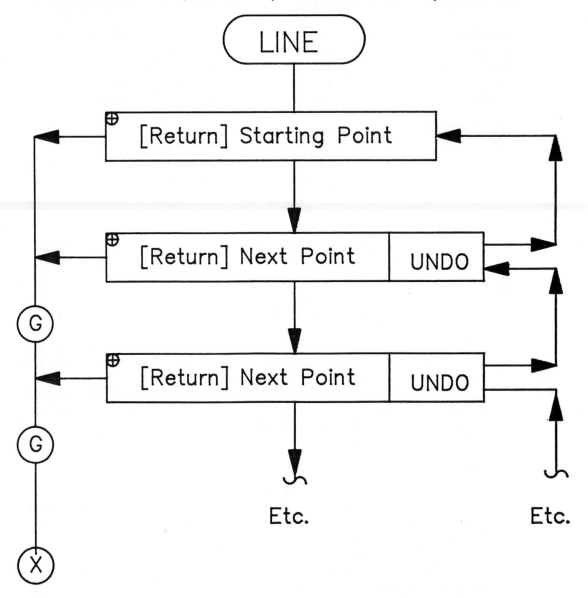

LINE

[Return] Starting Point

[Return] Next Point   UNDO

[Return] Next Point   UNDO

Etc.   Etc.

LINE Command—(See also Object Snaps.) To draw a line, enter *LINE*, then specify the starting point with the keyboard or with your puck or mouse. As you move the cursor, the line will *rubber band* to help you see where the line will actually go. Select another point for the endpoint of the first segment. AutoCAD saves you time when you are entering a series of connected lines by keeping the *LINE* command active, asking for new points until you press [Return]. Each line is treated as a separate entity, even when it's drawn in this fashion, as part of a series of connected lines.

The most recent line segment can be undone while you are still in the *LINE* command by responding to the *"To point:"* prompt with *U*. This detaches the line from the last point specified and leaves it rubberbanding from the previous point. *U* can be repeated to step back and erase several lines.

If you are creating a closed polygon with the *LINE* command, you can close off the last side by entering *"C"* at the *"To point:"* prompt.

To continue the most recently drawn line or arc, you can use a null response at the initial "From point:" prompt. AutoCAD will then put the start point for your line at the endpoint of the last such entity constructed. If the last entity was an arc, the direction of continuation is specified by the arc itself; you need only provide a distance for the continuation line.

LINETYPE Command—(See also LTSCALE.) Entities are normally drawn with a continuous line. However, the type of line used to draw arcs, circles, lines and polylines can be changed with the *LINETYPE* command. *LINETYPE* can be used to draw with lines stored in the standard acad.lin file, which contains the following:

TYPE OF LINE	LINE NAME
— — — — — — —	dashed
- - - - - - - - - - - - - -	hidden
- ----- - ----- - ----- -	center
----- - - ----- - - -----	phantom
—— · —— · —— · —— ·	dashdot
—— —— · —— —— · —— —— · ——	border
—— · · —— · · —— · · —— ·	divide

You can also use *LINETYPE* to create your own library file of linetypes or to load a linetype library you've already created.

You must load a linetype from a library file before you can assign it to a layer or entity in your drawing. Once you load a linetype, its definition becomes part of the drawing, just like a block. Your drawing will be automatically regenerated if you use *LINETYPE* to recreate and reload a new linetype and that linetype is currently assigned to layers in the drawing.

You begin any of these processes by entering LINETYPE. The initial prompt is:

?/Create/Load/Set:

These options are discussed in detail below:

Query (?)—This option is used to find out what linetypes are in your linetype file. Provide the file name when prompted or take the default file name by hitting [Return]. AutoCAD will respond with a listing of all the linetypes contained in that file.

Set—Set allows you to determine the linetype of each entity drawn thereafter, either as individual entities or by whatever layer they are on. You'll be prompted to provide the name of the new entity linetype:

New entity linetype (or ?) <current>:

You can press [Return] to use the current linetype, if you decide not to change. You can alternatively respond with *BYLAYER* or *BYBLOCK*. If you enter *BYLAYER*, objects will be drawn from then on with whatever linetype is assigned to the layer you are working on when you create them. *BYBLOCK* allows you to draw entities with a continuous line and when you *BLOCK* them and subsequently *INSERT* the block, the entities will acquire whatever linetype is active when you do the *INSERT*ion. Entering a question mark will cause AutoCAD to display the linetypes that are currently loaded.

Load—This response to the initial prompt allows you to load a library file of linetypes. Respond as prompted with the name of the linetype you want loaded and then the library file name that contains your choice.

Create—This allows you to make a new linetype. You will be prompted first for the name of the linetype you want to create and then for the name of the file where you want to store that linetype definition. Next, you'll be asked for a description of the linetype.

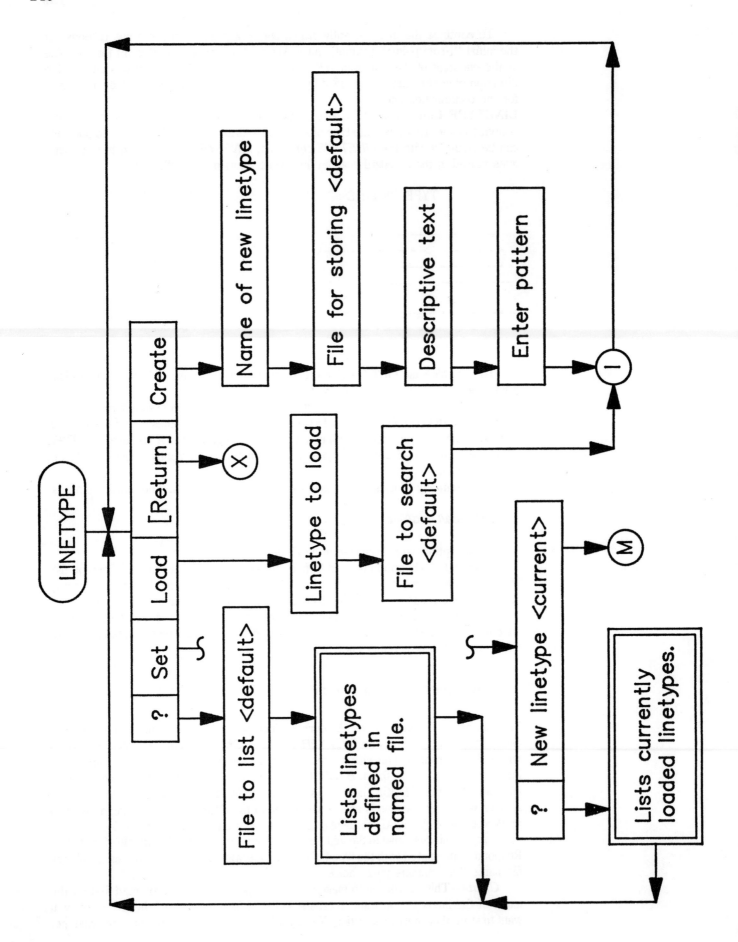

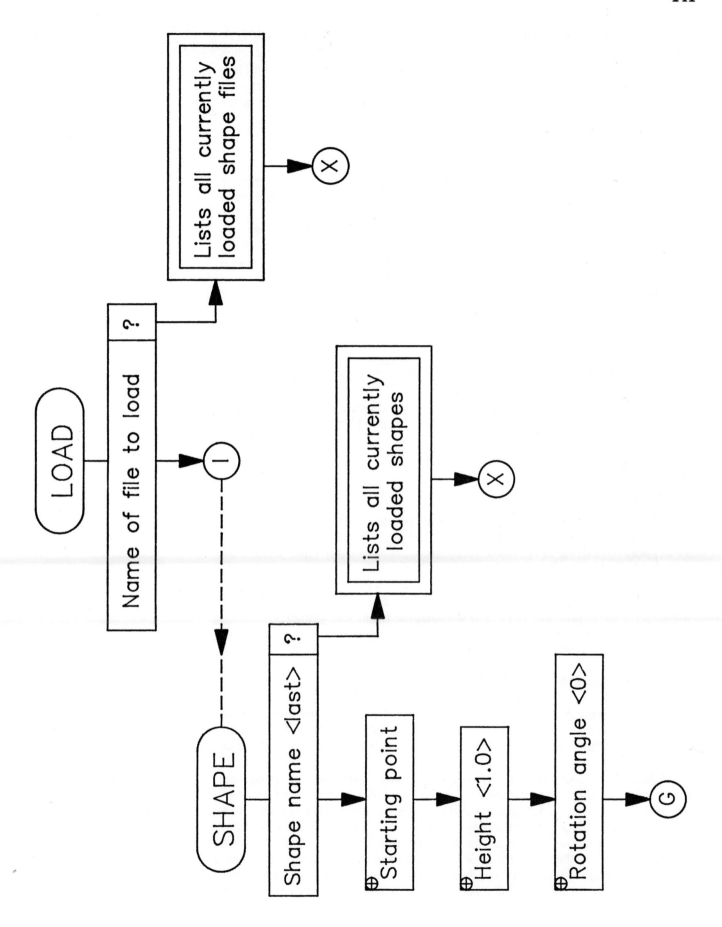

For example, suppose you want to create a linetype called "DITDITDAHDIT." You would type in: ..__. ..__. ..__. for the *description*. The description is just a rough text representation of the linetype, it doesn't mean a whole lot, and can be omitted. It only appears when you use the LAYER Ltype ? sequence of commands. After entering the description, you must enter a data line of up to 80 characters that contains the actual definition of the linetype. In our example it might look like this:

A,0,-.1,0,-.05,.1,-.05,0,-.2

The "A" is an alignment type that forces lines and arcs constructed with this linetype to end only in a dash for better visibility. There are no other types of alignment in AutoCAD as of Version 2.6.

The string of numbers after the A stand for blanks, dashes, and dots. A zero (0) is a dot. A dash is represented by a positive number whose value is the length of the dash in drawing units. A blank is represented by a negative number giving the distance to the next dot or dash.

The example has, after the *A*, a dot, a blank space one-tenth inch long, another dot, another blank half the length of the first, then a dash one-tenth inch long, then a one-twentieth inch space, another dot, and a two-tenths inch space. This is sufficient to define the linetype. An entity drawn with this linetype would have the pattern above repeated many times from one end to the other, depending on the length of the entity. The pattern would be squished together slightly, sufficient to force a piece of the dashed portion to lie at each end of the entity.

When you create a linetype library, it is stored as a separate file and can be edited using a text or word processor. The file name will automatically end in .lin. The entries in the file will look like this example:

*DITDITDAHDIT,..__. ..__. ..__.
A,0,-.1,0,-.05,.1,-.05,0,-.2

LIST Command—This is one of several AutoCAD commands that are extremely useful when you are having difficulties with a drawing. You can look at the information stored for an entity by entering LIST, and selecting the object. The entity type, position and layer will be listed, usually followed by additional information.

If the information stored requires more than a screen to display, you can use [CTRL] S to temporarily stop the scrolling and press any key to resume scrolling. [CTRL] C will abandon the display, and [CTRL] Q will send the list to your printer.

LOAD Command—In order to use a set of shapes in a drawing, you must first load the shapes. Enter *LOAD*; you'll be prompted as follows:

Name of shape file to load (or ?):

Enter the name of the shape file you wish to use. You don't need to include the identifier; .shx is assumed by AutoCAD. If you want a list of the Shape files that are accessible, respond with a question mark and the list of files currently loaded will be displayed.

LTSCALE Command—The dash in a linetype definition is expressed in drawing units that can be a specific unit of measure, say, inches. You might be doing some drawings where the units are miles, furlongs, or whatever. A dashed line with segments a half-inch long would not appear dashed unless you *ZOOM*ed way in on it. *LTSCALE* allows you to adjust the dashes so they are the scale you need for your particular drawing. Enter *LTSCALE* and then enter the scale factor you want, or accept the current value with another [Return]. When you change the linetype scale the drawing will be regenerated with the new scale, unless *REGENAUTO* is off. This scale factor is now a part of your drawing file.

M

Main Menu—This refers to the AutoCAD task selection menu that appears after the starting message (acad.msg). The Main Menu looks like this:

Main Menu:

0. Exit AutoCAD
1. Begin a NEW drawing
2. Edit an EXISTING drawing
3. Plot a drawing
4. Printer plot a drawing
5. Configure AutoCAD
6. File utilities
7. Compile shape/font definition file
8. Convert old drawing file

Enter Selection:

Enter the number corresponding to the desired task. If you enter 0, the system will return to DOS (or UNIX).

Entering 1 will start a new drawing. You will be asked for a drawing name which follows the DOS file name convention. (See DOS File Names.)

Don't add .dwg to the file name. Enter the desired name, along with a path if you don't want the drawing file stored in the present directory. If you precede the drawing name with a floppy drive designation (as in b:whatnot), the drawing will be stored and backed up on that drive. Initial settings or *drawing environment* will follow those of a prototype drawing selected when you configured AutoCAD. If no prototype was selected, AutoCAD will use acad.dwg as the prototype.

Alternatively, you can specify a different prototype by entering a new drawing name and a prototype at the same time. Example: Blimp=Goodyear. AutoCAD would then start a new drawing file called Blimp and use an existing drawing named Goodrich as the prototype. If you put an equals sign after the new drawing name but don't add a drawing name after it (Blimp=), AutoCAD assumes you wish to draw the Goodyear Blimp and doesn't use a prototype. Instead, default values will be used for all settings.

Choosing 2 will bring up an existing drawing into the editor. If you have been working in AutoCAD already, it will offer you the name of the last drawing worked on as the default. Just hit [Return] to call it back up.

If the drawing you want to work on is not in the same directory as AutoCAD, when prompted for the name of the drawing, precede it with the correct path. For example, \book\page will access the file called "page.dwg" in "book" directory.

Normally, AutoCAD will put you back into a drawing exactly where you left it, in the same zoom, with the same status, etc. If you want to get back into a different saved view, enter the drawing name thus: castle,rearelvn, giving the name of the view after the drawing name, separated by a comma.

(Note: When you call up AutoCAD, you can tell it what drawing you wish to edit by putting the drawing name after "acad." For example, entering "acad hogan" will make hogan.dwg the default drawing. This is particularly useful in scripts. See ACAD.)

Selection 3 will bring up the *PLOT* routine. AutoCAD will ask you which drawing you want to plot, and then continue the *PLOT* command. See Chapter 9, Plotting, for more information.

Selection 4 will enter the *PRPLOT* command routine. Furnish the name of the drawing you wish to plot on your printer. See the Chapter on Plotting for a further description of printer plotting.

Selection 5 is used to configure AutoCAD, that is, to tell AutoCAD what hardware you are using so that the proper drivers will be loaded. See Chapter 2, Configuring AutoCAD.

Selection 6 is the file utilities task. This operates similar to the *FILES* command.

Selection 7 compiles ASCII shape and font definition files into the form used by AutoCAD. Further description is contained under Shapes.

Selection 8 is used to convert old format drawing files to the latest version of AutoCAD. This is a one-way trip, unless you can locate a backwards translator. The conversion is automatic if you are putting the drawing into the drawing editor. The only time you need to use Selection 8 is when you are going to insert the translated drawing into another drawing, or when your old drawing utilized the *REPEAT* and *ENDREP* commands.

AutoCAD will retain a copy of the untranslated version of the drawing in an ".old" file. If you translate a batch of files using wildcard characters, the .old files will not be created.

Marker Blips—(See also *BLIPMODE*.) These are the small crosses that AutoCAD places on the screen wherever a point selection is made. These help to relocate points if you cancel a command or if you need to make further use of one of the locations. They also help to keep track of which entities have been selected so far. Doing a *REDRAW* will clean up the display, removing all blips.

MEASURE Command—(See also *DIVIDE*.) You can *MEASURE* an entity by placing markers along an object at specified intervals using the *MEASURE* command. This differs from the *DIVIDE* command in that *DIVIDE* measures the entity into a specified number of equal segments.

After entering *MEASURE*, select a single arc, circle, line or polyline by pointing. Next, either specify from the keyboard the distance you want used, or pick two points spanning the chosen distance using the cursor. Point entities will then be placed along the object.

Responding to the initial prompt with *Block* lets you enter the name of a currently defined block within the drawing. That block will be placed along the *DIVIDE*d object instead of marker points. You will then be asked if you want the block aligned with the object being measured. A *Yes* will result in the block being rotated so its horizontal lines are drawn tangent to the object being measured. If you respond with *No*, the block will be *INSERT*ed with no rotation. The Segment length is specified next; follow the prompt.

MENU Command—(See also the Section on Macros and Menus.) When you call an existing drawing up into the drawing editor, the last menu used in that drawing will

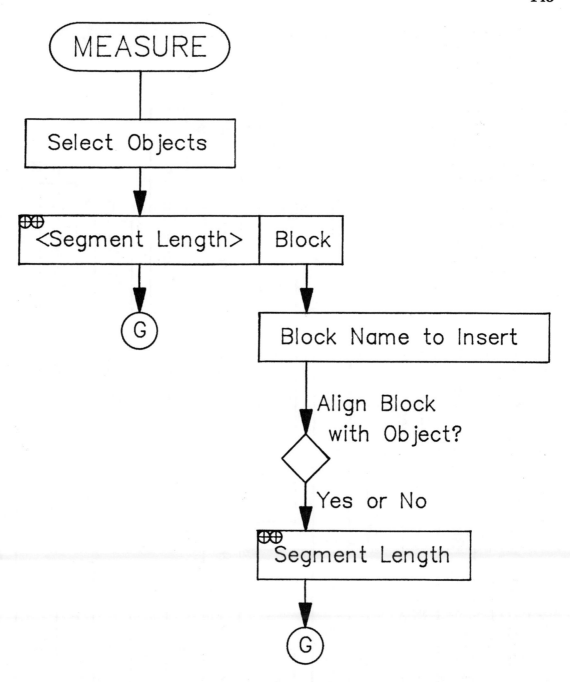

automatically be loaded. For new drawings, AutoCAD will load the default menu selected when you configured your system. To change menus, enter MENU. The prompt is:

Menu file name or . for none <current>:

To reload the present menu, hit [Return]. You might want to do this if you have just used SideKick or some other memory-resident text editor to modify the menu.

Enter the name of the new menu you wish to load. AutoCAD will load the newer of the source (.mnu) file or the compiled (.mnx) file. (If you are having difficulties with a menu, it might be best to delete the .mnx file and have AutoCAD recompile the (.mnu) file when it is loaded, making a new .mnx file.

If you don't want a menu, enter a period (.) at the prompt.

Don't forget to change your tablet overlay if the new menu contains a tablet section. See also the *TABLET* command.

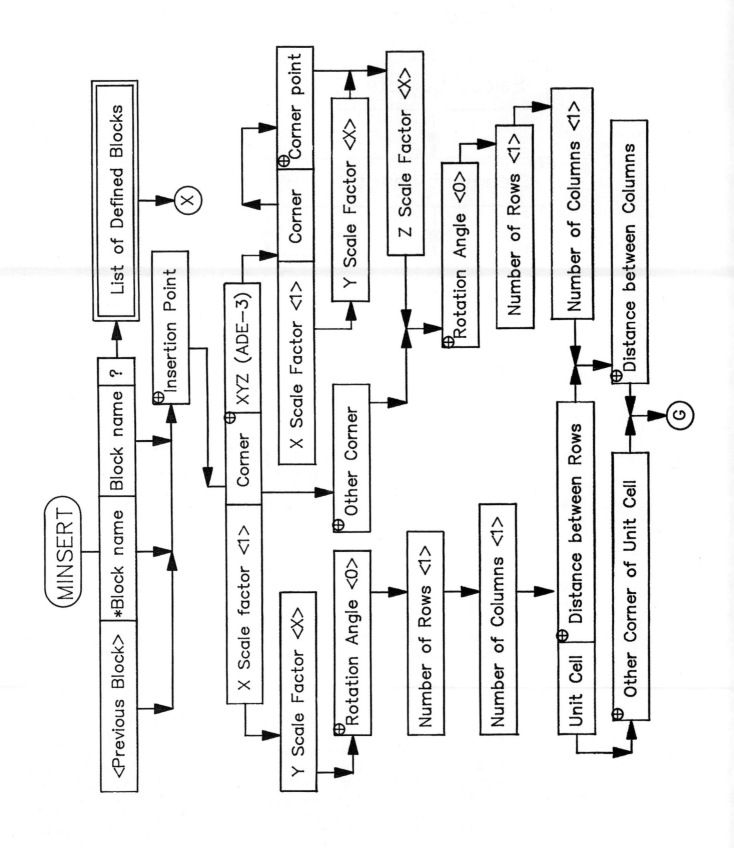

MINSERT Command—(See also INSERT and ARRAY.) This command is used to insert a rectangular array of a block at the same time that it is inserted. The initial prompt asks for the name of the block to insert. Responding with a question mark will give you a list of all the blocks defined in the drawing. If you enter the name of a block, you will be prompted for X and Y scale factors and a rotation angle, just as in *INSERT*. (See the *INSERT* command for details.)

After the rotation has been entered, you will be asked to supply the number of rows and columns and then the unit cell or the distance between rows. If you supply a row spacing, you will then be asked for the column spacing.

One peculiar feature of *MINSERT* is that if you rotate the block you insert, the entire array will be tilted by that same angle about the base point of the first item, leaving the block at an angle of zero with respect to the rest of the array created.

MINSERT's can't be *EXPLODED*. They also may not be created with an asterisk in front of the block name.

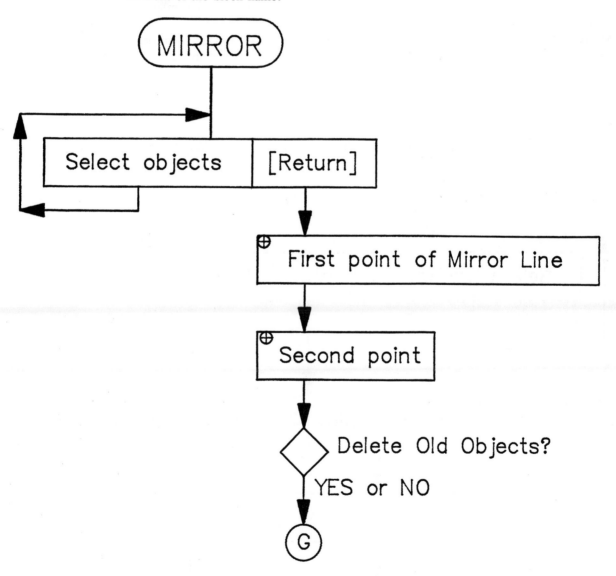

MIRROR Command—(See also Copy and Move.) ADE-2 allows you to make mirror images of existing objects. After entering MIRROR, choose the objects to be mirrored, using the usual methods of selection. Then, as prompted, select two points to determine the *mirror* line; objects will be MIRRORed symmetrically about this line. The length of the mirror line is not critical. What is important is the placement of the mirror line and its angle relative to the objects to be *MIRROR*ed.

After the mirror line is complete, you'll be given the option of having the original object(s) deleted or retained on the drawing. Usually you will choose to retain them on the drawing.

Mirrored Text—Rarely does anyone want text to appear backwards or upside down. Using the *MIRROR* command will also *MIRROR* any text or attributes contained in the selected objects. If you don't want this to happen, use the *SETVAR* command to reset the system variable, *MIRRTEXT*, to zero before you use *MIRROR*. See *SETVAR* for other system variable definitions.

Version 2.6 notes. The *MIRROR* command under Version 2.6 of AutoCAD can be used on 3D lines and faces, but is restricted to mirroring in the X-Y plane. Also, the *MIRROR* command can result in automatic redimensioning when used on associative dimensioned entities. The current variable settings will be used to regenerate the dimension set.

Mode—This refers here to a manner or style of drawing, or a type of drawing method, as in *ORTHO* on versus *ORTHO* off, Isometric versus Normal, sketching versus ordinary construction, and so forth. See also Toggles.

Mouse—This is a simple and inexpensive pointing device. It usually has three buttons and either an LED and sensor on the bottom, or a rotating sphere, like an upside-down trackball. It is cost-effective if you are only using AutoCAD occasionally but it is not a very nimble drawing implement. (As John Vitale says, "Did you ever try to draw with a brick?")

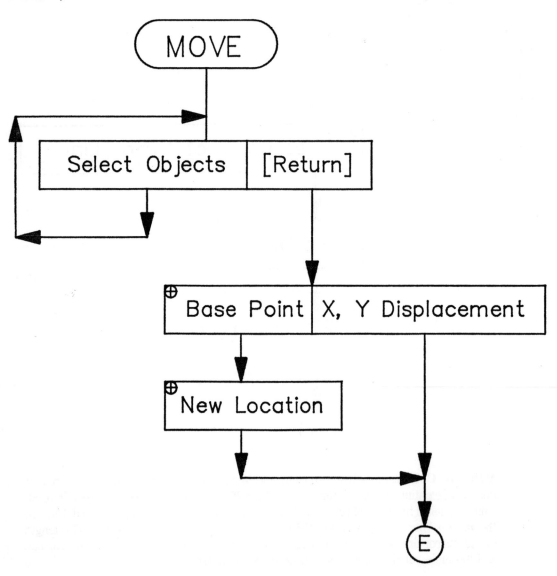

MOVE Command—(See also COPY and MIRROR.) An entity or group of entities can be moved to a new location on a drawing with the *MOVE* command. After entering MOVE, select the object(s) you want to move and hit [Return], then either enter two points, showing where to move from and where to move to, or enter an X,Y displacement distance pair at the first prompt and hit [Return]. The ADE-2 version lets you respond with *DRAG* instead of a displacement so you can visually move the object, using the puck or mouse.

    Version 2.6 notes. The *MOVE* command will work in the Z direction if ADE-3 is present.

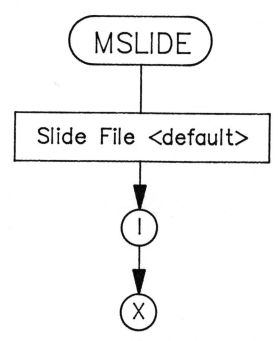

MSLIDE Command—(See also VSLIDE and the entry on Slides.) MSLIDE allows you to create *slides* or snapshot views of a portion of a drawing. First you cause the portion of the drawing you want to view to appear on the screen, using *ZOOM* and *PAN*. Then enter *MSLIDE*. You'll be prompted for the name of the slide file you want to create. You can simply press [Return] and accept the default, this will give the slide the same name as the present drawing, except with an .sld suffix. You might instead choose any other name conforming to the DOS file name convention.

Multi-line Text—(See TEXT Command.) Entering a null response for a starting point in the *TEXT* command will cause the text to appear directly below the last text entered in the drawing. All the text settings of the previous line will be repeated for the new line: angle, layer, color, height, and justification.

N-O

Named Views—AutoCAD supports the use of named views, that is, zoom and pan positions that can be restored to the display much faster than zooming out and back in. See the *VIEW* command.

New Drawing—(See Main Menu.)

Null Response—This refers to hitting the [Return] key without first typing anything in.

Object Pointing—(See Selecting Objects.)

Object Selection—(See Selecting Objects.)

Object Snap—(See also *OSNAP* Command.) Some constructions require accurately locating a point that is not on a snap point. For this type of work, AutoCAD has been provided with the ability to snap to certain features, as listed below. When prompted for a point, you must enter the first three letters (or more) of the appropriate object snap mode or modes. A snap target will appear on the display, showing the area within which AutoCAD is searching for a match to the requested snap mode. You can adjust the size of the target box by using the *APERTURE* command.

CEN	Center:	Seeks the center of a circle or arc whose circumference crosses the pixel (target) box.
END	Endpoint:	Snaps to the nearest endpoint of an arc or line.
INS	Insertion point:	Looks for the insertion base point of a block, shape, or piece of text.
INT	Intersection:	Looks for the intersection of lines, traces, arcs, or circles crossing the target box. Doesn't snap to arcs or circles that are parts of blocks.
MID	Midpoint:	Snaps to the midpoint of a line or an arc.
NEA	Nearest:	Snaps to the nearest point on a line, arc, or circle. Doesn't snap to arcs or circles that are parts of blocks.
NOD	Node:	Snaps to a point. Can be used to snap to points placed strategically in block definitions for easy attachments.
PER	Perpendicular:	Snaps to a point on a line, arc, or circle to form a perpendicular with the last point, if any. Doesn't snap to arcs or circles that are parts of blocks.
QUA	Quadrant:	Hunts for a quadrant point on a circle or arc.
QUI	Quick:	Used in combination with other snap modes, except

INTERSECTION. Stops searching as soon as the first item matching the other snap mode (or modes) is found.

TAN Tangent: Forms a tangent to an arc or circle, from the last point entered, if any.

NON None: Turns off object snap.

An example of how the snap modes are used:

AutoCAD Prompt:	*User Input:*
Command:	*LINE*
from point:	*0,0*
to point:	*MIDP*
of:	(select a line).
to point:	*TANG*
to:	(select an arc or circle.)

Note that the snap mode called for is only in effect for a single point. For running snap modes for more than one point, see the *OSNAP* command. Note also that while *ORTHO* is overridden by an object snap (if there is one), ordinary *SNAP* points are not.

OFFSET Command—This command can be used to make a duplicate of another object, such as a polyline, line, or arc, or circle, conforming to the shape of the original, but offset by a given distance. The initial prompt after entering *OFFSET* is:

Offset distance or Through <last value>:

Use the "Through" option if you want to indicate a point where you want the new object to pass through. If you know how far you want the offset duplicate to be from the original, you can enter that value at the prompt, either from the keyboard or by hitting two points with the puck.

The next prompt asks you to select an object to offset. This must be done by pointing.

You will next be asked for which side of the original you want the new object to appear, or for a point to draw it *through*, depending on which option you used above. A point in the right spot will satisfy the requirements of this prompt. After constructing the offset object, AutoCAD will loop back to the initial prompt and allow you to select another object to *OFFSET*.

Exit the command by hitting [Return].

There are a few nuances to the *OFFSET* command:

(1) Complicated curves, such as polylines, often don't have just one, unique *OFFSET* curve. The results of the *OFFSET* command may or may not match what you want. In that case, you can proceed in one of two ways: (a) Edit the resulting polyline using *PEDIT*. (b) Undo the *OFFSET* command, *EXPLODE* the original polyline, and start over, OFFSETting the pieces one at a time.

(2) *OFFSET*s for wide polylines will be measured from the centerline.

(3) If you ask for an impossible *OFFSET*, you will receive an error message indicating what the problem is.

(4) You might find that AutoCAD can't create an *OFFSET* for complicated entities, such as long polylines or sketches.

Old Drawings—(See Main Menu.)

OOPS Command—(See also *UNDO*.) When you *ERASE*, AutoCAD stores a list of the last batch of *ERASE*d entities. You can enter *OOPS* to restore that group to the drawing. *OOPS* won't restore any more than the last set of erased entities. *OOPS* will

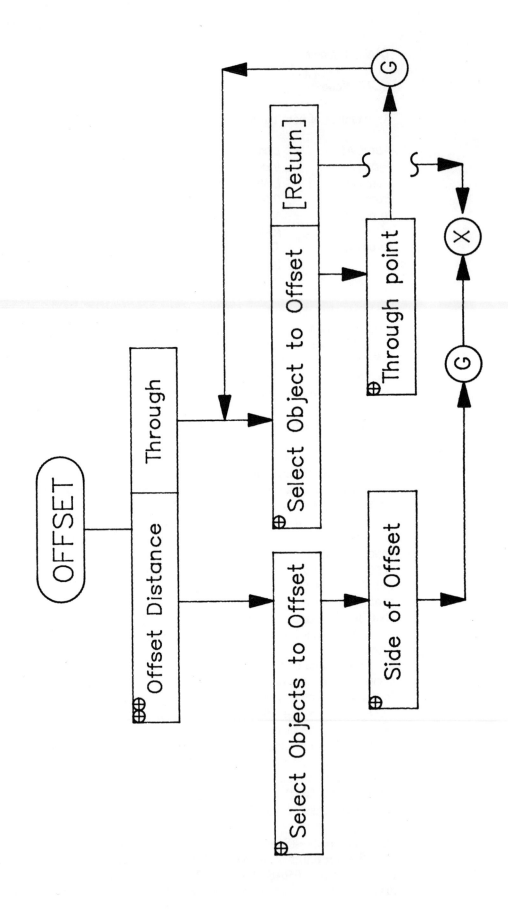

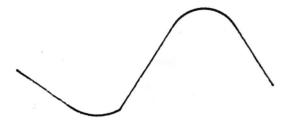

Before offset

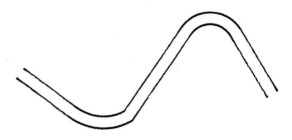

After offset

also restore objects erased with *BLOCK* or *WBLOCK.*

ORTHO Command—ORTHO makes sure that Lines and Traces drawn with a pointing device will be perpendicular or orthogonal to the current Snap grid. It is like drawing with a T-square.

The *ORTHO* function is a toggle, that is, when you enter *ORTHO*, you answer *ON* to turn *ORTHO* mode on, and *OFF* to allow drawing lines and angles.

See "Toggle Settings" for more information on other toggles. The control key to turn toggle *ORTHO* on, even during a command, is the F8 key, on most PC compatibles. *ORTHO* can also be controlled by the *ORTHOMODE* system variable, accessible through *SETVAR* and AutoLISP.

OSNAP Command—This command allows the use of object snap modes for more than one point. It turns on an object snap mode and leaves it on. Several snap modes can be invoked at the same time. Enter *OSNAP*, followed by a list of desired snap modes, separated by commas. To turn the snap modes off, enter *OFF* or *NONE* or nothing at the prompt. An example:

Command: OSNAP
Object snap modes: INS,ENDP,QUIC

The sequence above will cause subsequent points to snap to the nearest of an insertion or endpoint. The "QUICK" mode will prevent searching the entire database for the best matching objects; the search will be terminated as soon as any point with the correct snap mode is found within the target box. See Object Snap.

It should be noted that if no suitable object snap point is found within the target box, the crosshairs location is used instead, without any warning.

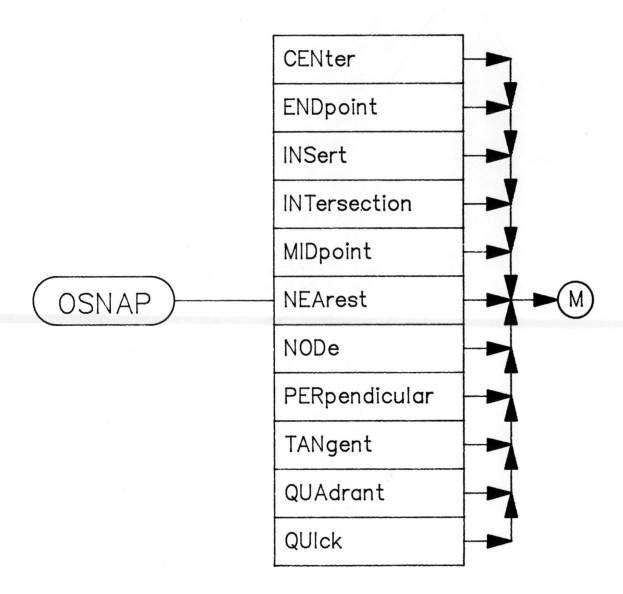

P

PAN Command—You can view a different part of a drawing, without changing the magnification, by using the *PAN* command. Enter PAN, then tell AutoCAD what direction to move the screen view by specifying the displacement with either an X,Y displacement pair, followed by two [Return]s, or by designating two points with the cursor. The display will move by the amounts in the X,Y pair, or, if you used the pointing device, will move so that the first point specified falls where the second point was entered.

*PAN*ning will often cause a *REGEN* if *REGENAUTO* is on.

The *PAN* command has a *transparent* form that allows using it without first exiting from another command you have already started. Put an apostrophe in front of the transparent command: *'PAN*. AutoCAD will then let you *PAN* before continuing with the other command.

Parallel lines—A line or sequence of lines parallel to an existing polyline or object can be constructed by the use of the *OFFSET* command. See *OFFSET.*

Path Names—Path names are directory names placed in front of file names to tell DOS or AutoCAD where to find those files. For example, you can include path commands in your autoexec.bat file telling DOS which directories to search in which order:

PATH C:\;C:\ARCHITEC;C:\JOHN\MISC;B:

DOS will then look for external commands first in the working directory, then in the root directory, then in the ARCHITEC directory, in the subdirectory called MISC in the JOHN directory, and finally in floppy drive B.

AutoCAD supports the use of path names in drawing names. For example, when naming a new drawing, if you include a path, AutoCAD will store the .dwg file as specified by that path:

/architec/smithous

This will store your drawing called "smithous" in the "architec" directory. Note that AutoCAD, unlike DOS, is not particular whether you use a forward slash or a backslash. Crafty buggers!

You can, alternatively, get into your working directory, where your drawings are stored, and invoke AutoCAD from there. To do this, you must have a path command like:

PATH C:\ACAD

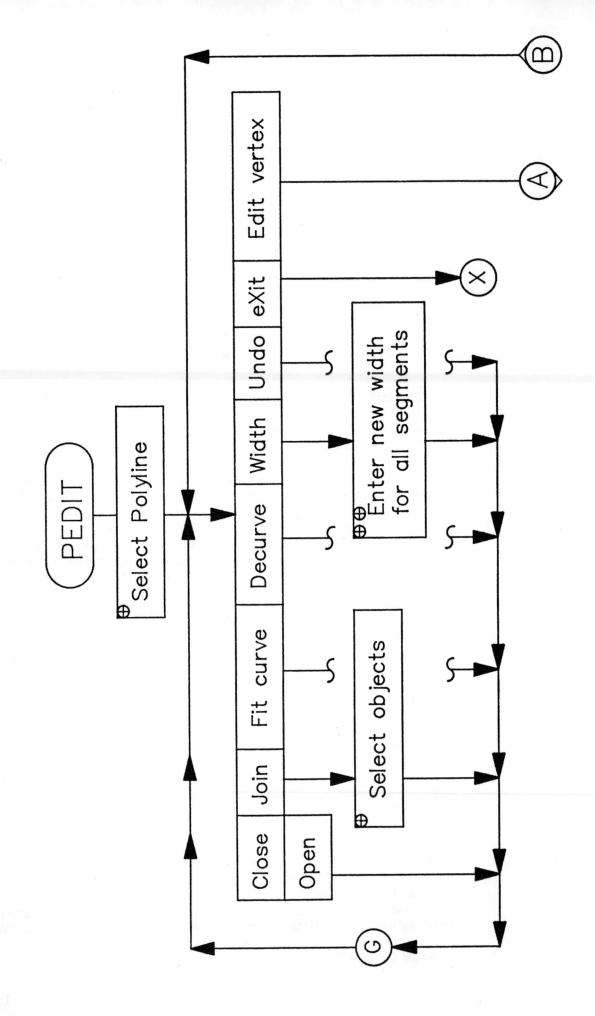

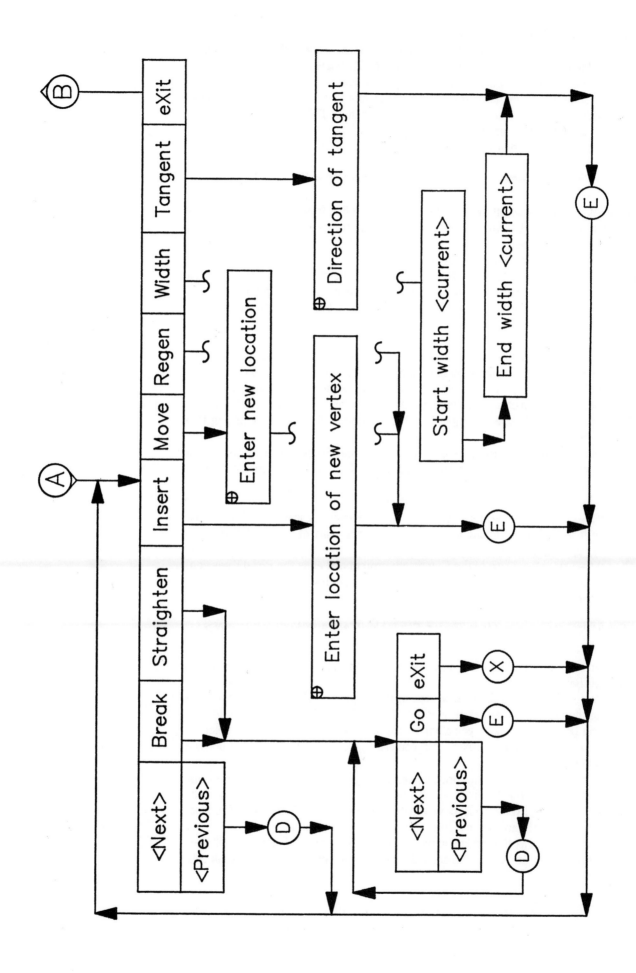

Pattern Filling—(See HATCH Command.)

PEDIT Command—This command is used for performing edits on polylines. Remember, though, that the *BREAK, FILLET* and *CHAMFER* commands can also be used on polylines for those specialized editing operations. Enter *PEDIT,* then select a polyline, as prompted. If you have selected an arc or line that is not part of a polyline, AutoCAD will ask you if you want to make it a polyline. This is useful for joining independent arcs and lines into a single polyline.

The main selection menu for PEDIT is:

Close/Join/Width/Edit vertex/Fit curve/Decurve/Undo/eXit <X>:

*(C) Close—*This closes off the polyline by drawing a line from the last point to the starting point. (If the polyline you selected is closed, the prompt will offer you the option "Open," instead of Close.)

(O) Open—(See above under Close.)

*(J) Join—*Any lines or arcs connected to an open polyline at either end will be added to the polyline, if selected at the next prompt (Select objects:). You can use the *LIST* command to determine whether all the selected objects have been added to the polyline. Another method is to change the width of the polyline temporarily.

If you can't get some pieces to join, *ZOOM* in tightly at the intersection of the two polylines and see what it looks like. Use a conventional *BREAK* command and put a line between the ends of the polylines using endpoint object snaps. Then select the new segment in *PEDIT,* convert it to a polyline, and join it to the other polylines.

*(W) Width—*You can change all segments of the polyline to a single, uniform width. Supply the desired width when prompted, either by keyboard input or by hitting two points with the cursor.

*(F) Fit curve—*This will smooth the polyline into a series of curved lines by converting each line to two arcs. If you wish to improve the fit, the Edit vertex option can be used to make alterations, or you can use Decurve, below.

*(D) Decurve—*This straightens out fitted curves.

*(U) Undo—*To back up one step, use Undo. This will undo the last *PEDIT* operation. You can use it repeatedly, working your way back to the start of the *PEDIT* session, if necessary, up to but not including the conversion of a line or an arc to a polyline.

*(X) eXit—*This returns you to the Command: prompt and ends the PEDIT session.

*(E) Edit vertex—*To make changes in a single vertex, use this option. The Edit vertex submenu looks like this:

Next/Previous/Break/Insert/Move/Regen/Straighten/Tangent/Width/eXit/ <N>:

The first vertex will be marked with an X. The sub-options under the Edit vertex option are amplified below:

{*N*} *Next—*This selects the next vertex in the polyline. "Next" means the next vertex along the polyline in the direction it was drawn. Next also becomes the default, so that hitting [Return] will move you along to the next vertex. The currently selected vertex will have the X placed on it. Note that you can't go completely around the polyline with this option.

{*P*} *Previous—*This selects the prior vertex in the polyline, that is, the earlier one in the original construction. "Previous" also becomes the default after it is used the first time, so that hitting [Return] will move you one more vertex in the previous direction. You can't go completely around the polyline with this option, either.

{*B*} *Break—*To break the polyline in two, take the "B" option. The break will start with the current vertex and end at the second vertex, as selected under the Break sub-submenu:

Next/Previous/Go/eXit <N>:

These choices under Break allow you to move the marker X along the polyline until you reach the desired break point. Hit "G" to perform the break from the current vertex to the vertex where you entered the Break choice. The closing segment will also be erased when you Break the polyline. "X" will return you to the Edit vertex submenu if you decide not to proceed with the Break.

{I} Insert—If you wish to add another vertex to your polyline, use this option. Move the marker X, using "Next" or "Previous", to the vertex just short of where you want to add the new corner and hit "I". You will be asked to show where you want the new vertex.

{M} Move—To move a vertex to a new spot, step the marker X along the polyline until you reach the vertex you want to move. Hit "M" and, at the prompt, enter the new location desired.

{S} Straighten—This is the same as the Break option, except that the space will be filled with a single line when you hit "Go". If you select just one vertex, any arc following that vertex will be straightened.

{T} Tangent—You can assign a tangent direction to a vertex by flagging it with the X and selecting "T". Then enter a tangent angle, as prompted, using the keyboard or cursor. Tangent directions are used to force the direction of the smooth polyline produced by curve fitting, at that vertex. Note that the polyline will retain any tangent direction data even after Decurving.

{W} Width—If you select the "W" option, you can set the starting and ending widths of the segment just beyond the marker X. Note the defaults at the starting and ending width prompts. The new width/taper will not be shown until the polyline is REGENed.

{R} Regen—To see the effect of any Width subcommand used, hit the Regen option, "R".

{X} eXit—This will put you back to the *PEDIT* menu.

PLINE Command—This command is used for the construction of "Polylines." A polyline is a continuous sequence of lines, arcs, or traces. AutoCAD treats polylines as a single entity for some operations, such as crosshatching.

After you enter *PLINE*, you will be asked to enter the starting point and then the current line width will be displayed. Next, AutoCAD will offer you the following choices:

Arc/Close/Half width/Length/Undo/Width/<endpoint of line>:

Respond with the initial letter of your choice, or enter another point for the continuation of the polyline.

(A) Arc—Selecting Arc will call up a new prompt for drawing various polyline arc types.

(C) Close—This closes off the polyline by drawing a line from the last point to the starting point, stepping out of the polyline command. Note that if you don't use the Close command, but draw a line to the starting point instead, the polyline is still considered *open* by AutoCAD.

(L) Length—By selecting the Length option, you can add a line of specified length to the polyline, in the same direction as the end of the polyline.

(U) Undo—This will go back one operation, eliminating the last segment and putting you in the polyline drawing mode corresponding to the prior segment.

(W) Width—This is used to permit changing the width of the polyline. You will be asked for a starting and an ending width, so that tapered line or arc segments can be drawn.

(H) Half width—Similar to the Width option, this permits specifying a distance equal to half the desired width. Why would you want to do this? Because your pointing device can easily enter the half width by selecting a point on the desired edge of the trace. (Remember: polyline traces are treated in the database and in object snaps and intersections as if they were a single line corresponding to their centerline.)

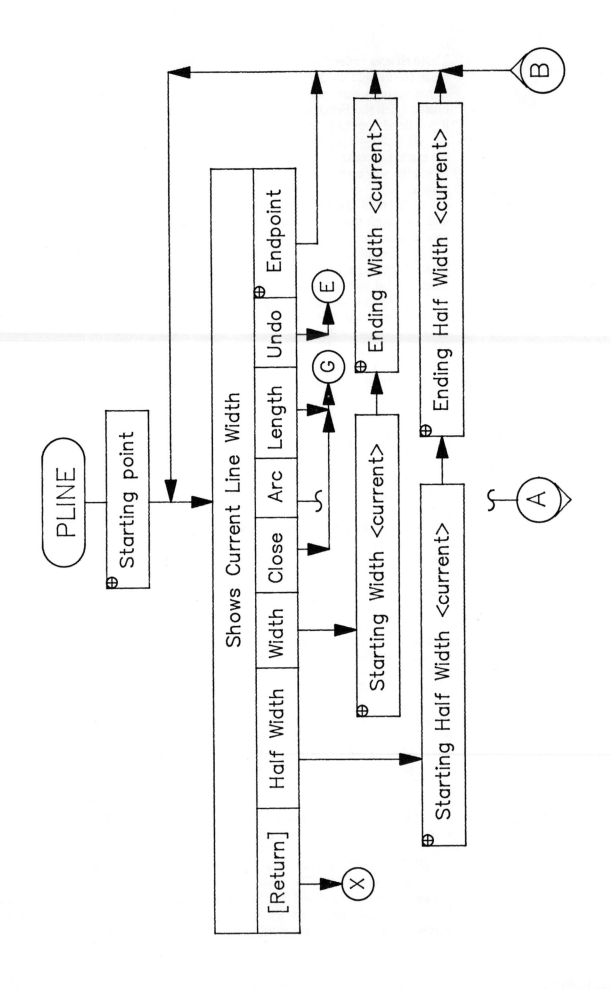

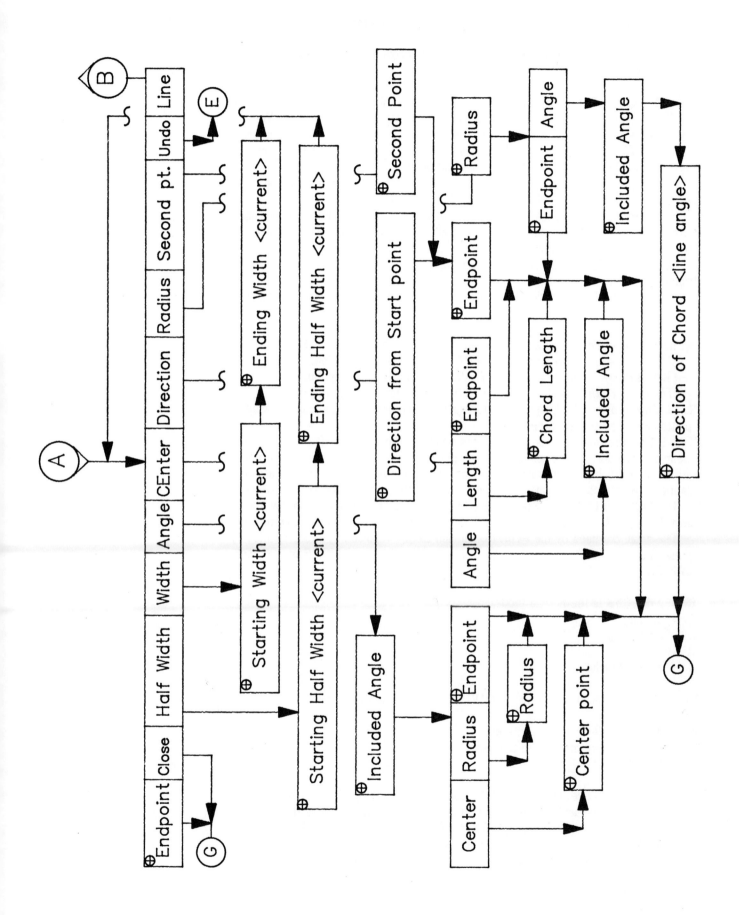

The submenu choices under the Arc option are as follows:

Angle/CEnter/CLose/Direction/Half-width/Line/Radius/Second pt/Undo/Width/<endpoint of arc>:

{*A*} *Angle*—This choice will cause AutoCAD to ask for the included angle of the arc. (Remember that AutoCAD likes to draw positive arcs counterclockwise.) You will then be asked for a center, a radius, or an endpoint, similar to the ARC command.

{*CE*} *CEnter*—Entering "CE" permits specifying a center point for the arc, followed by an included angle, a length, or an end point.

{*CL*} *CLose*—"CL" calls for closing the polyline with an arc instead of a straight line. Again, this will pop you out of the PLINE command.

{*D*} *Direction*—AutoCAD normally draws polylines in the smoothest way possible, constructing arcs tangent to the previous straight line segment. The Direction option allows you to specify a non-tangent direction, followed by an endpoint.

{*L*} *Line*—This exits the Arc mode of polyline construction and returns you to the straight line mode.

{*R*} *Radius*—After entering "R", you will be asked for the arc radius, followed by an included angle or the endpoint.

{*S*} *Second pt*—This allows you to continue drawing the arc as a three-point arc. You must supply the second and third points after you have entered "S".

{*U*} *Undo*—See above under the *PLINE* main menu Undo option.

{*W*} *Width*—As above under the *PLINE* main menu Width option.

{*H*} *Half width*—As above for the *PLINE* main menu Half-width option.

PLOT Command—(See chapter on Plotting.) This command sends your drawing to a plotter for execution on paper.

POINT Command—This command places points in the drawing. These points will appear as small dots on the screen, and will plot. If a point lies on top of a grid point, neither will be visible. Points are not very useful in themselves, but serve to assist in locating other objects. A point, for example, can serve as an object to snap to using "node" *OSNAP*s (ADE-2). A point placed in a block definition can also allow you to select that object by pointing to a part of it that would otherwise have nothing to *grab* it by.

The small dot used by the *POINT* command can be replaced by other entities by the use of the *SETVAR* command to adjust the system variables *PDMODE* and *PDSIZE*. *PDMODE*'s are as follows:

```
0 = a dot (this is the normal mode)
1 = nothing
2 = a plus sign
3 = an X
4 = an apostrophe
```

Add these numbers to the above *PDMODE*'s to modify the point marker:

```
32 = draw a circle around the marker
64 = draw a square around the marker
96 = draw both of the above
```

PDSIZE, if positive, is the size of the point blip in drawing units. If negative, it is the percentage of the screen size. Note that negative PDSIZE will cause the point blip to stay the same size regardless of how far in or out you zoom. See *SETVAR* Command.

If you have a large number of points you wish to remove, and you can't find them all, or you can't erase them because they are too small to locate among other objects, change *PDMODE* to 2, *REGEN* the drawing, and you will be able to see all the points and grab them by the ends of the crosses easily.

		+	×	'
0	1	2	3	4

⊙	○	⊕	⊠	⊙
32	33	34	35	36

⊡	□	⊞	⊠	⊡
64	65	66	67	68

◙	◘	⊕	⊠	◙
96	97	98	99	100

Version 2.6 notes: If ADE-3 is present, you can use the *POINT* command in all three dimensions.

Pointing Devices—The keyboard is not a particularly efficient input device, even for AutoCAD. A number of cursor-controlling devices can be configured for use with AutoCAD. The most important of these is the digitizing tablet. Second place goes to the mouse, with the TouchPen a distant third. Other devices are also supported by AutoCAD—see Appendix E.

Polar Arrays—The *ARRAY* command can be used to make either rectangular or circular arrays. The latter are referred to in later versions of AutoCAD as Polar Arrays. See ARRAY.

Polar Coordinates—See also Coordinates, *UNITS* Command Polar coordinates consist of a pair of numbers that describe the location of an object in terms of its distance from a fixed point (the *origin*) and its angle from the X axis.

POLYGON Command—This command permits drawing regular polygons in three different ways: Inscribed, Circumscribed, and Edge methods. Enter POLYGON and then enter the desired number of sides, from 3 to 1024. Read the prompt:

Edge/<Center of polygon>:

If you reply *E*, for Edge, you will then be prompted for two points defining an edge of the polygon. The polygon will be drawn counterclockwise, with one side lying exactly from one point to the other.

If you enter a point for the center of the polygon, the next prompt is:

Inscribed in circle/Circumscribed about circle (I/C):

Enter *I* or *C*. The new prompt will ask for the radius of the circle. Enter the radius from the keyboard or enter a point using the cursor. Radii from the keyboard will give a polygon with the first side aligned with the snap grid. If you enter a point to show where the radius lies, an inscribed circle will have a corner at that point. A circumscribed circle will have one edge centered at the radius point.

Polylines—A polyline is a series of objects consisting of lines and arcs connected end to end. The line width can vary, giving tapered lines and arcs, or the line can be like

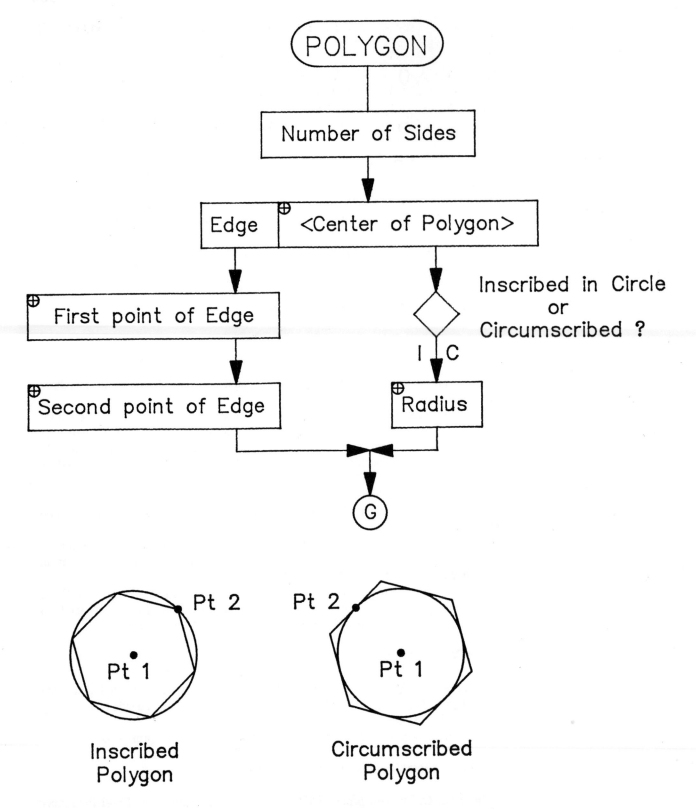

Inscribed Polygon

Circumscribed Polygon

a trace, or can be of various linetypes. Polylines are drawn with the *PLINE* command and edited with the *PEDIT* command or the *FILLET* or *CHAMFER* command.

Previous Selection Set—(See Selecting Objects.) When AutoCAD prompts *"Select objects:"*, you can enter *"P"* and the previous set of selected objects from the last command or from the *SELECT* command will be reused.

Printer Echo—If you wish, for some reason, to keep a running record of all AutoCAD prompts, input, and data output, you can turn on printer echo with [CTRL] Q. Everything that occurs in the prompt area will then be printed out continuously. Another [CTRL] Q will toggle printer echo off.

Prototype Drawing—(See also Configuring and Main Menu.) You can specify a standard or *prototype* drawing for AutoCAD to use in setting all of its parameters for any new drawings created. If you don't specify a prototype drawing of your own, AutoCAD will use acad.dwg as the prototype. The following table describes the settings used in acad.dwg:

APERTURE	10 pixels
AXIS	Off
BASE	0,0
BLIPMODE	On
CHAMFER	0
COLOR	BYLAYER
DIM Variables	(See DIM Command)
DRAGMODE	Auto
ELEV	Elevn 0.0, Thickness 0.0
FILL	On
FILLET	0.0
GRID	OFF, spacing (0,0)
Highlighting	Enabled
ISOPLANE	Left
LAYER	Layer 0 ON, Color 7, Cont. Linetype
LIMITS	0,0 to 12,9
LINETYPE	BYLAYER, CONTINUOUS
LTSCALE	1.0
MENU	acad.mnu
MIRROR	Text mirroring
Selectivity	3 pixel box
ORTHO	Off
OSNAP	None
PLINE	0 width
POINT	Display mode 0, size 0
QTEXT	Off
REGENAUTO	On
SKETCH	Increment .1, producing lines
SNAP	Off, Spacing 1 × 1
SNAP/GRID	Standard, base 0,0, rotation 0
STYLE	STANDARD, txt, var. height, width 1.0
TABLET	Off
TEXT	STANDARD, ht. 0.2, rotation 0
TIME	User elapsed time on
TRACE	Width 0.05
UNITS, linear	Decimal inches, 4 places;
UNITS, angle	Decimal degree
VIEWRES	Fast zoom on, Circle zoom 100%
ZOOM	To drawing limits

If you wish to use other settings for a prototype drawing, either create an entirely new drawing and make the necessary settings, or, if you only wish to make a few deviations from the acad.dwg, make a copy in DOS (named, say, proto.dwg), edit the copy as needed, and reconfigure from the AutoCAD Main Menu to make the proto.dwg the prototype drawing.

PRPLOT Command—Plotting can either be done from the Main Menu or from the Drawing Editor using the *PLOT* or *PRPLOT* commands. *PRPLOT* will dump a copy of

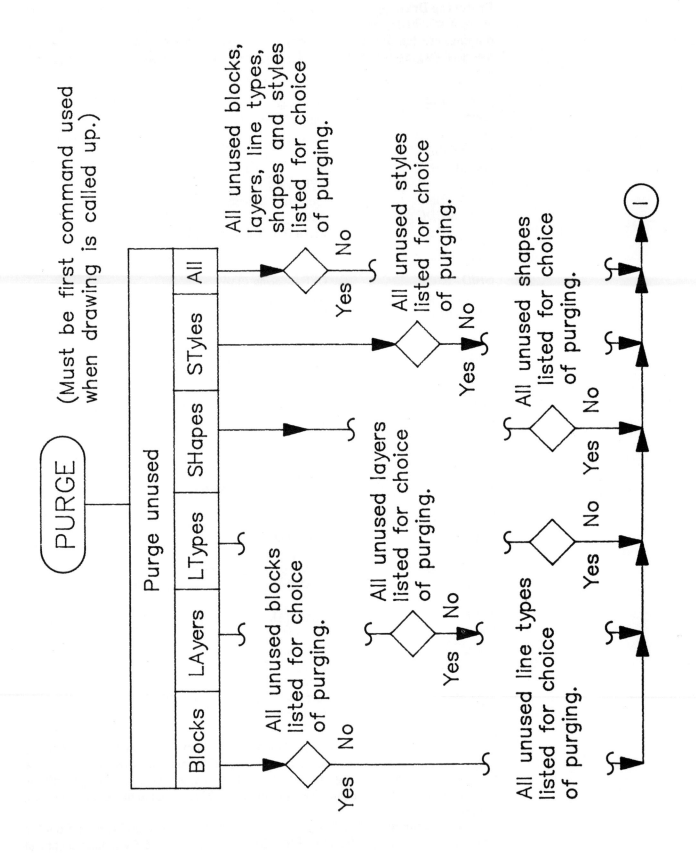

your drawing to a dot matrix printer. For general information on plotting, see the *PLOT* command. Specific data on printer plots is listed below:

You can't specify a plot size larger than *MAX*.

Printer plots go a lot faster if there is no border around the drawing. Turn it off as a separate layer before printer plotting.

For more information, see Chapter 9 on Plotting.

PURGE Command—PURGE allows you to delete unused named objects when you first enter the drawing editor. Enter *PURGE*. The initial prompt will be:

Purge unused Blocks/LAyers/LTypes/SHapes/STyles/All:

Select either the type of objects you want purged, or *A*ll to get rid of all of them. AutoCAD will name the unused things one at a time and let you verify whether each one should be purged.

Keep in mind the following:

§ *PURGE* only works if it's the first command you issue after entering the drawing editor

§ Some standard objects can't be purged, including layer 0, the *CONTINUOUS* linetype and the *STANDARD* text style.

§ *SH*ape lets you purge references to the Shape Files named in the *LOAD* command.

§ *PURGE* won't purge named Views, but *VIEW* allows their deletion.

§ *PURGE* removes only one reference level. For example, if you purge a layer containing a reference to a linetype, only the reference will be removed, not the linetype itself. The same is true for blocks, etc. Because of this, to purge ALL unreferenced objects from the whole drawing, you must use the PURGE command and then END. Get back into the drawing editor and repeat the above until you receive a message telling you there are no unreferenced objects.

Q-R

QTEXT—The time it takes to REGENerate a drawing is related to the number of vectors that must be displayed on the screen. *TEXT* contains many vectors and will slow your drawing *REGEN*s down considerably, depending on how much *TEXT* is in the view being displayed.

When *QTEXT* is turned on, the text in a drawing is replaced with a pair of parallel lines or a rectangle when the drawing is regenerated, depending on which version of AutoCAD you have. This reduces the effective number of display vectors and saves subsequent regeneration time.

When *QTEXT* is on and you enter new text, it will be drawn as actual characters so you can confirm content, spacing and placement; the next time you cause the drawing to be *REGEN*erated, the new text will be displayed in abbreviated form.

QTEXT is toggled by entering *QTEXT* and responding with either *ON* or *OFF*.

The *QTEXTMODE* system variable can also be controlled through *SETVAR* and AutoLISP.

Quick Text—(See the *QTEXT* Command.)

QUIT Command—You can return to the Main Menu without updating the drawing by entering *QUIT*. You will be asked if you really want to disregard all the changes you've made to the drawing. If you answer Yes, neither the .dwg nor the .bak file will be changed. Be sure to use the *QUIT* command if something really disastrous happens to the drawing while you are working on it. If you have been *SAVE*ing the drawing every half hour or so, the way you're supposed to, you will have only lost thirty minutes' work, max. You might want to try the *UNDO* command, but for really awful cases, where you have eradicated major pieces of the drawing beyond recovery, you will be better off with a *QUIT* and calling back up the .dwg file as it stood when you started your last half hour's work.

Radians—An angular measure. (See the *UNITS* Command.)

RADIUS Subcommand—(See *DIM* Command.)

Recovering Drawings—There are five kinds of lost drawings: (1) accidentally erased, (2) ones placed in the wrong directory, (3) drawings on disks that have been formatted, (4) drawings garbled by faulty media or other mishap, (5) drawings with editing changes lost when the system locks up or when power fails.

(1) Erased drawings can be recovered if their erasure is discovered immediately. Norton Utilities™ can resurrect erased files if nothing else has been stored over

them. If you think you have just erased something important, whip out your Norton and take a peek. There are some other programs on the market that make it very difficult to accidentally erase a file. They intercept the DOS commands that eliminate files and warn you if something is going to be killed.

(2) Norton's File Find utility can locate files anywhere on a floppy or hard disk, even if they have been tucked away in some strange and forgotten sub-sub-subdirectory like C:boondock\remote\farout\. This usually happens when somebody gets directory-fever on a multi-user machine.

(3) Accidentally formatting a hard drive or floppy has been known to happen. One early version of a well-known program for the Macintosh occasionally grabbed the hard drive instead of a ram drive and did a Data-In-Garbage-Out number on it. Some early DOS versions would respond to a format command where no drive was specified by doing the same thing, totally without warning. When this happens, you are usually out of luck. Norton has a program that will recover formatted disks, if you have installed and been running under the program before the accidental format.

(4) Drawings that are still on disk, but which have lost pieces of data or header information will often not respond to the drawing editor. You will get a message like: "yurt.dwg is not an AutoCAD drawing." These can sometimes be recovered by the following process:

(a) Call the drawing up in AutoCAD.
(b) Before the drawing editor has finished loading, hit [CTRL] C.
(c) Immediately after the Command prompt appears, do a *DXFOUT*.
(d) Call the *DXF* file up in an ASCII text editor and look for obvious glitches. (It helps to have a good *DXF* file for a similar drawing on hand for comparison, or for borrowing from, to restore missing or damaged header information.)
(e) Restore a faulty or missing header by copying one from a similar, valid drawing.
(f) Correct any obvious errors, like objects inserted at infinity, etc.
(g) Start a new drawing and do a DXFIN with the corrected DXF file.

If that procedure doesn't work, and if the header looks good, save a master copy of the DXF file and try working with copies where you have lopped off part or all of the last part of the file. You can sometimes find the glitch in the file by cutting off various chunks of the file until you find the maximum size piece that works. The glitch will be just beyond that point.

(5) When you make an unscheduled exit from drawing editor because of a system lockup or power failure, you will find that AutoCAD has created several files, some of which will have the same name as the drawing. Make backup copies of the .dwg, .bak, .$$$, and ef.$ac files before doing anything. Then try renaming each piece as a different drawing, such as, notsohot.dwg, backup.dwg, dollar.dwg and eee-fff.dwg. Call each of these up in the drawing editor and see what is in it. You might find part or all of your drawing in these files. Use the most complete file.

If your drawing is split up between these files, insert the pieces into the most complete file. If none of the above techniques recover your drawing, go get the backup floppy with the most recent version and continue from where you left off in that file. You say you don't have a backup on a separate floppy? Try gnashing your teeth and chanting this mantra one hundred times "Siam, Oh watta gu!"

One last desperate move if you can't find any backup copy at all: Find a disk that previously had an older version of the drawing or a .bak file for it. Run Norton on it and see if you can unerase the ghost of the file. You might find, depending on how much activity you have had on your hard drive, three or four erased versions of the drawing. Give each one a different name when using Norton's UnErase feature. Use the most recent version as the starting point for your replica.

Rectangular Arrays—(See *ARRAY* Command.)

Redefining Blocks—When you wish to redefine a block, insert a copy of it with the *INSERT* command, using an asterisk in front of the block name. Then make any desired changes and use the *BLOCK* command on the corrected version. Because the block already exists, you will be asked if you wish to redefine it. Answer *Y*, for yes, and continue with the blocking process. Normally, this will cause the drawing to *REGEN*, unless *REGENAUTO* has been toggled off. As soon as the drawing regenerates, all occurrences of that block (where inserted without an asterisk) will be altered to conform to the new version.

REDO Command—(See also *UNDO.*)—This command reverses the action of the previous *UNDO*, even if that *UNDO* undid more than one step.

REDRAW Command—*REDRAW* [Return] will cause AutoCAD to redraw the screen, removing marker blips, etc. [CTRL] C will abort *REDRAW. REDRAW* will return the screen to normal after viewing a slide.

There is a transparent form of the REDRAW command that can be used during the progress of another command. Enter *'REDRAW.*

Reference, Circular—(See Circular Reference.)

REGEN Command—*REGEN* [Return] causes AutoCAD to redraw the screen and regenerate the whole drawing, based on recalculation of where everything is in the drawing database and what portion of the drawing is on the screen. *REGEN* takes much longer than *REDRAW. PAN, VIEW* Restore, and *ZOOM* will also regenerate the drawing under certain conditions. [CTRL] C will abort *REGEN*, but will allow you to continue to work on the portion of the drawing showing. You can, for example, Window *ZOOM* into an area of a partial *ZOOM* All.

You will rarely use the *REGEN* command. You might use it if *REGENAUTO* is *OFF* and you have changed a number of *BLOCK* or *TEXT* Style definitions and wish to see what the drawing really looks like. You also could use *REGEN* to restore normal text to the drawing after you turn *QTEXT* off.

REGENAUTO Command—Whenever you make a change in a drawing that changes the way it should appear on the screen, AutoCAD will automatically *REGEN*, that is, recalculate the drawing database so that the screen will show what it really looks like. This is a lengthy process in a large drawing. Sometimes this is not necessary, as when you are making a number of changes and don't need to see what the intermediate steps look like. To turn off the automatic *REGEN*, enter *REGENAUTO*, then *Y*.

The following commands can result in an automatic *REGEN:ATTEDIT, BLOCK, INSERT, LAYER, LTSCALE, PAN, STYLE, ZOOM.*

If a *REGEN* is called for by a *PAN* or *ZOOM*, you will be asked to approve the *REGEN* before it proceeds, if *REGENAUTO* is off.

REGENAUTO can be toggled back on by the use of the same command.

You can still cause a manual *REGEN* by using *PAN* or *ZOOM* with fast zoom off, or by entering *REGEN*, or by a *VIEW* Restore.

Regeneration—(See *REGENAUTO* and Quick Zoom.)

Relative Coordinates—(See Coordinates.)

RENAME Command—RENAME allows you to change the name of a *BLOCK*, a named *VIEW*, a *LAYER, LINETYPE* or *TEXT* style. Enter *RENAME*. The initial prompt will be:

Block/LAyer/LType/Style/View:

Select the kind of object you want to rename. You will be asked first for the old name and then for the new name. Names must follow the AutoCAD naming convention.

Keep in mind that AutoCAD won't allow you to change some standard object names, including layer "0" and *CONTINUOUS* linetype. You can rename the *STANDARD* text style. Shape names can NOT be changed with *RENAME*. Shape names can only be changed by getting into the ASCII file where they are defined, by altering their names there.

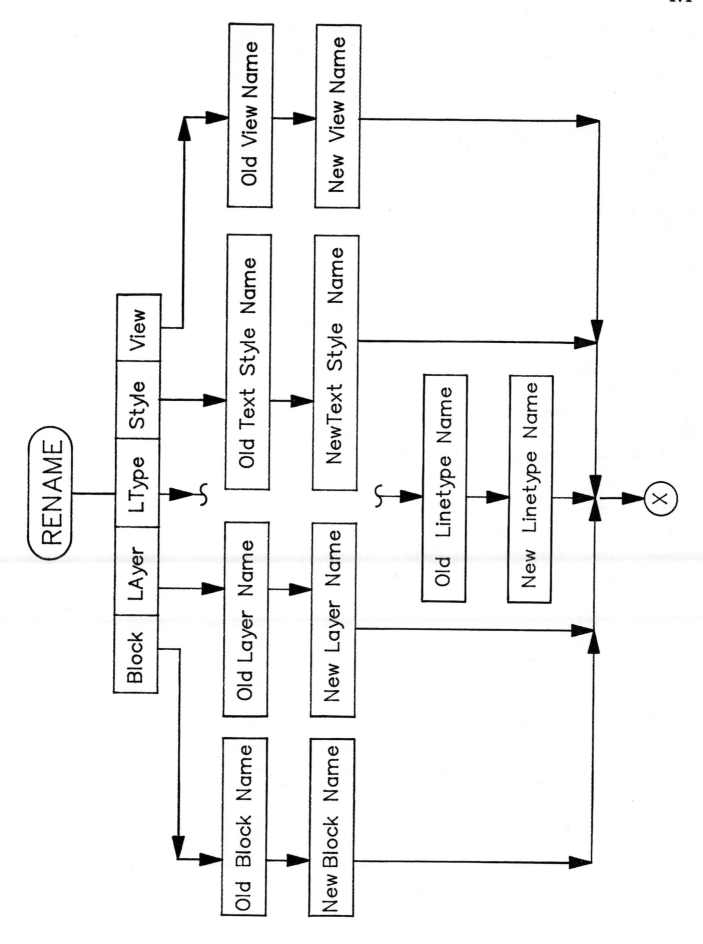

172

REPEAT/ENDREP Command—This related set of commands is no longer supported by AutoCAD. Older versions of AutoCAD allowed you to record a construction and then *REPEAT* it for a number of rows and columns. This has been superseded by the *ARRAY* and *MINSERT* commands. *REPEAT* and *ENDREP* are likely to result in a drawing requiring a translation to process in AutoCAD's most recent versions. Do not use *RE-PEAT* and *ENDREP*.

Rescaling—Normally, a drawing that is not the right scale can be proportioned during the *PLOT* process to fit your paper and to appear at a different scale. If this is not sufficient, you can rescale the drawing by using the *SCALE* command and window selecting the entire drawing. There is a sample macro to do this contained in the Macros and Menus Chapter.

RESUME Command—If a script has been halted with a [CTRL] C or a Backspace, it can be restarted by entering *RESUME*. *RESUME* can be used *transparently* in the midst of another command by prefixing it with an apostrophe. (See Transparent Commands.)

[Return] Key—This key is used to enter commands and data to AutoCAD. Some keys for this function are labelled "Enter." In this book, wherever it says to "enter" information, a [Return] is understood to be included in that action. Note that the space bar will also enter commands in AutoCAD, except for entry of actual text.

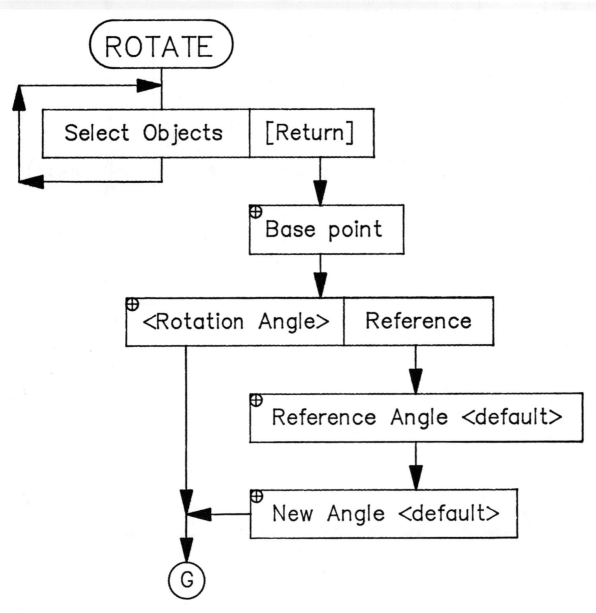

ROTATE Command—The orientation of an entity can be changed by rotating it around a specified base point using the ROTATE command. After entering *ROTATE*, you will be asked for a base point. This can be anywhere in the drawing. The next prompt will ask you:

<Rotation angle>/Reference:

You can respond with a rotation angle. A positive number will rotate the object counterclockwise, a negative number will rotate it clockwise.

Suppose you know what the current rotation of an object is and you know what you want it to be. Rather than calculate the amount of rotation to adjust the object by, you can enter an *"R"*, and then supply the present angle at the *"Reference angle:"* prompt and the desired angle at the *"New angle:"* prompt. If you don't know the old angle, you can point to two points on the object's centerline or other definitive axis, and AutoCAD will calculate the angle for you.

You can also drag the rotation of the object, adjusting the angle until it looks correct.

Version 2.6 notes: The *ROTATE* command, under AutoCAD Version 2.6, will cause any associative dimension entities to be regenerated with any resultant changes, using the latest settings for the dimensioning variables. Also, if ADE-3 is present, you can use ROTATE on 3D lines and faces; only the X and Y coordinates will be altered, however.

RSCRIPT Command—When script files are begun explicitly, by the use of the *SCRIPT* command, as opposed to automatically by inclusion of the script name on the acad line from DOS, you can cause the script to loop back and restart itself by putting *RSCRIPT* at the end of the file. Remember that in this case the script can't interact with the Main Menu. (See *SCRIPT* Command.)

S

SAVE command—(See also END, QUIT.) You should update the disk file of the drawing you are working on every half hour or so, depending on how reliable your system is. Use the *SAVE* command to save your latest revisions without exiting back to the main menu. If you wish to save under a different file name, respond to the "File Name:" prompt with the new name. Otherwise, just hit [Return] to save under the original name. The previous copy of the .DWG file will become the .BAK file and the old .BAK file will be erased.

SCALE command—(See also *ROTATE*.) This command allows changing the size of objects already in a drawing. The X to Y ratio of the objects will remain the same, as will the location of the base point.

Enter *SCALE*, then select objects as prompted. Next, define a base point. Objects selected will grow or shrink in size about that point. The options are then to enter a scale factor or to give a "Reference" size. The scale factor can be entered from the keyboard or dragged with the puck. If you wish to increase or decrease an object to a particular size, you may choose the "Reference" option by entering *"R"*. You will then be prompted for the old length and the new length desired; either or both of those lengths can be defined by use of the puck.

Version 2.6 notes: You can re*SCALE* dimension entities under Version 2.6 of AutoCAD without having to repeat the *DIM* command. The entire dimension set will be recalculated and regenerated using the latest dimension variable settings.

Screen—This refers to the CRT (Cathode Ray Tube), monitor, or display device being used to view the drawing. (See Appendix D.)

Screen menus—(See Menus.)

SCRIPT Command—(See also *RSCRIPT* Command.) This is the command used to start up a script while editing a drawing. All the commands stored in the .scr file selected will be executed in sequence. (See Chapter 6, Scripts, plus the entry below.)

Scripts—(See also Menus.) Scripts are pre-recorded sequences of commands stored in EDLIN, similar to menus, and run by the *SCRIPT* command. (They can also be called up along with AutoCAD by entering the command, in DOS, acad [space] name of default drawing [space] name of script. See *ACAD*.) They can be used to do presentations or to perform a standard sequence of drawing tasks.

Unlike menus, scripts can contain a pause command *(DELAY)* that halts execution of the script for a specified number of milliseconds, up to 32,767 milliseconds. *DELAY*s in presentation scripts are necessary to slow AutoCAD down to allow viewers to see what is happening. *DELAY*s in script files used for drawing allow the operator to read prompts or messages or the text screen. Two special commands are used within scripts to toggle between the text screen and the graphics screen: *TEXTSCR* and *GRAPHSCR*, respectively.

Scripts can be made to loop in an endless cycle for presentations: If the script was invoked when AutoCAD was called up, placing *END* or *QUIT Y* at the end of the script will cause it to repeat. (A zero [0] on the next line after the *END* command will exit AutoCAD and halt the script.) Otherwise, if the script was called by the *SCRIPT* command, *RSCRIPT* at the end of the .scr file will cause the script to loop back to the beginning. Also, one script can call another.

Scripts run somewhat faster if the *UNDO* feature is turned off. (See *UNDO* Command for information on how to do so.)

To stop a script during execution, enter [CTRL] C or a backspace. This will halt the script at the end of whatever command is in progress. To restart the script, enter *RESUME*.

Errors in scripts—Script entries must follow the same protocols as menu items. A space or a blank line in a script will be interpreted as a [Return]. Semicolons don't function as [Return]s. Control characters don't work, either. Entries must provide the proper information needed to complete execution of any commands invoked. If an error in the script causes it to stop, it can be restarted in the Drawing Editor with *RESUME*. If it stopped while a command was in progress, enter '*RESUME*, the transparent form of the command. (See Transparency).

An example of a script file called 1701a.scr follows. It is designed to get into several drawings and rotate an existing block located at X=6, Y=6 in each drawing. If the operator stays around to watch the process and doesn't like the looks of the rotation, a [CTRL] C during the *DELAY* will stop the script.

Script item:	What it does:
2	
spock	(name of drawing called up)
ROTATE 6,6 6,6 10	(turn existing item at 6,6 by 10 degrees)
DELAY 3000	(pause to give a chance to halt script)
END	(end and save the drawing)
2	(call the next drawing from the Main Menu)
scotty	(name of drawing called up)
ROTATE 6,6 6,6 10	(turn existing item at 6,6 by 10 degrees)
DELAY 3000	(pause to give a chance to halt script)
END	(end and save the drawing)
2	(call the next drawing from the Main Menu)
chekhov	(name of drawing called up)
ROTATE 6,6 6,6 10	(turn existing item at 6,6 by 10 degrees)
DELAY 3000	(pause to give a chance to halt script)
END	(end and save the drawing)
0	(exit AutoCAD)

SELECT Command—This command lets you create an object selection set for later use. You can access this selection set by responding *P* (for previous) when prompted to *"Select objects."* To create a pre-selected group of objects, enter *SELECT* and go through the selection process as outlined below in "Selecting Objects."

Why would you want to do this? Suppose you are *ZOOM*ed in tightly on the lower left corner of a big drawing and you intend to copy many small items there into the upper right corner, after you *INSERT* some blocks among and around the small items. If you do the *INSERT*ions before the *COPY* command, you won't be able to *COPY* all the small objects with a Window selection, the fastest method. You also don't want to *COPY* first,

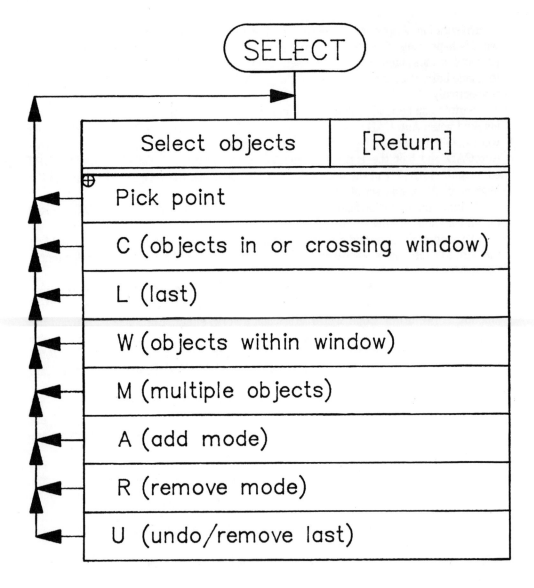

because you'd have to *ZOOM* out or *'PAN* to the far corner and back, which takes more time.

The solution: Use the *SELECT* command to create the selection set for the *COPY* command. Do an ID command to find a Base point for the *COPY* command, too. Write down the Base point coordinates. Then go ahead and *INSERT* the other items amongst the ones selected. Get over to the far corner with *PAN* or *VIEW*, and run the *COPY* command. Enter *P* when asked to select objects. Provide the Base point from the keyboard.

Selecting Objects—When AutoCAD prompts you to *Select objects* it's asking you to create a collection of entities called a selection-set. You can add to and subtract from this collection. The crosshairs on the screen are replaced with a small object selection target box. (This object selection target size can be changed; enter *SETVAR* and then *PICKBOX* to increase or decrease the box. (See the *SETVAR* command.)

You can use more than one of the methods of selecting objects described below. Each selection method will bring back the "Select objects:" prompt and allow you to add to the selection set with another method or with the same method again.

Objects that have been added to the selection set will be highlighted or shown with dotted lines. You can respond to the "Select objects:" prompt in any of the following ways:

Question Mark (?)—When you enter a question mark, you will be prompted with a list of possible responses: *pointing, Window, Multiple, Crossing, Last, Previous, Undo, Remove, Add, null,* and [CTRL] C.

(pointing)—When you bring the display crosshairs over an object and press the pick button on the puck, it selects the entity that crosses the target box. If you hit at the intersection of two items, usually the *LAST* one created will be selected, unless you used the *BREAK* command, or you did a *WBLOCK*, or . . . Take no chances, pick away from intersections if you only intend to select one of the lines. It's impossible to predict which one will be selected. If you want to select a polyline, solid, or trace, point to its edge rather than its filled region.

Multiple objects—Enter *M* at the *"Select objects:"* prompt to add multiple objects to the selection set. This mode of selection differs from the others in that AutoCAD will not search through the drawing database for the selected objects until you press [Return]. Then AutoCAD will do a single search for objects that were selected. This will proceed much faster than if you had picked out the objects by pointing, one by one.

Multiple objects that intersect can be selected two at a time by first entering *M* and then specifying the intersecting point twice.

Windows—Objects can be selected by putting them in a *'window'*. Enter *W* and respond with two points that are the opposite corners of a rectangle around the objects. A box will be drawn around the objects chosen. If the box encloses only a part of a visible object, the object will not be selected. If the entire visible part of an object "hangs over" beyond the screen limits is within the box, the object will be selected.

Crossing—By entering *C*, all objects within or crossing the window boundary will be selected. In all other respects, this option works the same way as the Window method.

Last object—Choosing *L* will result in the selection of the most recently created object.

Previous object(s)—AutoCAD remembers your most recent selection set and allows you to reselect it with *P*. Keep in mind that if you delete objects from the drawing by *ERASE* or *UNDO*, *P* will bring up an empty selection set.

Undo—*U* allows you to take out something you've just added to the selection set. You can step back through the set, removing each group of most recently added entities with a "U."

Remove—*R* is a toggle that allows you to take objects out of the selection set instead of adding them. After you enter *R*, the objects you select will be removed from the selection set.

Add—Entering *A* toggles *Remove* off and puts you back into Add mode. Note that you are in Add mode when you start selecting objects.

(null)—Either a space or a [Return] at a *"Select objects:"* prompt lets AutoCAD know you're finished with entity selecting.

[CTRL] C—[CTRL] C aborts the selection process. The selection set will be discarded and the highlighted objects will become unhighlighted.

SETVAR command—(See also Toggle Settings.) AutoCAD stores certain program settings in the drawing and others in the acad.cfg file. Most of these settings are changed as you use the function keys or commands such as *SNAP, GRID, COORDS, LIMITS, OSNAP,* and so forth. The latest versions of AutoCAD also allow you to access these variables directly by use of the *SETVAR* command or through AutoLISP.

To change system variables, enter *SETVAR*, the name of the variable you wish to change, and then provide the desired setting. Changing the 3D elevation with *SETVAR* is shown as an example:

Prompt:	Response:
Command:	*SETVAR*
Variable name or ?:	*ELEVATION*
New value <current>	*3.5*

If you enter a question mark instead of a variable name, the names and current settings of all system variables will be displayed. Note that some variables are read only.

Altering some variables will not result in an immediate change in the appearance of the display. You might have to do a *REDRAW* or maybe a *REGEN* to update the screen to match the system variables. *AXISUNIT, GRIDUNIT, SNAPANG, SNAPBASE,* and *SNAPUNIT* require a *REDRAW* when you are done, if you want to see the result immediately. Otherwise wait for the next *REDRAW* or *REGEN*.

The *SETVAR* command can be used "transparently" under Version 2.6. (See Transparent Commands) When you are in the middle of another command, you can change a system variable by entering 'SETVAR. Notice the apostrophe before the command. You will be put into *SETVAR* mode, with a different prompt, until you reset the variable. Nifty, huh?

The following list, updated to Version 2.6, shows the names of the system variables, what they do, their type (i.e., integer, real number, string variable, or X,Y coordinates). All system variables are saved in the drawing, unless noted otherwise with an asterisk (*).

NAME	TYPE	WHAT IT DOES
ACADPREFIX	STRING	The directory path (read-only) specified by ACAD environment variable
AFLAGS	INT	Attribute flags bit-code for ATTDEF Command (sum of the following): 1 = invisible, 2 = constant, 4 = verify
ANGBASE	REAL	Angle 0 direction
ANGDIR	INT	1 = clockwise angles, 0 = ccw
APERTURE *	INT	Object snap target height, in pixels
AREA	REAL	Area computed by AREA, LIST, or DBLIST (read-only)
ATTMODE	INT	Attribute display mode (0 = OFF, 1 = normal, 2 = ON)
AUNITS	INT	Angular units mode (0 = decimal degrees, 1 = degrees/min/secs, 2 = grads, 3 = radians, 4 = surveyors' units)
AUPREC	INT	Angular units decimal places
AXISMODE	INT	1 = Axis ON, 0 = OFF
AXISUNIT	COORD	Axis spacing, X and Y
BLIPMODE	INT	1 = Marker blips ON, 0 = OFF
CDATE	REAL	Calendar date/time (read-only) (special format; see below)
CECOLOR	STRING	Current entity color (read-only)
CELTYPE	STRING	Current entity linetype (read-only)
CHAMFERA	REAL	First chamfer distance
CHAMFERB	REAL	Second chamfer distance
CLAYER	STRING	Current layer (read-only)
CMDECHO	INT	1 = AutoLISP command function echo ON, 2 = echo OFF. (ADE-3)
COORDS	INT	0 = coordinate display is updated on point picks only. 1 = display of absolute coordinates is continuously updated. 2 = distance and angle from last point are displayed when a distance or angle is requested.
DATE	REAL	Julian date/time (read-only) (special format; see below)
DISTANCE	REAL	Distance computed by DIST, LIST, or DBLIST. (read-only)
DRAGMODE	INT	0 = no dragging, 1 = ON if requested, 2 = Auto
DRAGP1 *	INT	Regen-drag input sampling rate
DRAGP2 *	INT	Fast-drag input sampling rate

DWGNAME	STRING	Drawing name (read-only)
DWGPREFIX	STRING	Drive/directory prefix for drawing (read-only)
ELEVATION	REAL	Current 3-D elevation (ADE-3)
EXPERT	INT	Suppresses these "are you sure?" prompts: 0=none, 1="About to REGEN, proceed?" "Do you want to turn the current layer off?", 2=as above PLUS "Block already defined. Redefine it?" "A drawing with this name already exists. Overwrite it?", 3=as above plus LINETYPE redundancy prompts.
EXTMAX	COORDS	Upper right "drawing uses" extents (read-only)
EXTMIN	COORDS	Lower left "drawing uses: extents (read-only)
FILLETRAD	REAL	Fillet radius
FILLMODE	INT	1=Fill mode ON, 0=OFF
GRIDMODE	INT	1=Grid ON, 0=OFF
GRIDUNIT	COORDS	Grid spacing, X and Y
HIGHLIGHT	INT	1=Object selection highlighting ON, 0=OFF (ADE-3)
INSBASE	COORDS	Insertion basepoint (set by BASE command)
LASTANGLE	REAL	The end angle of the last arc entered (read-only)
LASTPOINT	COORDS	Reference point for @X,Y,Z relative coords
LIMCHECK	INT	1=Limits checking ON, 0=OFF
LIMMAX	COORDS	Upper right drawing limits
LIMMIN	COORDS	Lower left drawing limits
LTSCALE	REAL	Global linetype scale factor
LUNITS	INT	Linear units mode (1=Scientific, 2=Decimal, 3=Engineering, 4=Architectural)
LUPREC	INT	Linear units decimal places or denominator
MENUECHO	INT	0=Menu input is echoed and prompts are displayed normally. 1=Menu input not echoed (but ^P in a menu toggles echo ON). 2=Prompts are suppressed if input is coming from a menu item. 3=Menu echoing and prompts are both suppressed. 4=Disable ^P toggle of menu item echo.
MIRRTEXT	INT	1=MIRROR reflects text, 0=retains text direction
ORTHOMODE	INT	1=Ortho mode on, 0=OFF
OSMODE	INT	Object snap modes bit-code (sum of as many of the following as needed at once): 1=endpoint 2=midpoint 4=center 8=node 16=quadrant 32=intersection

NAME	TYPE	WHAT IT DOES
		64 = insert point
		128 = perpendicular
		256 = tangent
		512 = nearest
		1024 = quick
PDMODE	INT	Point display mode
PDSIZE	REAL	Point display size
PERIMETER	REAL	Perimeter as calculated by AREA, LIST, or DBLIST (read-only)
PICKBOX *	INT	Object selection target height, pixels
QTEXTMODE	INT	Quick text mode, 1 = ON, 0 = OFF
REGENMODE	INT	REGENAUTO 1 = ON, 0 = OFF
SCREENSIZE	COORD	Graphics screen size in pixels, X & Y (read-only)
SKETCHINC	REAL	Sketch record increment
SKPOLY	INT	0 = SKETCH generates lines, 1 = polylines (ADE-3)
SNAPANG	REAL	Snap/Grid rotation angle
SNAPBASE	COORD	Snap/Grid origin point
SNAPISOPAIR	INT	Current isometric plane (0 = Left, 1 = Top, 2 = Right)
SNAPMODE	INT	0 = snap mode OFF, 1 = snap mode ON
SNAPSTYL	INT	0 = Normal, 1 = Isometric
SNAPUNIT	COORDS	Snap spacing, X & Y
TDCREATE	REAL	Time and date of drawing creation (read-only) (special format; see below)
TDINDWG	REAL	Total editing time (read-only) (special format; see below)
TDUPDATE	REAL	Time and date of last update/save (read-only) (special format; see below)
TDUSRTIMER	REAL	User resettable elapsed timer (read-only) (special format; see below)
TEMPPREFIX	STRING	The directory name for placement of temporary files (read-only)
TEXTEVAL	INT	0 = Text entry taken as typed, 1 = Text starting with (or ! is taken as an AutoLISP function (ADE-3)
TEXTSIZE	REAL	Text height default value
TEXTSTYLE	STRING	Current text style name (read-only)
THICKNESS	REAL	Current 3-D thickness (ADE-3)
TRACEWID	REAL	Default trace width
VIEWCTR	INT	Center of current view (read-only)
VIEWSIZE	REAL	Current view height, in drawing units (read-only)
VPOINTX	REAL	X component of current 3-D viewpoint (read-only) (ADE-3)
VPOINTY	REAL	Y component of current 3-D viewpoint (read-only) (ADE-3)
VPOINTZ	REAL	Z component of current 3-D viewpoint (read-only) (ADE-3)
VSMAX	COORDS	Upper right corner of virtual screen (read-only)
VSMIN	COORDS	Lower left corner of virtual screen (read-only)

SH Command—(See SHELL Command, External Commands)

SHAPE command—(See also *LOAD* command and Shape Definition.) To place shapes into your drawing, enter *SHAPE*, then enter the name of the shape you want. Next define the height and rotation angle, using the cursor or the keyboard, similar to text insertion. Shapes must be LOADed before they can be inserted with the *SHAPE* command.

Shapes—See also the *LOAD* command and the special section on Shape Files, Appendix B)

Shapes are very similar in operation to blocks. Shapes are harder to define than blocks, but they are faster to regenerate and take less storage area. Text utilizes predefined shapes stored in ''.shx'' files. Note that shapes can only be composed of lines, circles, and arcs.

Before inserting shapes, you must LOAD the .shx file that contains them. The .shx file must be compiled (Main Menu Task 7) from the .shp file produced by using a text editor to define the shapes.

Each .shp file can contain up to 255 shape definitions.

Defining a shape file is very much like teaching a robot to print. You have to tell the robot when to pick up the pen, when to put it down, how far to move it, etc. This is a very exacting job, but is fun once you get the hang of it. If you need additional fonts, beyond what AutoCAD provides, or special shapes, you can make them yourself. You can also purchase third-party text fonts and shape-maker packages if you don't have time to make your own.

SHELL Command—(ADE-3) (See also External Commands.) Although AutoCAD provides the ability to do certain file operations via the *FILES* command, there are times when it is necessary to do other DOS operations. It is inconvenient to END the drawing and get back into DOS, do what you want to do and then call up AutoCAD and your drawing again. AutoCAD has provided the *SHELL* command to permit doing some things from DOS without exiting the Drawing Editor.

Enter *SHELL*. The Command prompt will change to:

DOS command:

You can now do such things as *DIR*ectory commands, *COPY*, file *COMP*arisons, *PRINT* files, run EDLIN, and do anything you would do from DOS, with a few exceptions. Generally, the less you do in this mode the better, since there is the very real possibility of an operation overwriting your AutoCAD work in RAM. Also, you will find that some of the things you want to do mysteriously can't be done. Some pertinent warnings:

Don't run any other programs that need a disk swap, if you are working on floppies.

Don't use *CHKDSK*. AutoCAD has been left hanging, with open files. *CHKDSK* will find these and say you have lost clusters. Especially, don't use *CHKDSK/f*, it will trash these files.

PRINT and several other DOS commands stay resident in RAM when you run them. This could create a problem if AutoCAD is trying to use the same RAM. To get around this, run this type of DOS command once before getting into AutoCAD, if you think you're likely to want to run it from within.

Don't run any program or do any DOS operation that resets serial ports.

Don't try to run AutoCAD a second time from DOS! To return to AutoCAD, you must use the command ''EXIT,'' which seems strange, but is how you get back into your drawing.

If AutoCAD has not left enough memory to run the SHELL command, you can use a variant of it, the SH command. This requires a lot less RAM to function, but it is only able to run internal DOS commands, such as *DIR, COPY, VERIFY, REN*ame, and *MKDIR*. See your DOS book for which commands are kosher here.

SKETCH Command—AutoCAD will let you do freehand drawing from a tablet or with a mouse. Well, sort of. It doesn't produce a smooth, artistic curve, but it will make a drawing with a fair amount of speed, that can be edited by means of other AutoCAD commands. Using *SKETCH* effectively takes some practice.

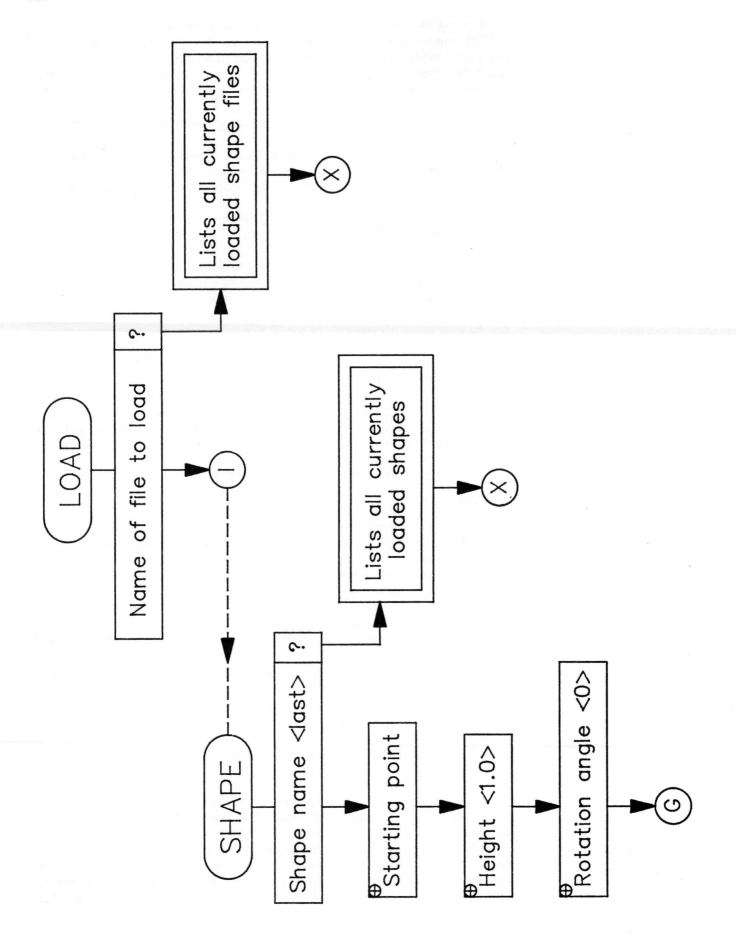

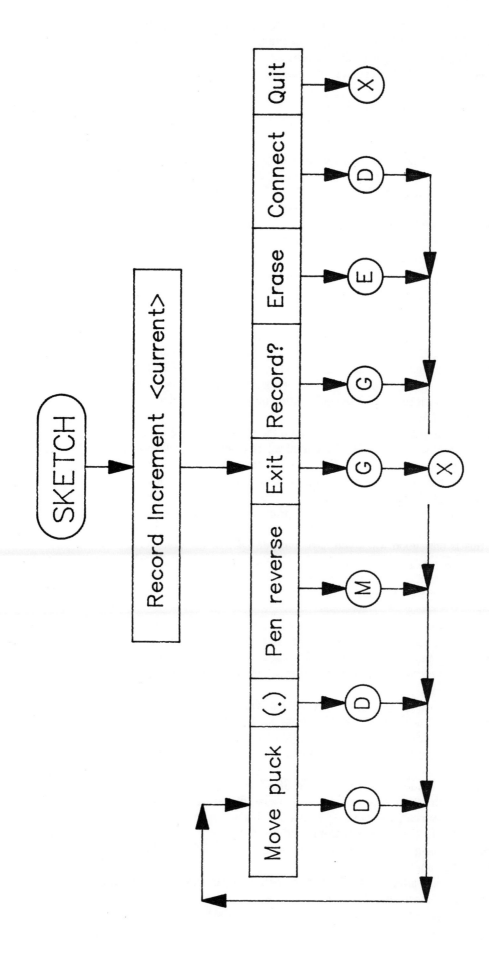

You should also be aware that when you are *SKETCH*ing, you are chewing up a lot of storage space. *SKETCH* puts in beaucoup tiny segments, rather than a smooth curve, as you will soon notice from the spidery lines produced. You can make the lines a little smoother by making the segments shorter and shorter, but the storage space gets bigger and bigger.

Enter *SKETCH*. The starting prompt will be:

Record increment <current>:

Enter a number. The "record increment" is the distance you must move the puck in order for a segment to be drawn. Don't pick a number smaller than your current SNAP setting, if you intend to use snap while *SKETCH*ing. An 8½ by 11 drawing would probably need a record increment of about .05 to .1 for optimum performance. This is definitely an area for some personal experimentation.

Negative record increments can be entered. The minus sign tells AutoCAD to give you a beep if you are moving the puck too fast.

The next prompt after entering the record increment is:

Sketch. Pen eXit Quit Record Erase Connect .

These seven (yes, there ARE seven) options remain on the prompt line most of the time while you are in *SKETCH* mode. The puck (or whatever device you are using) corresponds to an imaginary pen used to sketch the lines. The pen must be *DOWN* to draw, and *UP* to move without making more lines. The pen starts in the *UP* position and a *P* must be entered to lower it (or just hit the pick button on your pointing device.) *P* also raises the pen if it is DOWN.

After you have lowered the pen, every time you move the puck a distance corresponding to the "record increment", another small segment will be drawn. You will leave a line behind you wherever you move the cursor. Hit another P (or pick button) to raise the pen; you can then move the puck to another area (without leaving a trail), lower the pen, and start a new piece of line.

Note that the period (.) is one of the choices in the prompt line. This option lets you put a straight line where you are working, from the last segment to wherever the cursor is. Obviously, this is only good when you have the pen *UP*. (If the pen were down, the last segment would be right under the pen.) This is very useful if you reach a part of your sketch where you need to do a sequence of straight lines and don't have a steady hand, or don't want to waste space on the extra bytes needed for the small increments.

The Erase option allows you to delete from the end of a *SKETCH* line back as far as you want. Hit an *E*, and then show AutoCAD where you want to terminate the erase by placing the crosshairs there and hitting a *P* or the pick button. AutoCAD will lift the pen and take out the segments of the line back to the point selected. Hit *E* again before erasing if you change your mind.

When you have finished a line or lines, if you decide that what you have sketched is what you want, you can Record the lines with the *R* option. Every line, or piece of a line, will be recorded into the drawing database. After you have done this, however, you will no longer be able to use the *SKETCH* command editing options, Erase and Connect.

On the other hand, if you decide that what you have *SKETCHED* so far is all junk, rather than Erase it (which can take a long time to do, because of the way AutoCAD changes the display during Erasures), you can Quit with a *Q*. This will drop all the lines done so far and put you back to the AutoCAD Command prompt.

When you are done sketching, enter an X to record all the lines *SKETCH*ed and eXit back to the Command prompt.

If you want to continue a line after you have lifted the pen, you can pick up where you left off by choosing the Connect option, *C*. AutoCAD will ask you to show where to connect, but you can only connect to the end of the last erasure or the last line drawn.

Notes—(1) Slower computers might not be able to follow the motion of the puck fast enough to draw a line every record increment. Try using a negative record increment to get better accuracy on slow machines. AutoCAD will then honk at you if you move too fast. Slow down if the drawing is not putting down segments accurately enough, or increase the record increment. If the disk drive lights up, on the other hand, stop right where you are and wait for the system to catch up.

(2) You can toggle to Tablet mode and digitize a drawing placed on top of your tablet by using *SKETCH.* This is not very efficient in terms of memory requirements, but is fairly fast and can be cleaned up later if you need to condense the file a little.

(3) If you are drawing with a tablet in Tablet mode, remember that unless you are in a *ZOOM* All position, the cursor is not necessarily on the screen. You must *ZOOM* to the region you wish to draw in.

(4) You will also find that you can't access the screen menus in Tablet mode, because AutoCAD makes that area of the tablet available for working on the right hand part of your drawing. Your tablet menus will still work, however, as will your button menus.

(5) You can easily exceed the capacity of a floppy disk if you do a very big drawing using *SKETCH.* It is a good idea to stop *SKETCH*ing from time to time and do a *STATUS* to see how much room you have left, if you are working on a floppy.

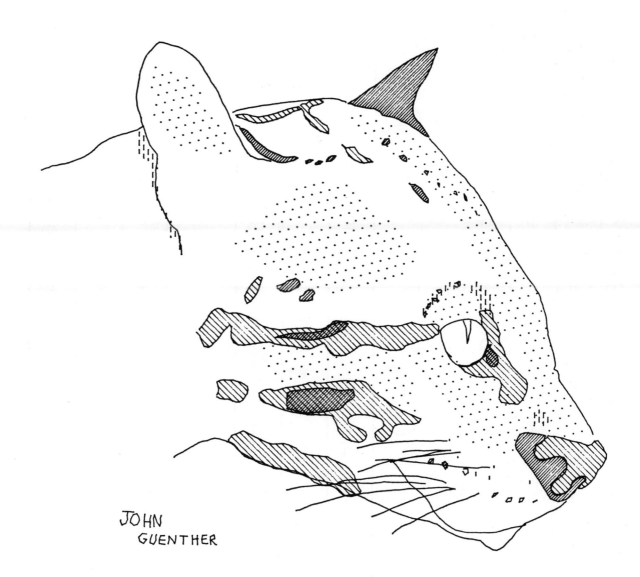

JOHN
GUENTHER

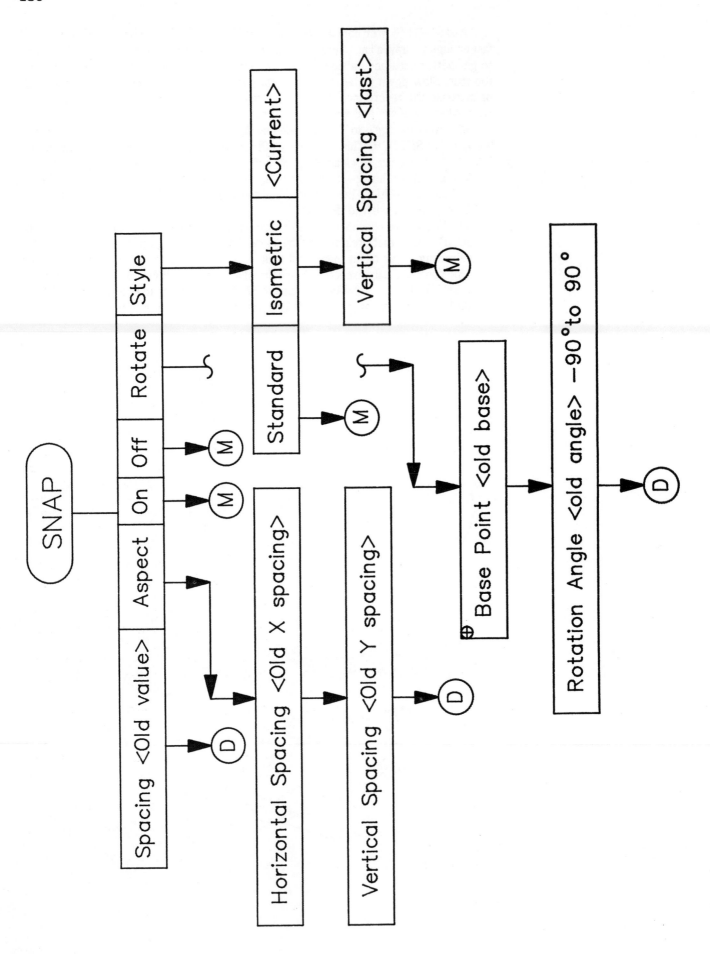

SNAP command—(See also the *GRID* command and the *OSNAP* command) You sometimes draw on graph paper to evenly space or align objects. This is why AutoCAD provides the *GRID* command. AutoCAD also makes it easy to "draw on the lines" by forcing points to lie only on the grid intersections. If you have the cursor reasonably close to the desired point, AutoCAD will "snap" the cursor right to the nearest grid point.

NOTE: the *"SNAP"* grid and the *"GRID"* grid don't have to be the same! You might decide that a quarter inch grid spacing is too dense (or AutoCAD could decide for you by refusing to display it). You can set the visible *"GRID"* grid to one inch spacing and the invisible *"SNAP"* grid to quarter inch.

Enter *SNAP,* then read the initial prompt:

Snap spacing or ON/OFF/Aspect/Rotate/Style < current >:

The *SNAP* command is used both to toggle *SNAP* on and off and to set the size and type of grid. A number entry will set the snap spacing. *OFF* will toggle snap off. *ON* will restore the snap spacing to whatever the last setting was. Note that the F9 key or the *SETVAR* command can also be used to toggle snap on and off.

Options—The Aspect subcommand allows using a different spacing in the Y direction than in the X direction. Enter *A* and supply the X and Y spacing values, as prompted.

The Rotate subcommand lets you turn the *SNAP* grid about its origin or base point. Enter *R* and supply a value between −90 and +90 degrees.

The Style subcommand is used to set AutoCAD to draw in isometric mode. Enter *S* and then *I* to call up an isometric grid with matching snap and crosshairs. (Responding with *S* instead of *I* restores the grid to standard.) You will then be prompted for the vertical spacing desired; enter a number. See Isometric Grid for more information.

Note—An approximate isometric grid can be simulated for earlier versions of AutoCAD by creating a rectangular array of points with an X separation twice the Y separation. Put this array right on top of the normal snap points and turn off the normal grid. Isometric sketches will then snap to those points, producing a drawing that will be very close to a true iso, if you're careful not to hit the intermediate, non-iso snap points. The array of points should be on a layer all by itself so it can be turned off before plotting.

SOLID Command—You can produce filled-in figures with line (not arc) edges in AutoCAD. (*SOLID*'s are not available in all other CAD systems and therefore might not translate, should that be necessary. Don't use *SOLID*s if there is any chance you will later have to convert the AutoCAD file to, say, Auto-Trol.)

The procedure for making *SOLIDS* is a little tricky, because you do not draw a *SOLID* by enclosing it with lines, the way you normally would make figures. You have to define the *SOLID* in pieces. Each piece will be four sided or three sided. You lay out each piece by specifying two edges within which the pen will go back and forth, filling the area in.

A simple example: to do a *SOLID* square, enter a point at the upper left corner, then the upper right, then the lower *LEFT*, and finally the lower *RIGHT*.

Enter *SOLID*. AutoCAD will prompt you for four points, enough for two edges. If you are defining a triangular piece, just hit [Return] when prompted for the fourth point. After the fourth point, AutoCAD will start over asking for a "third point", allowing you to define another three or four sided piece attached to what you have already laid out.

Points for defining the edges can be entered with the cursor control device or typed in from the keyboard.

The following is an example of input for a one inch square at the origin:

Prompt:	Response:
Command:	*SOLID*
First point:	*0,1*
Second point:	*1,1*

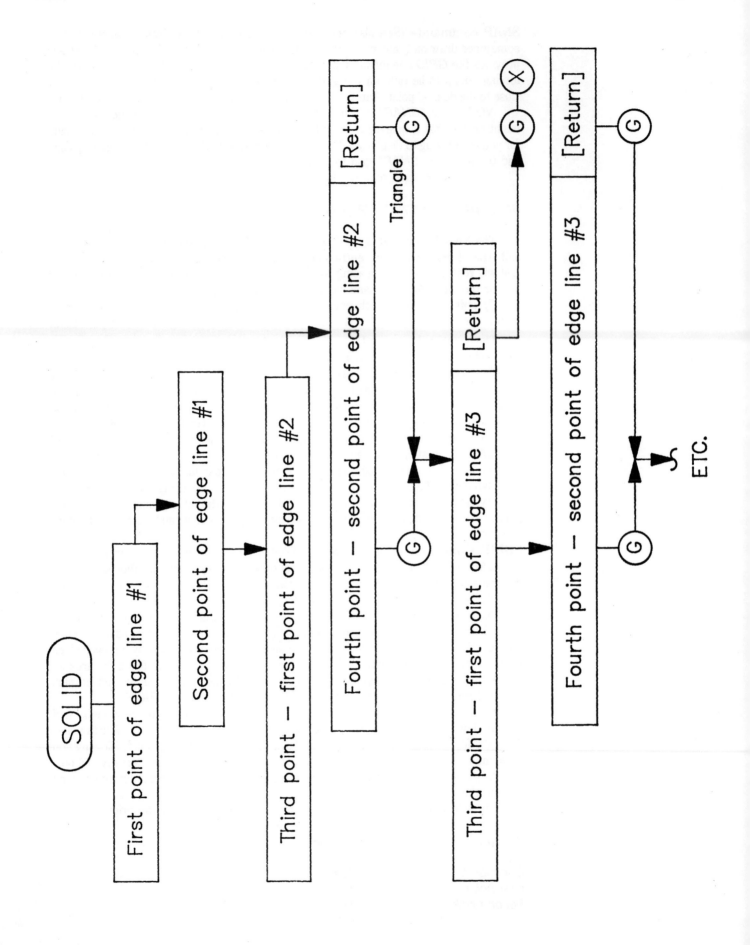

Third point:	0,0
Fourth point:	1,0
Third point:	[Return]

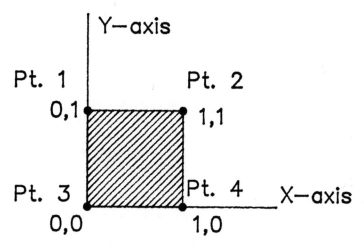

Here is another example, an isosceles triangle sitting on the X-axis:

Prompt:	Response:	
Command:	SOLID	
First point:	1,0	
Second point:	2,0	
Third point:	1.5,1	
Fourth point:	[Return]	This ends the triangle.
Third point:	[Return]	This ends the command.

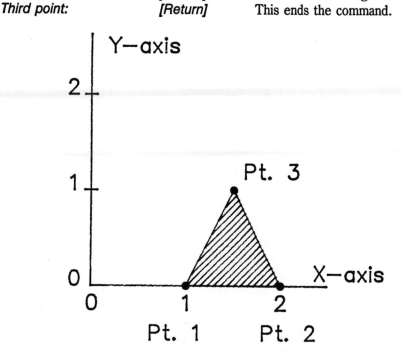

A final example. You tell me what this will look like:

Prompt:	Response:
Command:	SOLID
First point:	1,2
Second point:	2,2

Third point:	*2,3*	Here's where it gets tricky!
Fourth point:	*1,3*	
Third point:	*1.5,4*	
Fourth point:	*[Return]*	
Third point:	*1,5*	
Fourth point:	*2,5*	
Third point:	*[Return]*	

In order for *SOLID*s to be filled in, you must have *FILL* on. See *FILL*. It is faster to have *FILL* off for normal drawing and turn it on only to view the finished drawing. Do a *REGEN* after turning FILL on.

Standard Drawing—This is a prototype or template drawing that is accessed by AutoCAD when starting a new drawing. Various settings from the standard drawing will be used to set up the new drawing.

Standard Menu—AutoCAD is shipped with a standard menu, acad.mnu. Upon registering your copy of AutoCAD, you will receive a digitizer tablet overlay for operating the tablet portion of the menu.

STATUS command—The status command will display the following information on the screen:

Drawing name	*Number of entities*	*Toggle settings*
Limits	*Extents*	*Display range*
Snap resolution	*Grid size*	*Current layer*
Current color	*Current linetype*	*Elevation*
Snap modes	*"Free RAM"*	*Free disk space*
"I/O page space"		

Whenever you are having mysterious things happening in a drawing, the first thing you should do is use the *STATUS* command. Study the resulting display carefully; you might be able to diagnose the problem in a few seconds. An example: one operator complained that whenever he tried to do a *ZOOM E,* the system locked up. A *STATUS* revealed that his drawing extended to minus infinity! (I still don't know how he managed to insert an entity that far out in left field.) *WBLOCK*ing the good area salvaged the drawing.

Status Line—At the top of the AutoCAD screen you will see a line consisting of something like:

Layer: Bolting Ortho Snap Tablet Fill   X=4.553 Y=3.876

This line tells you what layer you are drawing on, and the names of any drawing modes (such as *SNAP, ORTHO, FILL*) that are currently *ON*. The coordinates can be toggled by hitting the F6 key to give either (1) a constant update of where the cursor is, or (2) to only show where the cursor is when you pick a point, or (3) to show polar coordinates of the cursor location relative to the previous point.

STATUS Subcommand—(See *DIM* Command)

STRETCH command—(ACAD 2.5.) This is a modification of the *MOVE* command that causes the objects moved to remain connected to their neighbors. Any interconnecting lines will be stretched as needed, along with any arcs, polyline segments, pieces of traces or solids that cross the window used to define what is to be moved. Note that a window must be used to select the objects to be moved. Usually a "Crossing" window is best. Lines, etc., that you want stretched can be selected individually. Don't use more than one window, or the first window will not be moved.

Generally, the *STRETCH* command will move only the endpoints located within the window, leaving the outside endpoints fixed and stretching the line and arcs in the direction defined by the base point and new point entered, similar to the *MOVE* command.

Version 2.6 notes: This command will alter the z coordinates of an entire object if you have ADE-3 and provide a z displacement. Also, if you *STRETCH* an associative dimensioned object, the dimension set will be recalculated and regenerated according to the latest dimension variables.

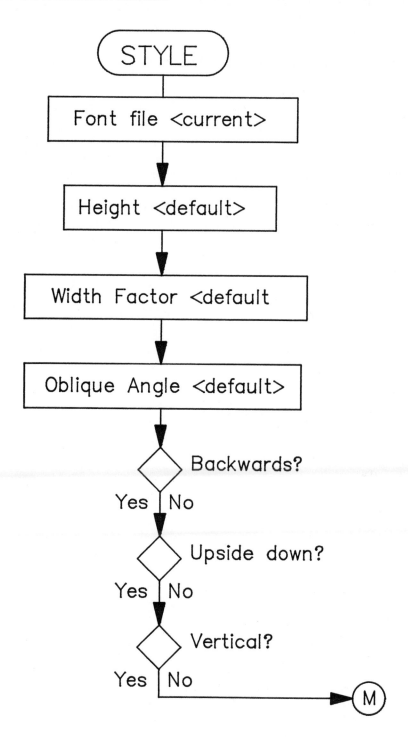

STYLE Command (See also *TEXT.*) AutoCAD is shipped with (currently) five different text fonts: txt, simplex, complex, italic, and monotxt. Each of the fonts can be cloned and modified to produce other *"STYLEs"*. You can change the height, width ratio, obliquing (italic) angle, or make the style upside-down, or backwards, or vertical. AutoCAD also creates a *"STYLE"* called *STANDARD* when you start a new drawing. It consists of an unmodified version of the txt font.

To create a new *STYLE*, enter *STYLE*, and then provide, as prompted, the name you wish to use for the *STYLE*, the font file you are starting with, the height, width factor, and so forth. When you are done, the new style will be the default *TEXT* style.

The initial prompt in the *STYLE* command is:

Text style name (or ?) <current>:

If you enter a question mark, AutoCAD will list out all of the currently defined styles. Hit F1 to return to graphics.

If you enter the name of an existing style, you can modify that style without changing any text previously inserted using it, *unless* you change the font file used to generate it or change the orientation (horizontal or vertical). To create a new style, enter a new style name of up to 31 characters, following the AutoCAD naming convention.

You will next be asked for a font file. Enter the name of one of the five AutoCAD fonts, or other font, if you have made or bought others. Don't append the extension ".shx" to the font file name.

Enter the rest of the *STYLE* data as prompted. Notice that the defaults, which can be accepted by hitting [Return], will correspond to the values for *STANDARD* or, if you have entered the name of an existing STYLE, the values for that *STYLE*. This makes it easy to make a few modifications to an existing *STYLE* very rapidly.

STYLE Subcommand—(See *DIM* and *SNAP* Commands)

T

TABLET Command—Your tablet (See Appendix E) can be used either as a screen pointing device, as a means for entering commands without typing them, or as an input device for copying (digitizing) drawings.

The options under the *TABLET* command are as follows:

ON/OFF/CAL/CFG

ON and *OFF* toggle the tablet mode on and off. If you have not calibrated the tablet before turning it on, it will not work properly.

CAL is used to calibrate the tablet for digitizing.

CFG is used to tell AutoCAD where the tablet menus are located on the tablet.

Digitizing—Digitizing, or tablet, mode is invoked via the *TABLET* command and is toggled with the F10 key. Several steps are necessary to digitize a drawing:

(1) Take the drawing and divide it up into smaller pieces or "boxes", as necessary to fit the digitizer, by drawing a series of horizontal and vertical coordinate lines, evenly spaced and somewhat closer together than the dimensions of the active area of your tablet. (If your drawing is smaller than the tablet, this step is unnecessary.) These boxes will be used in calibrating the tablet (see below).

(2) Fasten the drawing over the digitizer so that it will not move around as you slide the puck over it. (If you are going to do a lot of digitizing, you might want to devise a special table with the digitizer sunk into it, flush with the surface.) Make sure that the origin point of the drawing is somewhere in the lower left corner of the active part of the tablet and that the first box is completely within the digitizing area.

(3) Enter the *TABLET* command. Select the option *CAL* to calibrate the tablet.

(4) Use the puck or stylus to enter the first known point, as prompted. This will be the origin (0,0).

(5) The prompt will ask for the true coordinates of that first point. Enter 0.0 from the keyboard.

(6) Use the puck to enter the second known point at the upper right corner of the first box.

(7) Use the keyboard to enter the true coordinates of the second point. For example, if you have divided a 36″ by 24″ drawing into twelve 9″ by 8″ boxes, the second point will be 9,8 (assuming you wish to copy the drawing full scale.)

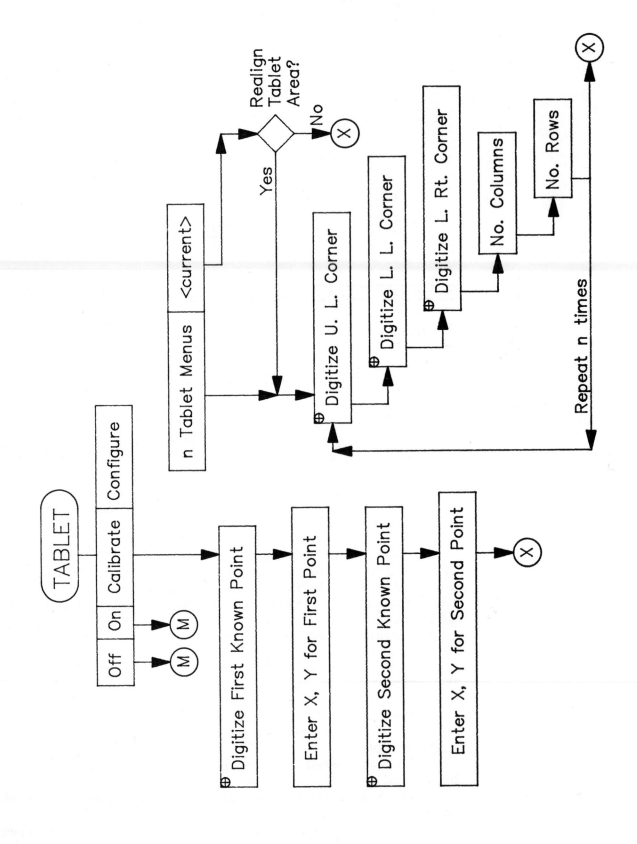

(8) You may now "trace" the drawing into AutoCAD by using the puck and the keyboard to enter each object. For example, enter the LINE command and then hit the two ends of one of the lines on the drawing with the puck. You will now have a line on the drawing with the puck. You will now have a line on the screen if you are in the zoom all position. If you are not in the zoom all position, the lines are still there, you just won't be able to see them until you zoom back. Remember, in Tablet mode, the digitizer surface corresponds to the limits of the whole drawing, rather than the current view on the display.

(9) When you have finished the first box, move the drawing to locate the second box over the digitizer surface and recalibrate the tablet as in steps (3) through (7) above. Repeat as needed to complete the drawing.

Digitizing is an art. You may have to do considerable experimentation with different scale drawings, *SNAP* and *ORTHO* settings, menu devices, and menu development to arrive at an optimum procedure.

Larger digitizers help, but are expensive, typically costing about $1000 per square foot. A better alternative might be photodigitizing—using a camera to produce a pixilized drawing. See CAD/Camera™. Photodigitizing requires very little labor. The drawback is that the output files are huge: a circle will be stored as a series of leetle bitty lines, chewing up disk space well into the megabytes for a large drawing. Some manual cleanup can be necessary to replace awful looking text and to cut the file size down to what will fit on a floppy, or what can be efficiently transmitted by modem.

If you have only a monochrome system, you can do reasonably efficient cleanup of photodigitized drawings by using the *CHANGE* command to push text and circles, etc., to a layer with a dashed or dotted linetype. Then, using a special cleanup menu, draw continuous lines on a new layer, on top of the entities that are dashed. When you have traced over all the items you have decided to clean up, turn off all layers except the dashed one, and erase the duplicated items. When done, turn on the other layers again to plot. Manual cleanup is somewhat easier if you have a color system.

Tablet Menus—(See also Chapter 5, Macros and Menus.) One nice thing about tablets is that they are usually big enough to hold several hundred commands or macros at one time. Different menus can be loaded with the *MENU* command, often by calling them up from cells within the present menu, and the overlay changed to suit. Another neat thing is that tablet menus, unlike screen menus, can contain little symbols to give the operator a clue as to what block or command lurks within. (The AutoCAD-supplied menu, for example, has a little firecracker to symbolize the *EXPLODE* command.)

Tablet menus have some disadvantages: they leave less room on the tablet for screen pointing, making point entry a bit goosier, and they require taking your eyes off the screen to pick up the command. Neither of these factors is very serious: neither will slow you down as much as poor planning of a drawing.

The *TABLET* command *CFG* option is used to lay out the location(s) of menu(s) on the tablet. After you enter *CFG*, AutoCAD will ask how many menus you want on the tablet. Any number from zero to four will be accepted. Then you will be allowed to align the menus by picking points corresponding to three corners of each menu area: upper left, lower left, lower right. Last, you must tell AutoCAD how many columns and how many rows are in each menu area.

A final choice is offered at the end of the *CFG* routine. If you want to change the live area of the tablet used to control the cursor, answer Yes when asked if you want to respecify the pointing area. Two more points will be required to define the live area: digitize the lower left and upper right corners.

Template File—(See Attributes, *ATTEXT* command.)

Temporary Files—(See also File Size.) Larger drawings can't fit into RAM all at once, so AutoCAD creates some temporary files for storing parts of the drawing on disk. Normally they go into your working directory or wherever the drawing is that you are working on. These files usually get deleted as you *END* your drawing. When you configure

AutoCAD, you can tell where to stash these files, other than where your drawing is located. For example, you could specify:

d:\ stuff

Make sure that any drive \ directory you specify actually exists and that there is at least enough room in it to hold your complete drawing, or more, if the *UNDO* function is currently ON.

For faster execution of AutoCAD, it is good practice to create a RAM disk and use that as the *drive* for storage of the temporary files. This is especially effective for large drawings. If you are on a network, the files should be stored on your local node.

Make sure that any drawing files, as opposed to temporary files, that are created on a RAM disk get stored onto your hard drive before turning your computer off.
TEXT Command—(See also *DTEXT, STYLE* commands.) This is one of the most powerful commands in AutoCAD. Power, however, means complexity, and this command *is* complicated.

To do text in a drawing, enter TEXT. The initial prompt is:

Start point or Align/Center/Fit/Middle/Right/Style:

Next, for left-justified text, choose a starting point for the bottom left corner of the first line of text. If you do not want left-justified text, enter instead the letter corresponding to the desired type of justification:

Type	Stands for	Description
A	"aligned"	Adjusts text to fit exactly between two baseline points. The text height will be scaled to match the width.
C	"centered"	Centers the text around a single baseline point.
F	"fitted"	Same as aligned, but text height will not be automatically scaled.
M	"middle"	Same as centered, but definition point is dead center in the text itself.
R	"right"	Right justifies.

The two other choices at this level in the *TEXT* command are "S" and a null response. Use the null response (a [Return] without entering anything) if you just wish to continue the last text entry with additional lines of text; the new text will have the same style, size, and justification as the old.

Use the "S" choice to select a different text style before continuing with the *TEXT* command. The default *STYLE* that is used by AutoCAD when you start drawing is "STANDARD." (See the *STYLE* command.)

After you have responded to the initial prompt and provided any necessary baseline definition points, you will be asked to select a text height. (Exception: Aligned text) The height can be entered by either (a) moving the cursor up from the baseline point a distance corresponding to the desired height and entering a point, or (b) entering a number from the keyboard, or (c) taking the default height shown in brackets in the prompt. The default height will be the same as the last height used for that style of text. Similarly, you will next be prompted for a text angle. (Exceptions: Aligned and fitted text).

Finally, you will be prompted to enter the text itself. When you have finished your first line of text, hit [Return]; the space bar will not function as a [Return] when entering text.

The later versions of AutoCAD permit using control codes in text strings. The

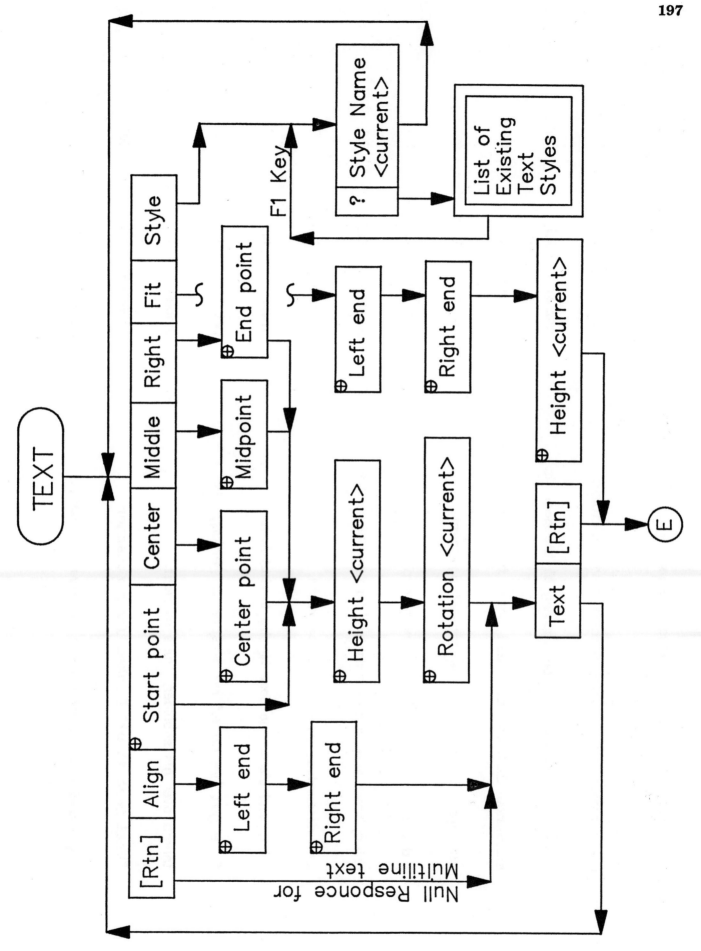

(Expert from A. Conaw Doyle's "Engineer's Thumb.")

Font	width factor	obliquing	
txt	1.0	0.0	One morning at a little before seven o'clock,
simplex	1.0	0.0	I was awakened by the maid tapping at the door, to
complex	1.0	0.0	announce that two men had come from Paddington,
italic	1.0	0.0	and were waiting in the consulting room.
txt	0.9	0.0	I dressed hurriedly, for I knew by experience that
simplex	0.9	0.0	railway cases were seldom trivial, and hastened downstairs.
complex	0.9	0.0	As I descended, my old ally, the guard, came out of the
italic	0.9	0.0	room, and closed the door tightly behind him.
txt	1.0	10°	'I've got him here,' he whispered, jerking his
simplex	1.0	10°	thumb over his shoulder; "he's all right."
complex	1.0	10°	"What is it, then?" I asked, for his manner
italic	1.0	10°	suggested that it was some strange creature...

following list shows the more useful control codes. Remember that combinations of these can be used.

%%o	Toggles overscore on and off
%%u	Toggles underscore on and off
%%d	Draws degrees symbol
%%p	Draws plus or minus symbol
%%c	Draws circle diameter symbol
%%%	Draws a percent sign
%%nnn	Draws special character number nnn

A few added notes on *TEXT*:

The text editing capabilities of AutoCAD are rather primitive as of Version 2.6. For this reason, there are programs to convert WordStar™, ASCII, Lotus™, etc., files into AutoCAD text in the form of .DXF files. One noteworthy example is AutoWord. See Chapter 7 on Third-party Software for more information about AutoWord.

One problem area is how to delete a line of text in the middle of a paragraph and insert a corrected line. The spacing of multiple lines of text (using the null response at the initial prompt to pop you back into *TEXT* entry mode) does not necessarily correspond to the snap grid, making it difficult to accurately position the inserted line. There are four ways to get around this:

(a) Select a text height that will cause each successive line to lie on a snap point.

(b) Insert lines of blank text on top of each line of the original text, starting with the first line (this is easy to hit because of the snap point), filling in text only for the line where the deletion took place.

(c) Insert the new line as close as you can get it and then move it in drag mode until it looks good to the eye.

(d) Use the *CHANGE* command to alter the contents of the line of text. Enter *CHANGE*, select the text line, hit [Return] five times, type in the new text string, and hit [Return] again.

TEXTSCR Command—(See Scripts.) This command is used for flipping back to the text (alpha) screen from the graphics screen. It can be used transparently. See Transparent Commands.

Thawing—(See *LAYER* Command.)

Three-Dimensional Drawing—(ADE-3) AutoCAD has limited 3D drawing capabilities, but should suffice for some applications. See the following commands: VPOINT, ELEV. For Version 2.6 and higher, see also *3DLINE, 3DFACE*. You will also find that for Version 2.6 and up, you can specify and read out points in all three dimensions for these commands: *BASE, DIST, ID, INSERT, POINT*.

The z coordinate of any entity can be changed with these commands for Version 2.6 or higher:

COPY
MOVE
STRETCH

Under 2.6, you can also work with *3DLINEs* and *3DFACEs* using the following commands. Only x and y coordinates will be altered, however, leaving the z values the same:

ARRAY
MIRROR
ROTATE

Additionally, four other commands can be used with 3D lines and faces:

SCALE
CHANGE
INSERT
EXPLODE

3DFACE—(ADE-3) This is the three dimensional equivalent of the *SOLID* command. Each vertex (corner) can be given a different z coordinate, producing a surface or a planar entity in space.

Unlike the *SOLID* command, the points outlining the edge of the *3DFACE* can be entered in the usual order, clockwise or counterclockwise. Also, the *3DFACEs* are never filled.

The following object snaps work with *3DFACE*'s: *Endpoint, Midpoint,* and *Intersection*.

3DLINE—(ADE-3) This command allows you to create a line that lies outside the X-Y plane. It is used in the same way as the line command, except that you can enter a third coordinate for every point, from the keyboard, giving the z elevation of that end of the line.

If you are using a mouse or puck to enter X and Y coordinates, the z coordinate for the *3DLINE* command will be set at whatever the current elevation is. See the *ELEV* command. To reset the elevation during the creation of a *3DLINE*, use the transparent form of the *SETVAR* command: *'SETVAR*. You will be asked to enter a new value for the elevation, and then the *3DLINE* command will be resumed.

Relative 3D coordinates will work, as in: @2,2,5. Polar coordinates are only good in 2D work and would probably be very awkward in 3D, anyway.

3DLINEs are always continuous linetype and can't be extruded.

You can also use object snaps with *3DLINES: Endpoint* and *Midpoint*. Note that the way object snap works with these entities depends on whether the new construction is 2D or 3D. Object snapping to a *3DLINE* while forming another 3D object will result in a z component determined by the *3DLINE*. If you are generating a 2D entity, the z coordinate will be the current elevation.

Here is an example of the generation of a *3DLINE* going from the origin to 5,5,5. The elevation is set to 5 using *'SETVAR* so that the final point can be input using the puck:

Command: 3DLINE
From point: 0,0,0
To point: 'SETVAR > >Variable name or ?: ELEVATION
> >New value for ELEVATION <0.0000>: 5
Resuming 3DLINE command.
To point: 5,5

TIME Command—This command is excellent for tracking drawing progress and productivity and for benchmarking drawing methods. Entering *TIME* will show you the current date and time from the system clock, the date and time of creation or translation of the drawing, the date and time of the last *SAVE* (or *END*), the number of hours spent so far creating the drawing, the elapsed time on a resettable timer, and the status of that timer (on or off).

Options under the *TIME* command are: *Display, On, Off,* and *Reset.* "Display" updates and repeats the list above. "On" and "Off" turn the resettable timer on and off. "Reset" zeroes out the resettable timer. None of these affect the timer that keeps track of total editing time on the drawing.

Toggle Settings—(See also *SETVAR* command.) AutoCAD drawing modes can be turned on and off by either direct commands or by use of the function keys or "mode toggle control keys." The keys have the advantage that they can be invoked during the execution of a command. The list below gives the toggles and the key(s) controlling them, where applicable:

TOGGLE	FUNCTION KEY	CONTROL KEY
Snap	F9	[CTRL] B
Grid	F7	[CTRL] G
Ortho	F8	[CTRL] O
Qtext	none	none
Axis	none	none
Tablet	F10	[CTRL] T
Fill	none	none
Coords	F6	[CTRL] D
Printer Echo	none	[CTRL] Q
Isoplane	none	[CTRL] E

TouchPen™—(See Appendix H.) This is a screen entry device that consists of a thin screen placed over the CRT and a pointer cabled to a board inside the chassis. It can be used to select screen menu items and to enter points. For some applications it is fast, but fatiguing if used for very long. The advantage is that, with properly constructed menus, you need never take your eyes off the screen.

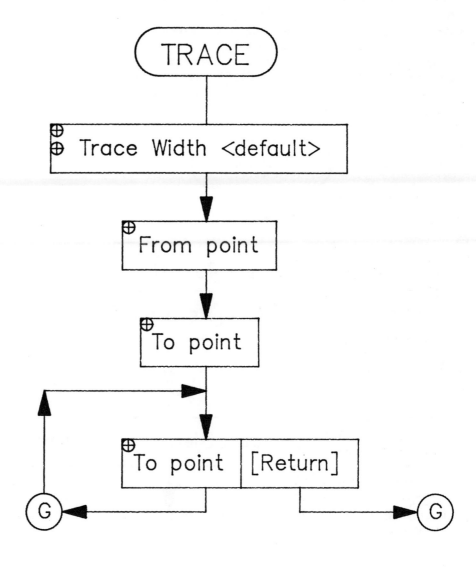

TRACE Command—(See also Polylines, and *FILL.*) The trace command is for making fat lines of uniform width. You can, of course, plot some lines thicker than others by changing pens. If you don't have the right width pens, or if you don't want to stop in the middle of a plot, you should use the *TRACE* command.

TRACE works just like the *LINE* command, except that you are prompted for a trace width following entry of "*TRACE.*" Keyboard entry or two points entered with your puck can be used to define the width. You will be asked for a starting point and a point to go to. The first line will not show until you enter a third point or until you hit [Return]. As you enter more points, a double line will be constructed on the screen. As is the case with *SOLIDS,* the lines will not be filled in unless *FILL* is on. It is faster to work with *FILL* off. For fat lines of varying width, see the *PLINE* command.

Transparent Commands—Certain commands in AutoCAD can be entered in midstream. That is, they can be invoked during the use of another command. These are called "transparent commands." To distinguish these commands from input to the command in progress, you must place an apostrophe (') in front of them. Such commands will not work if AutoCAD is waiting for entry of a text string.

Prompts resulting from transparent commands are prefixed by > > to help keep you aware of which command you are providing input for.

Commands that can be used transparently include:

```
'GRAPHSCR    (Same as toggling F1, Flip Screen, for graphics)
'HELP        (Lets you get help for the command you're using)
'PAN         (Fast zoom mode must be ON) *
'REDRAW      (Cleans up the marker blips screen)
'RESUME      (Restarts a halted script)
'SETVAR      (Lets you look at or reset system variables)
'TEXTSCR     (Same as toggling F1, Flip Screen, for text)
'VIEW        (To save or recall a view of the drawing) *
'ZOOM        (To move in or out) *
```

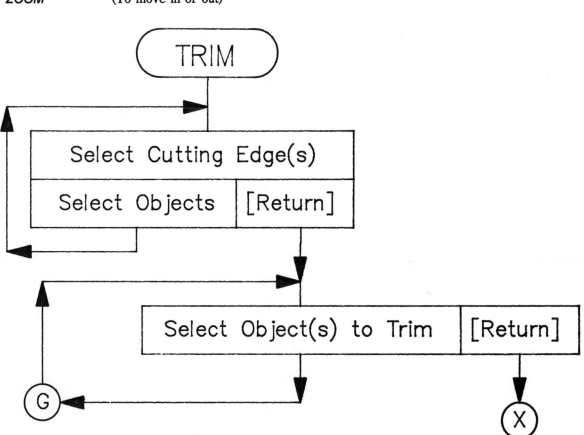

Notes Version 2.6: For transparent use of *PAN, ZOOM,* and *VIEW,* Fast zoom mode must already have been invoked with *VIEWRES,* and no use of these three commands can be made that will cause a regeneration. This rules out all 3D use of these commands, except for *VIEW* Save. *ZOOM* Extents and *ZOOM* All are also verboten, since they too involve a *REGEN.* You might, however, be able to *VIEW* Restore a saved view of the drawing corresponding to the *ZOOM* All position, if that doesn't cause a *REGEN.* Don't try to use transparent *ZOOM, PAN,* or *VIEW* during another *ZOOM, PAN, VIEW,* or a *VPOINT* command.

TRIM Command—(ADE-3) This is a refinement of the *BREAK* command. It is sometimes difficult to terminate a line or other item exactly at the point where it hits another object. In this command, a "cutting edge" is defined as an object you wish to be the stopping point for one or more lines. Cutting edges can be lines, arcs, circles, or the centerline of polylines.

Enter *TRIM,* then select cutting edge(s). Hit [Return] and select objects to be trimmed by hitting individual points. (Window and Last won't work here.) Be careful to point only to the pieces that you wish to eliminate. An object can serve as both a "trimmor" and a "trimee" if selected at both prompts.

Version 2.6 notes: When you trim linear dimensions created under Version 2.6's associative dimensioning, the dimension set will automatically be recalculated and updated using the current dimensioning variable settings.

Before trimming

Select cutting edges

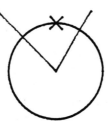

Select objects to trim

After trimming

U

U Command—(See also *UNDO*.) This is a step-at-a-time *UNDO* command. It eliminates the effect of the most recent command only.

UNDO Command—The *UNDO* command allows you to back up several steps in the creation of the drawing. It also lets you mark progress points that you can return safely to if you blunder, and group commands together for later *UNDO*ing as a group.

The options under *UNDO* are as follows (Sub-options in parentheses):

C	"Control"	Permits turning off *UNDO* (pick suboption "One") or both *UNDO* and *U* ("None"). Also toggles *UNDO* and *U* back on ("All").
A	"Auto"	Toggles on and off automatic grouping of menu macros so that they can be *UNDO*ne at one step. (Yes/No)
n	(a number)	Backs up by that number of steps. This is usually much faster, if a little riskier, than using the *U* command the same number of times. A number *UNDO* will not pass a Mark (See below.)
M	"Mark"	Puts a mark in the file, letting you *UNDO* back to that point later. See "Back", below. Marks do not work inside of Groups.
B	"Back"	*UNDO*es everything back to the last Mark and removes that Mark.
G	"Group"	Starts a command Group that will be *UNDO*ne all together by *U* or *UNDO*.
E	"End"	Ends a command Group. Groups can't be nested; starting another Group ends the previous Group.

General notes: Some commands are not affected by *UNDO*. Most of them are fairly obvious: *HELP, DIST, STATUS*, etc. Others are: *END, MSLIDE, DXFOUT, IGESOUT, SAVE, WBLOCK.*

UNDO has the equivalent of an *OOPS: REDO* will put back the items removed by one previous *UNDO* command if entered immediately after the *UNDO.*

*PLOT*ting or *PRPLOT*ting resets the *UNDO* file, eliminating all Groups and Marks. After each *UNDO*, AutoCAD displays the name of the command that is *UNDO*ne.

Note that line segments created during a single use of the *LINE* command will all be undone as a single group. Script actions will also be undone as a single group.

It can save multiple regenerations if you tell AutoCAD to *UNDO* a specific number of operations instead of stepping backwards one at a time. Of course, you have to know how many steps you wish to remove to do this.

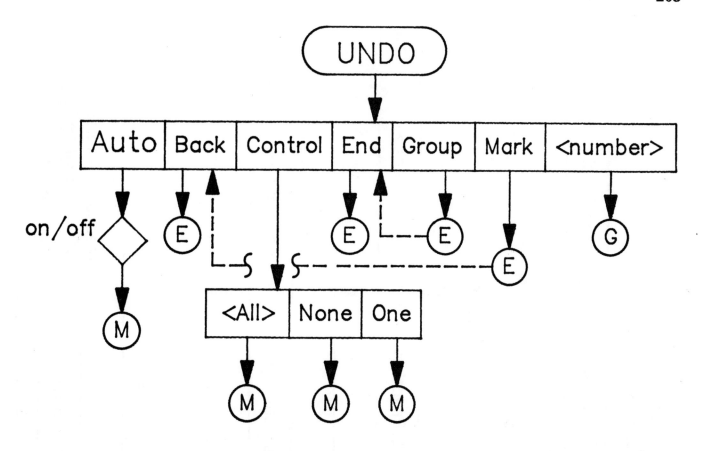

U Sub-Command—(See *LINE* Command.) During entry of lines, a *"U"* response to the *"To point:"* prompt will detach the last entered point and allow you to reposition the prior segment.

UNDO Sub-command—(See *DIM* Command.)

UNITS Command—(See also Prototype Drawing, Angles.) To change the system of numerical notation, enter *UNITS*. The choices are:

Menu Selection	System	Example	Drawing Unit
1	Scientific	2.543E+02	inches
2	Decimal	254.300	inches
3	Engineering	21'–2.3"	inches
4	Architectural	21'–2 19/64"	inches
5	Fractional	254 19/64	any

Enter the number corresponding to the system you wish to use. You will then be prompted for either the number of decimal places or the smallest fraction you wish displayed. After the linear units format has been selected, a second menu will appear covering angular formats:

1	Decimal degrees	54.667
2	Degrees/minutes/se-conds	54d40'
3	Grads	60.741
4	Radians	0.9541
5	Surveyors units	N35d20'E

UPDATE Subcommand—(See *DIM* Command.)

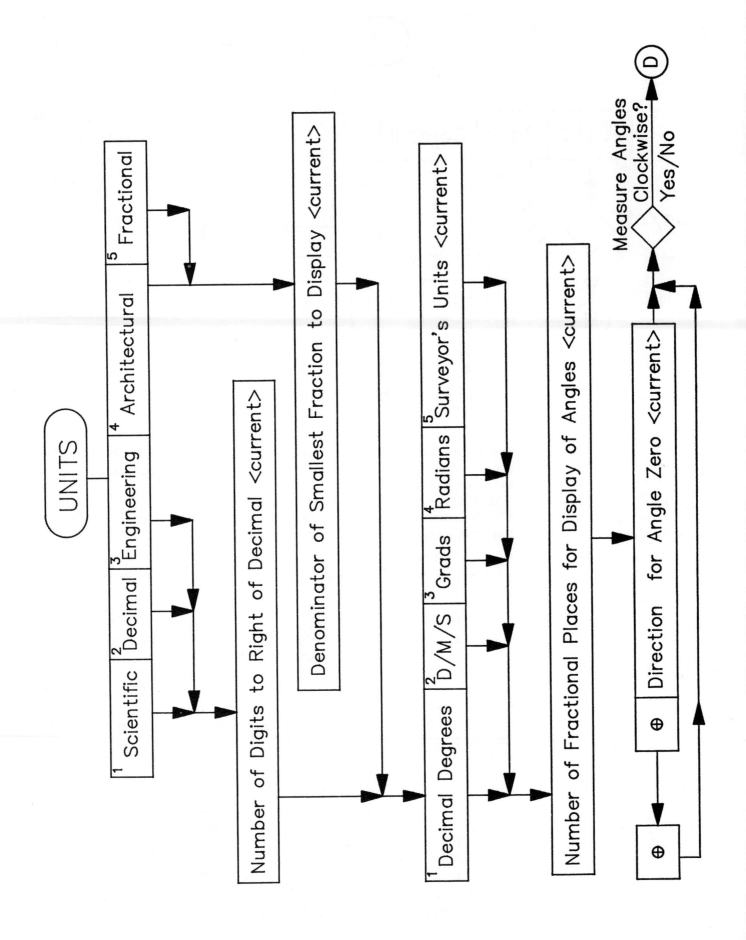

V

VIEW Command—(See also *MSLIDE*.) This is a very useful command where multiple passes are necessary to edit a large drawing. This command can replace the *PAN* and *ZOOM* commands for returning to a previous area where you must *ZOOM* in closely to draw details.

When you have finished working on one part of the drawing, enter the *VIEW* command. The options are: *Delete, Restore, Save, Window,* and *?.*

Saving the view you have just worked on will allow you to return to that same view later, without having to *ZOOM* or *PAN* to it. (See the Section on CAD Efficiency, Chapter 4.)

"Restore" is selected if you wish to return to a previously saved view.

"Window" lets you specify two points determining a view that may or may not be on-screen at the time you create the view.

Enter a question mark (?) if you want to see what views have been saved so far.

Views no longer needed can be deleted by entering D for "Delete."

Views can be plotted (See PLOT) or called up when using the main menu to select editing an existing drawing (See Main Menu.)

The names used for views can have a maximum length of 31 characters. The same set of characters can be used as for drawing names.

Under Version 2.6 of AutoCAD, VIEW can be used in the middle of another command, as long as the other command is not waiting for text. Enter *'VIEW*, with a leading apostrophe. See Transparent Commands.

VIEWRES Command—The *VIEWRES* command speeds up *ZOOMs* and *PANs* by eliminating regeneration, when possible. Graphics data for much of the drawing are held in a virtual screen and used to *REDRAW* the new view during a *ZOOM* or *PAN*. If the new zoom exceeds the virtual screen limitation, a regen will be necessary, at the usual speed.

Enter *VIEWRES,* and then *Y* or *N* at the prompt. *Y* will turn on fast zoom mode, *N* will toggle it off.

The last prompt in the *VIEWRES* command asks for a "circle zoom percent" from 1 to 20,000. Circle zoom percentages below 100 gain added speed at the expense of a little less accurate generation of circles and arcs *on the display only.* At the very worst, circles will appear as octagons on the display. Plotting is not affected. Circle zoom percentages above 100 increase the number of straight lines used to simulate a true circle on the screen; this slows regeneration down somewhat.

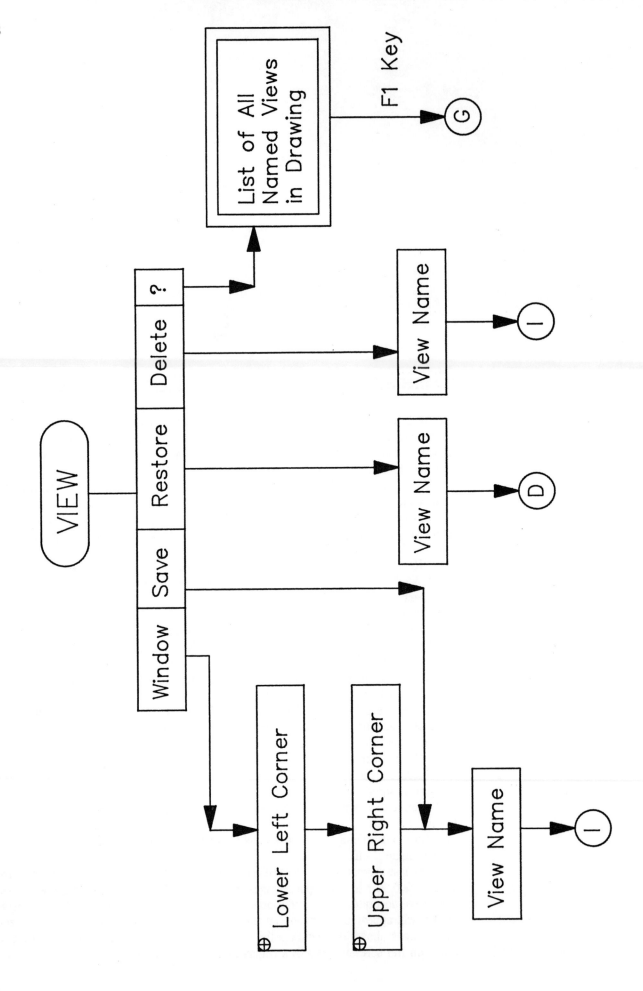

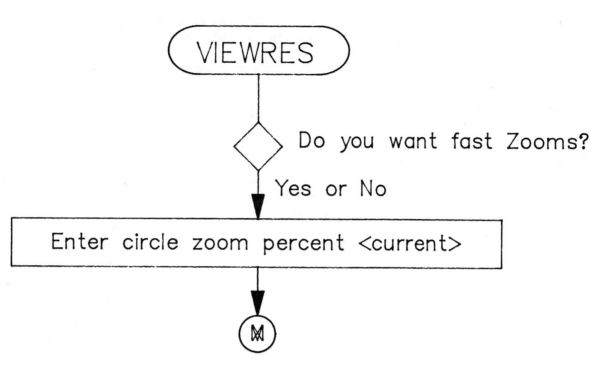

VIEW Restore is the same as a *ZOOM*, for the purposes of *VIEWRES*, and is also sped up.

VPOINT Command—The direction from which a three-dimensional AutoCAD drawing is viewed is set by use of the *VPOINT* command. The initial prompt calls for X, Y, and Z values (example: 1,1,1) for where the viewer is located. The viewer is looking back towards the origin (that is, X=0, Y=0, Z=0). A plan view would correspond to 0,0,1.

If you respond to the initial prompt with [Return], a "compass" and the "axes tripod" will be shown.

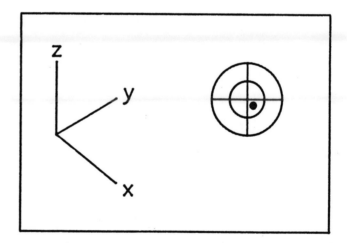

The compass is a representation of a sphere of radius equal to one, opened up at the south pole and flattened out. The outer ring of the compass corresponds to the southern hemisphere, the inner ring the northern hemisphere. If you move the puck or mouse, it will cause a spot to move around on the sphere, showing where the observer is situated on the surface of the sphere. The origin lies at the center of the sphere, with the X-axis pointing to the right, Y-axis pointing toward the top of the screen, and the Z-axis pointing out of the screen.

As you move the spot, the "axes tripod," consisting of the positive legs of the X, Y, and Z-axes, will shift around, continuously showing how it would appear to the viewer from the viewpoint shown on the surface of the sphere.

Pressing the select button on your puck will set the viewpoint to match the spot location. Hitting [Return] will take the default viewpoint, i.e., the current viewpoint.

Note that there is no perspective. Everything constructed in 3-D can be thought of as lying in a very small sphere at the origin. Zooming in on details is possible, but you can't zoom back to any particular distance; the direction of the viewpoint is all that can be set by *VPOINT.*

VIEW Restore or *ZOOM* Previous will alter the viewpoint to what was in effect when the *VIEW* Save or *ZOOM* command was used.

VSLIDE Command—(See also *MSLIDE.*) *VSLIDE* will call up a previously made slide (an .sld file). Slides appear on the display very quickly and can load even faster if they are "preloaded." To preload a slide, enter: *VSLIDE *slidname.* When you wish to view the preloaded slide, enter *VSLIDE.* This is particularly handy in scripts, where the preloading can be done while a previously called slide is being viewed.

REDRAW will restore the current drawing. Editing commands will not affect the slide but will affect the current drawing, so watch what you do when a slide is on-screen.

WXYZ

WBLOCK Command—(See also *BLOCK*.) *WBLOCK*ing is similar to *BLOCK*ing, except that a *WBLOCK* is exported from the current drawing to a file created when the *WBLOCK* command is used.

Enter *WBLOCK*, then reply to the prompt with the output file name (no .dwg suffix is needed.) The next prompt asks for a block name. Options are:

[Enter]—You will then be asked to select objects and an insertion base point. All objects selected will be exported to the new drawing. To recreate them in the current drawing, enter an *OOPS*.

(Name a block)—A copy of a block that has previously been created in the current drawing will be exported to the new drawing.

=—The new drawing and the exported block have the same name.

*—The current drawing will be written to the new file, less any unused block definitions.

Note that the new drawing can be reinserted back into the current drawing later, if desired. WBLOCKing and reINSERTion is one way of cutting a drawing back down to a reasonable size to reduce zoom and pan times; later reinsertion combines both parts of the drawing for plotting.

Window—(See Selecting Objects.)

X/Y/Z Point Filters—(Version 2.6.) If you want to enter some coordinate components (X and/or Y and/or Z) for an entity with the puck, and others from the keyboard, or some with one object snap and the others with a different snap, you can tell AutoCAD the dimensions you are giving it, enter them, change devices or snaps, and then AutoCAD will prompt you for the missing component. An example will make this clear:

You are going to run a line from the origin to a point in space 5 inches above a circle in the X-Y plane, using the Version 2.6 command, *3DLINE:*

Prompt:	Response:	Notes:
Command:	*3DLINE*	
From point:	*0,0,0*	The origin
To point:	*.Z*	Period, plus coordinate filter
of	*5*	The height in Z direction

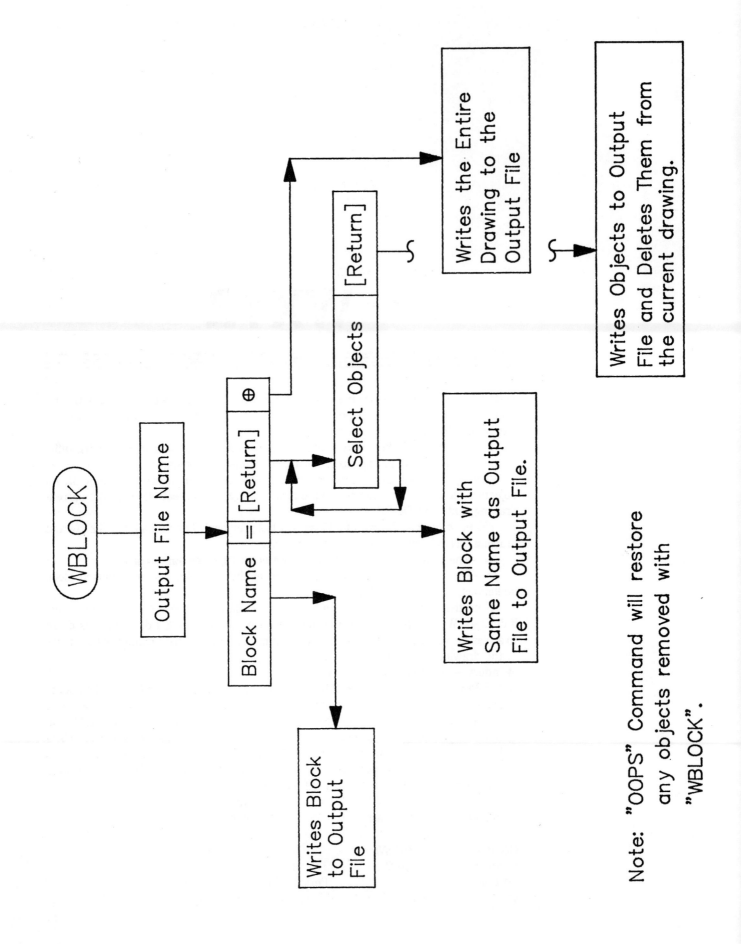

Note: "OOPS" Command will restore any objects removed with "WBLOCK".

AutoCAD now knows that you are only providing the z coordinate for the endpoint of the *3DLINE*. AutoCAD reminds you that something is missing:

(Need X,Y)	*CENTER*	One-shot object snap
of	*(a point)*	Hit the circle
To point:	*[Return]*	The *3DLINE* is now complete.

Notes: Don't try to use filters with *TANGENT* and *PERPENDICULAR* object snaps.

If you want to change the Y coordinate of a location after you've entered it, reenter the Y filter: ''.Y'' and give the new value.

ZOOM Command—This command is used for zooming in and out. After entering "*ZOOM*", the initial prompt will read:

All/Center/Dynamic/Extents/Left/Previous/Window/<scale(X)>:

(1) Enter "*A*" to zoom out to the current limits of the drawing. The display will then show the entire drawing, except for any layers that have been turned off or frozen.

(2) Enter "*E*" to zoom to the current extents of the drawing. If you don't have very much in the drawing, this will be a fairly close-in *ZOOM*. When your drawing is almost done, the "*ZOOM E*" view will be very close to the "*ZOOM A*" view.

(3) *ZOOM* "W" is used for *ZOOM*ing into a drawing, although occasionally it might be used (with the keyboard) to *PAN* if you know the coordinates of the area you wish to *ZOOM* in on. Hit "*W*", then select the corners of a window. The windowed area will be blown up to fill the screen. (NOTE: Because the proportions of the display are not necessarily the same as the window specified, you will probably see somewhat more of your drawing than just the windowed area.

(4) "*C*" will cause AutoCAD to ask for a point, followed by a height or magnification. The display will *ZOOM* in to place the specified point in the center of the display, with the height filling the screen or with the magnification requested. A magnification is indicated by an "*X*" after the number, for example, 5X means make everything displayed five times bigger than the current size; magnifications less than one make things smaller.

(5) "*L*" is a left-corner *ZOOM*. AutoCAD will put the lower left corner of the drawing in the lower left corner of the display. You will be prompted for a height or magnification, similar to *ZOOM C*, above.

(6) *ZOOM* "P" will restore the previous *ZOOM* to the display. AutoCAD keeps track of the five latest *ZOOM*s and will backtrack through all of them, if requested.

(7) Enter "*D*" for dynamic *ZOOM* (ADE-3). (Colors of the boxes will be as shown below in parentheses. If you don't have color, look for the type of line defining the box.) This allows you to *PAN* a view box around within a rectangle (white) representing the drawing extents. If you keep the view box within a second, precalculated rectangle indicated by four (red) corner lines, the drawing will REDRAW instead of REGEN as the display changes.

You can toggle from dynamic *PAN* to dynamic *ZOOM* by hitting the pick button on your puck. You can then drag the view box size, making it larger or smaller with horizontal movement of the cursor, showing the limits of the new *ZOOM*. You can also move the box up or down with vertical motion of the cursor. If you wish, you can toggle back into PAN mode with the pick button. When you press [Return], AutoCAD will *ZOOM* to the limits of the view box as it currently is set. Again, the *ZOOM* will be much faster if performed within the precalculated rectangle.

If you decide to stay in the present view, hit [CTRL] C. The view will return to where you started, as shown by the green rectangle.

(8) Entering a drawing scale followed by an "*X*" will cause the display to *ZOOM* in by that factor. See above under Center *ZOOM*.

ZOOM can be used transparently under Version 2.6 of AutoCAD. See Transparent Commands.

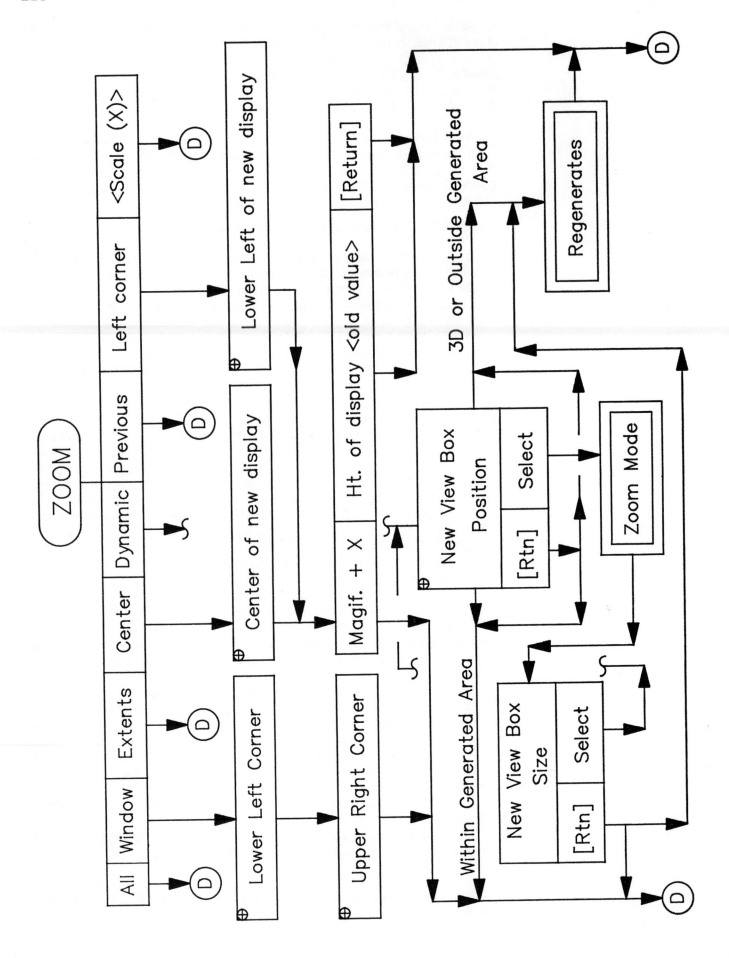

Section 3

Hardware and Software Considerations

This section contains a variety of things. Some, like Appendix D, E, F, and G, you'll only need when you buy new hardware or want to upgrade your existing system.

Appendix A contains the AutoCAD history of revisions through version 2.6. You'll need this information from time-to-time.

Appendix B, Shapes, and C, Custom Hatch Files, are advanced applications.

Appendix H is a summary of AutoCAD commands—located so it's easy for you to find.

Appendix I is a review of AutoCAD Release 9.

Appendix A

Revisions to Releases

AutoCAD has undergone several generations of updates. This book is more or less written around versions 2.52 and 2.6. If you have an older version, you might find some of the information herein doesn't apply to you. To help you see what you are missing, below is a summary of the important revisions made in each release.

Commands are shown in all caps:

Ver. 2.0 (October, 1984)	Ver. 2.1 (May, 1985)	Ver. 2.5 (June, 1986)	Ver. 2.6 (February, 1987)
LINETYPE	BLIPMODE	UNDO	3DFACE
LTSCALE	CHAMFER	REDO	3DLINE
LAYER Ltype	PEDIT	SETVAR	FILMROLL
STYLE	PLINE	VIEWRES	XYZ Filters
QTEXT	DXBIN	TIME	monotext
DXFIN	GRAPHSCR	DTEXT	assoc. dimensions
DXFOUT	TEXTSCR	EXPLODE	plot to file
SCRIPT	PRPLOT	TRIM	AREA totaling
RSCRIPT	pen changes	EXTEND	3D COPY
ENDSV	path names	STRETCH	3D MOVE
SAVE	prototype.dwg	OFFSET	3D STRETCH
MSLIDE	file copy	ROTATE	2.5D ARRAY
VSLIDE	line splitting	SCALE	2.5D MIRROR
OSNAP	VIEW Window	POLYGON	2.5D STRETCH
VIEW	Pline fillets	ELLIPSE	more AutoLISP
MIRROR	3D level 1	DIVIDE	DXF upgrading
named layers	ELEV	MEASURE	
LINE undo	VPOINT	DONUT	
polar COORDS	HIDE	AutoLISP	
attributes	LAYER Freeze	Dynamic ZOOM	
isometric	LAYER Thaw	Big Fonts	
grid rotation	variables	vertical text	
dragging	select hilite	ext'd memory	
submenus	curve fits	auto drag	

217

Other changes have been made in each of these versions, but those listed above are the most important, depending on the application. Some "improvements" have been less than a total success, but for the most part, every new release has been well worth the extra update fee.

Generally, every release has run faster than the previous version. The tendency to lock up in certain operations has apparently been eliminated.

Some of the added features above for each version were subject to having the proper ADE. For more information, see ADE in the Glossary.

Appendix B

Shapes

One particularly nifty feature of AutoCAD is its ability to do *shapes*. Shapes are similar to blocks, but they are more efficient to store. Shapes are more challenging to create, but if you want to define your own text fonts, you'll have to learn to do shapes.

Shapes are defined by creating an ASCII file containing explicit directions as to how each shape is to be drawn. Text fonts are also stored in these .shp files. Up to 256 shapes

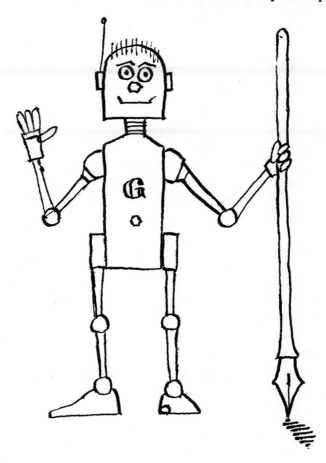

can be contained in an ordinary .shp file. Special "BIGFONT" .shp files can contain up to 65,535 shape definitions, should you desire to do Japanese or ancient Egyptian characters.

Blocks are easy to make. You draw what you want, tell AutoCAD, in effect, "make this thing into a block called 'deelybobber'," and there you have it. Making a shape is more like telling a 5-inch-high robot how to draw: "Put the pen down on the paper, Gort. Walk 3 inches northwest. Pen up, Gort. Go 2 inches east. Pen down. Now walk 2 inches south. Very good, Gort, you're done."

STANDARD VECTORS, OR GORT STEPS OUT

The basic instructions for moving Gort around the paper are contained in the Standard Vector chart, of Fig. B-2. Each vector is a distance and direction, starting from wherever Gort is standing. Each vector has its own code, as indicated on the chart.

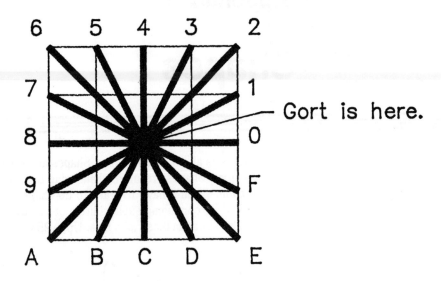

"Standard Vectors"

You have probably recognized the vector codes as being hexadecimal (base 16 arithmetic) numbers. It is not accidental that there are sixteen Standard Vectors. By putting another number in front of the vector code, you can tell Gort how many *paces* to take in that direction. (The length of Gort's pace is a variable, that you will learn to set later.) For example, if you tell Gort "01C", he'll take one pace downwards (*South*). An "020" will make him step two paces to the right (*East*). Or "0EE" will send him fourteen paces Southeast.

GORT SQUARE DANCES

Just for an example, to move Gort around in a square, you would give him these commands: 014,010,01C,018,000. Each of the first four numbers corresponds to one of the Standard Vectors, above. The last number, 000, is just the way we tell Gort "Very good, we're all done with that shape."

GORT IS BILINGUAL

Gort speaks both hexadecimal, and decimal. But you have to tell him what language you are using. If you are speaking hexadecimal, start the number with a zero: "01A" or "0EE", and so forth. If you want to speak decimal, the same messages would have no leading zero, and would be: "26" and "238", respectively.

GET IT UP, GORT

As Gort moved above, he had the pen down, and left a square on the paper. Gort has his pen down automatically at the start of every shape. If you want him to raise the pen, you have to tell him "002", for "pen up." To put the pen back down, he has to be told "001". There are some other messages we can give Gort:

Message:	Meaning:
000	Very good, you're done with that shape.
001	Put the pen point down on the paper.
002	Raise the pen, Gort.
003	Divide your standard pace by the next number.
004	Multiply your standard pace by the next number.
005	Remember where you are, Gort.
006	Go back to where you were.
007	Do a little dance defined by the next number.
008	Go an X and Y distance, as given by the next 2 bytes.
009	Do X and Y distances until I tell you "Enough".
00A	The next 2 bytes are an eighth-circle.
00B	The next 5 bytes are a fractional arc.
00C	The next 3 bytes are a X, Y, bulge arc.
00D	Do a bunch of bulge arcs, till I say "Enough".
00E	Follow the next command only if you're doing vertical text.
0,0	Enough.

GORT GOOSE-STEPS

The usual height of a shape is the length of Gort's standard pace, that is, the length of standard vectors 0, 4, 8, or C. This will not do for many shapes, so we tell Gort to decrease or increase his pace by dividing (003) or multiplying (004) by the next

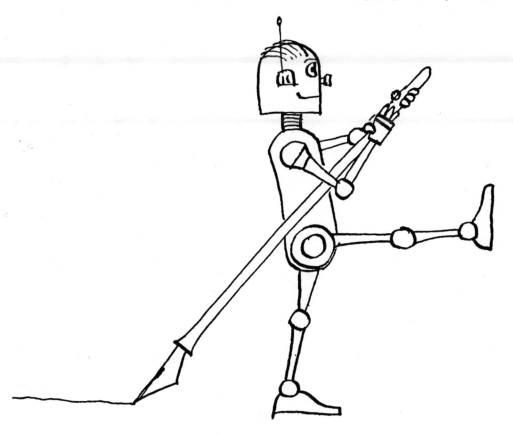

numerical message, the pace-factor. The pace-factor can be any integer from 1 to 255 (hexadecimal 001 to 0FF). If you give Gort directions to increase his pace several times in a shape, the factors are cumulative. He always multiplies or divides his present pace length by the new factor. It's often a good idea to tell him to go back to his original pace at the end of every shape.

GORT LOOKS BACK

You can tell Gort to remember where he is with the "005" message. There are only three problems with Gort's memory: (1) His memory is a *stack*: You have to tell him to go back to the last place he memorized ("006") before you can send him back to the one before that, and so forth. (2) The stack is only 4 pieces high: Gort can remember only up to four places where he's been. (3) You have to clear the stack: If you tell Gort to remember where he is, don't forget to tell him to go back there. He has to forget everything he remembers, otherwise his "Where-was-I?" memory gets full, resulting in the cryptic message, "Position stack overflow in shape 123."

GORT DANCES

In the middle of doing a shape, Gort can be told to do some other shape from the same file. Tell him: "007", followed by the number of the shape you want him to insert in his current shape. He'll dance around according to the instructions contained for the other shape and then continue what he was doing. Be careful, though. Gort will start the other shape with his pen up or down, depending on where it is currently. He will not automatically put the pen down for the *subshape*.

GORT TIP-TOES THROUGH THE VECTORS

The sixteen directions of the Standard Vectors aren't enough to do fine text or shapes. If you tell Gort "008", he will interpret the next two messages as being the

X and Y distances, respectively, of where you want him to go next. He will go directly in that direction by the shortest route. The X and Y distances are limited to a range of −128 to +127, (in hex, that would be −080 to +07F.) If you want Gort to go up and to the right a little less than 45 degrees, for example, you would tell him: "008,004,003". This would move him 5 paces roughly Northeast (36.87 degrees).

If you need to make directions a little easier to follow in your documentation, you can put parentheses around X,Y pairs. The example immediately above would appear: 008, (4,3). This is to help you, not Gort. Gort understands.

GORT DOES THE FLAMENCO

You can send Gort on a path consisting of all non-standard vectors with the "009" command. Every successive pair of numbers will then be interpreted as an X,Y pair, until Gort hits a zero-zero pair: (0,0). At this point he will return to normal message mode.

GORT GOES IN CIRCLES

So far, Gort has only done straight lines. You can also send him in circles, or in eighth-circles, with the octant arc message: "00A" or "10". This will be followed by two more commands defining how big the arc radius is and which octants are involved. The radius message is any number from 000 to 0FF (0 to 255). The octant identification message is more complicated: the first character is a + or a −, depending on whether you want Gort to go counterclockwise or clockwise. The second character is a zero, if you're speaking hex. The third character is the starting line, as explained in the figure below, and the fourth is the number of total octants Gort is to sweep through. A zero means 8 octants.

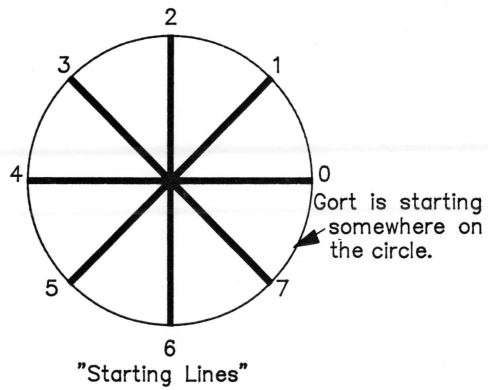

"Starting Lines"

When doing arcs, you have to imagine that Gort is standing on the circumference of a circle, at one of the 8 starting lines shown on the figure above. The direction you want him to go will be defined by which starting line you tell him he's on at the start of the octant arc command, and whether the octant identification message is positive or negative.

Let's send Gort in a big circle centered to the Southeast, going clockwise:

Message to Gort: "00A,0FF, − 030"

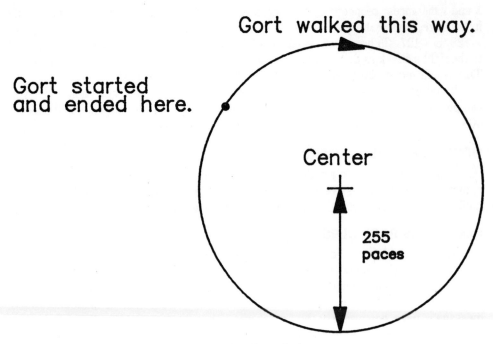

Give Gort this message to make the shape below:

Message to Gort: "00A,008,020,00A,004,024,00A,004, – 024,000"
Same thing, decimal: "10,8,32,10,4,36,10,4, – 36,0"
Ditto, with parentheses: "10,(8,32),10,(4,36),10,(4, – 36),0"

(to help YOU understand)

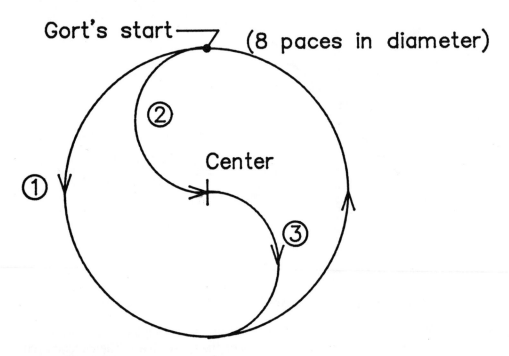

SON OF GORT GOES IN CIRCLES

Octant arcs are useful, but many times you will need more or less than a complete eighth of a circle. You will tell Gort how many degrees his start and stop positions are from starting lines, how big a radius to use, where the starting line is, and how many octants or partial octants are required. The radius can be more than 255 units, because a special field has been added to indicate a larger radius.

The command for fractional arcs is "00B" or "11". When Gort hears this, he will expect five more messages to define the arc: (1) How many Gort-degrees the beginning of the arc is from the starting line before the start point, (2) How many Gort-degrees the end of the arc is from the last starting line crossed, (3) A zero (for radii less than 255) or another number from 001 to 0FF corresponding to the highest 8 bits of the radius, (4) The lowest 8 bits of the radius, and (5) the octant identification message as defined above for octant arcs.

To calculate Gort-degrees, take the actual angular distance in degrees from the starting line to the endpoint of the arc, multiply by 256 and divide by 45.

An example of a Gort message string to do a 259-unit-radius arc from 35 degrees to 175 degrees: "00B,199,228,001,003,004". These commands mean:

00B Here comes a fractional arc, next five numbers
199 Start offset: (35-45*0)*256/45 = 199
228 End offset: (175-45*3)*256/45 = 228
001 High radius bits: INT(259/256) = 1
003 Low radius bits: 259-256 = 3
004 Octant identifier: counterclockwise, starting in the first octant, four octants involved.

REVENGE OF GORT GOES IN CIRCLES

Another way to tell Gort to make an arc is the "Bulge Specification" command: "00C". This is very similar to the X,Y displacement, above, except that, instead of moving in a straight line, Gort moves in an arc specified by the Bulge Factor, the last of three messages defining the arc.

The *Bulge Factor* is calculated by dividing the height of the arc above the chord by the length of the chord and multiplying by 254: BF = 254 * (H/C). If the Bulge Factor is negative, the arc is generated clockwise. A B.F. of 127 gives a semicircle. A B.F. of 0 is a straight line connecting the endpoints.

A sample Bulge Specified arc with a height of one-fourth diameter, tilted up at a 45 degree angle, chord length about 14.14 units, drawn clockwise:

Message to Gort: 00C,00A,00A, – 040.
Alternatively: 12,(10,10), – 64

GORT DOES MORE BULGE ARCS

In order to let Gort do a series of Bulge Specified arcs, give him the "00D" message. He will then take the next numbers in groups of three, executing an arc for each group, until he runs into a 0,0 pair.

GORT WRITES VERTICAL TEXT

The special message "00E" or "14" is used when a set of text shapes might be used for either vertical lettering or horizontal lettering. It allows sticking extra command sets into each letter shape so that Gort will go to the right place to start each letter when doing vertical text. This place will obviously be different if Gort is doing horizontal instead of vertical text.

If you are defining a letter in such a font, first give Gort "Pen up" (002), the 00E command, a 008 (for an X,Y displacement), followed by a X and Y pair sufficient to move the pen from where the last vertical letter left off to the normal start point for the new letter. Tell Gort "Pen down" (001). At the end of the letter, move Gort to where the next horizontal letter would start (pen up, of course), and add "002,00E,008," followed by a X,Y displacement pair that will put the pen at the top of the next vertical letter. A 000 ends the shape definition.

When Gort executes the letter in horizontal text, he will ignore the X,Y displacement commands immediately following 00E. If he is doing vertical text, the first 00E command takes him from the vertical endpoint of the last letter to the horizontal startpoint of the new letter. The second 00E command takes Gort from the normal (horizontal) endpoint of the letter to the vertical text endpoint of the letter.

In addition to the above information for Gort, each shape within the .shp file must have a header line starting with an asterisk (*), giving the shape number (1 to 255), the number of bytes used to describe that shape, and the name of the shape. Lowercase names are ignored by AutoCAD. This is handy for naming text shapes.

*Example: *11,4,GORTCIRC*
00A,008,020,000
[empty line if end of .shp file]

You can have more than one line of numbers defining the shape, if necessary. Be sure you have an empty line as the last line of the .shp file or it won't compile. This is true in spite of what's shown in the AutoCAD manual.

To use a shape file, you must run it first through AutoCAD's shape compiler, Option number 7 on the Main Menu, to form a .shx file.

Text font files must start with a special header line:

*0, 4, font name
u.c. height,l.c.descender length,horiz/vert identifier, 0

The second line of the header includes the height of an uppercase letter (in vector lengths), the length of lowercase descenders (in vector lengths), a vertical text indicator

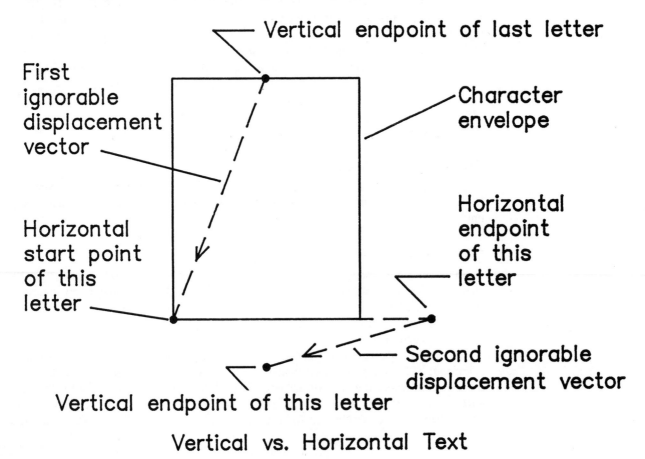

Vertical endpoint of last letter

First ignorable displacement vector

Character envelope

Horizontal start point of this letter

Horizontal endpoint of this letter

Second ignorable displacement vector

Vertical endpoint of this letter

Vertical vs. Horizontal Text

code (0 for horizontal only, 2 for both vertical and horizontal usage), and a 0 to terminate the shape.

The shape numbers for each text shape must be the ASCII code for that character. Tables of ASCII characters can be found in most printer manuals, computer textbooks, and in Norton's Utilities. Codes 32 through 126 are the only characters used, with four exceptions:

You will need a shape corresponding to ASCII code 10, the Line Feed. It is a message telling Gort to drop down a line with his pen up. An example of this would be:

*10,5,lnf
002,008,(0,12),0

The *degrees, Plus-or-minus,* and *Circle Diameter* symbols can also be used, and correspond to shape numbers 127, 128, and 129, respectively. To put special characters into a text line, type in "%%127", "%%128", or "%%129". There is also a shorthand version of each: "%%d", "%%p", and "%%c". Generally, special user-defined shapes can be put into text lines by prefixing the shape number with "%%".

A good way to make your own text font is to take one of the fonts supplied with AutoCAD and modify the uncompiled .shp file to match your requirements.

If you wish to do a large font file, with more than 256 characters, you must start the shape definition file like this:

*BIGFONT nnnn, rrrr, beg1, end1, beg2, end2, . . .

The first field, nnnn, must contain the rough number of text shapes, plus or minus 10 percent. The limit is 65,536.

The second field, rrrr, must tell AutoCAD how many ranges of escape code numbers follow.

The third field, beg1, is the first (lowest) hexidecimal escape code that will let AutoCAD know that the next byte is part of a bigfont character. AutoCAD will then use both bytes to select the proper character.

The fourth field, end1 is the highest hex escape code for an escape character. You may use more than one range of hex codes, but you must tell AutoCAD what the upper and lower limits are for each range, as indicated above. Each set of escape codes must be sequential within the range you specify.

An example of a 1000 character text font file:

*BIGFONT 1000,1,0A0,0AF

To call up a big font file using the STYLE command, enter the name of the font file thus: txt,nameofbigfontfile.

Appendix C

Custom-Hatch Patterns

If you aren't satisfied with the 41 standard crosshatch patterns provided with AutoCAD, it is possible to create others with very little effort, once you understand the process.

First, remember that hatching consists of straight lines, not arcs. The patterns drawn during crosshatching are made up of line segments generated by solid or broken lines repeated at intervals across the object being hatched, stopping when they reach an edge.

Second, you'll need to be fairly proficient at trigonometry to make the more interesting patterns. If it's been a while since you calculated any triangles, you might want to dive into one of your old math books to get back up to speed.

Third, some pointers when creating hatch patterns:

§ Don't try to make hatch patterns late in the day, when you are tired. It takes concentration to do the geometry and file structuring. You'd be surprised how many mistakes you can make in creating just one, simple pattern.

§ Avoid interruptions. Anything that breaks your concentration can take a long time to recover from.

§ For your ASCII .pat file, lay out everything in neat columns using extra spaces as needed to get your data to line up. It's much easier to spot missing commas or data if you do this. The extra spaces will be ignored, so go ahead and make things easy on yourself.

§ Don't use graph paper for laying out patterns that don't match the grid exactly. That is, if you have hatch pattern intersections that don't lie exactly on the graph paper intersections, use plain paper instead. The graph paper can easily fool you as to where the lines go.

§ Borland's SideKick™ is a good tool for developing hatch patterns. Because SideKick is memory-resident, you don't have to exit AutoCAD to get back into the ASCII text editor. This can save quite a bit of time. For the sake of your graphics monitor, however, you should *never* invoke SideKick from the graphics screen. Always flip to the text screen before getting SideKick up (by [CTRL][ALT]).

Here is a typical hatch pattern definition:

*ansi31,ANSI Iron/Brick/Stone masonry
45, 0,0, 0,.125

228

Refer to the Crosshatch Sampler in the Glossary Section, (under HATCH), as you read the information below, to see what these patterns look like and how the definition .pat file creates them.

The first entry for ANSI31 consists of an asterisk (*) to indicate the start of a pattern definition, then the pattern name, and some descriptive text. The text can say anything you wish, it doesn't appear anywhere else except in the .pat file that you create for a new hatch pattern. If you decide to omit the text, then also omit the last comma.

The second entry in this file defines a single unbroken line and gives its angle (45 degrees), a point that it passes through (the origin, 0,0 in this case), and how far it is from the next repetition of itself. The X,Y distance given between repetitions of this line (0,.125) is measured as if the line were the X-axis. Why there is an X component to this last parameter will be clear in a minute.

```
*ansi32,ANSI Steel
45,     0,0, 0,.375
45, .177,0, 0,.375
```

The .pat file entry for ANSI32, is only slightly more complicated than ANSI31. It has a second line at the same angle as the first. Refer to the Crosshatch Sampler to see why. A single line won't suffice because there is a gap between the lines of the pattern.

Note that the second line passes through a different point: 0.177,0. This defines how far the second line is from the first, measured on the regular X,Y coordinate system.

```
*ansi33,ANSI Copper alloys
45,     0,0, 0,.25
45, .177,0, 0,.25, .125, −.0625
```

ANSI33 is similar to ANSI32, except that one of the pair of lines defining it is a dashed line. The third entry for ANSI33, above, has an extra pair of numbers: .125, −.0625. These two numbers represent pen-up and pen-down distances, respectively. Negative numbers in this last field are gap distances, positive numbers are segment lengths. A zero (0) indicates a dot.

```
*ansi36,ANSI Marble, Slate, Glass
45, 0,0, .21875,.125, .3125, −.0625,0, −.0625
```

ANSI36, above is an example of a hatch pattern with dots. Note the last four numbers in the last entry: .3125, −.0625,0, −.0625. These give the lengths of the segments in the dashed line making up the hatch pattern for ANSI36. They stand for, respectively, a $\frac{5}{16}$ inch dash, a $\frac{1}{16}$ inch gap, a dot (0), and another $\frac{1}{16}$ inch gap.

In this same example, note also that the X distance in the offset field is not zero, as it was in the other examples so far. In this case, each succeeding occurrence of the dashed line is shifted $\frac{7}{32}$ of an inch to the right, in the same direction as the line itself.

(Remember, the fourth and fifth numbers in a line definition are measured using a different coordinate system than normal. The X component of the offset is measured parallel to the line itself, and the Y component is measured perpendicular to the first occurrence of the line.)

Now look at a more complicated example:

```
*square,Aligned square pattern
0,   0,0, 0,.125, .125, −.125
90, 0,0, 0,.125, .125, −.125
```

This pattern is made up of two line systems at an angle of 90 degrees to each other. Each defining line passes through the origin (0,0), is offset from its counterpart by $\frac{1}{8}$ inch, and has $\frac{1}{8}$ inch repeating segments with $\frac{1}{8}$ inch gaps. The result is the Square pattern as shown in the Sampler.

Have you got the hang of it? Fine. Try creating the "Honey" pattern as shown in the Sampler. Another interesting example is given below for your study.

*adam,octagons

0,	0.0,0.0,	0,2.4142,	1,−1.4142
135,	0.0,0.0,	0,3.4142,	1,−2.4142
45,	1,0,	0,3.4142,	1,−2.4142
90,	−0.7071,0.7071,	0,2.4142,	1,−1.4142
45,	−0.7071,1.7071,	0,3.4142,	1,−2.4142
135,	1.7071,1.7071,	0,3.4142,	1,−2.4142
−45,	1,0,	0,3.4142,	1,−2.4142
−45,	1.7071,0.7071,	0,3.4142,	1,−2.4142
225,	0.0,0.0,	0,3.4142,	1,−2.4142
225,	−0.7071,0.7071,	0,3.4142,	1,−2.4142

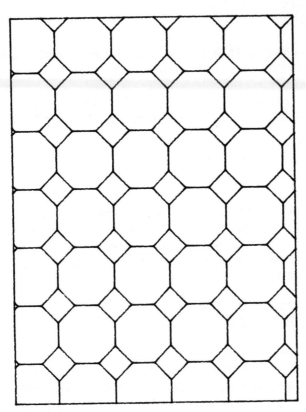

Appendix D

Display/Graphics Cards

AutoCAD can be used with many different video display cards and monitors.

RESOLUTION

Screen resolution, the clarity of the image on the monitor, is directly related to the number of addressable pixels or light emitting entities that make up the graphics and/or text on the screen. The more pixels per square inch of screen, the crisper the image.

On a monochrome monitor, all of the pixels are addressable for projecting an image. On a color monitor each pixel is dedicated to a certain color. This means that when you compare a monochrome monitor with a color monitor of the same resolution, the color image will be fuzzier because some of the pixels are devoted to another color. To get the same clarity from a color monitor it is necessary to use a higher resolution screen.

If you want your display in color, remember that the more color variation you want, the higher screen resolution you'll need. If the resolution is not high enough, graphics displayed might appear with jagged edges, this will not only look peculiar, but could result in premature operator fatigue and frustration: You will have to zoom in more closely to see drawing details. This means more zooms per drawing and more time waiting for the drawing to regenerate.

The trick is to match the graphics board and the CRT to get the desired resolution. A high resolution video screen will do no good if the graphics card will not support it or vice versa. The safest approach is to buy your CRT and graphics board from the same source, after seeing a demonstration.

DUAL SCREEN DISPLAYS

Dual screen setups have some special considerations. The second display unit requires a separate display adaptor board for text. AutoCAD can put graphics on one screen and text, that is, command entries and prompts, on the other, eliminating the need to flip back and forth. Two screens are most useful when you're debugging custom menus, they allow you to see the record of the progress of each macro.

Before you make a large investment in graphic cards and high resolution monitors, it is well worth your time to investigate the options available to you. Many articles about graphic cards and/or monitors have been written in computer trade magazines. You can find some of these in your local library. Computer dealers might be an additional source of useful information.

The table below also will help. If it is hard to visualize the screen resolution figures given below, visit a computer dealer and ask for a demonstration of different screens that match the resolutions listed.

When reading articles and/or talking to a computer salesperson, these translations of computerese might be helpful:

EGA is short for enhanced graphics adaptor.
CGA stands for color graphics adaptor.

Remember, buying the most expensive components does not assure the system will operate at its full potential. Buy only as much as you need.

Card	Configuration	Color(s)	Resolution (maximum)
Micro-Display Genius	single screen	monochrome	728×1004
Hercules Graphics Card	single screen	monochrome	720×348
Profit Systems Multigraph I	single screen	monochrome	720×348
Hewlett-Packard Multi-Mode	single screen	monochrome	640×400
STB Chauffeur	single screen	monochrome	640×352
IBM Enhanced Graphics	single screen	monochrome	640×350
STB Super Res 400	single screen	4	640×400
IBM Enhanced Graphics	single screen	4	640×350
Conographic Model 40	single screen	16	640×400
Control Systems Transformer	single screen	16	640×400
Persyst BOB	single screen	16	640×400
Sigma Designs Color 400	single screen	16	640×400
Tecmar Graphics Masters	single screen	16	640×400
IBM Enhanced Graphics	single screen	16	640×350
IBM Enhanced Graphics	single screen	16	640×200
Wyse Technology WY-700	single/dual	monochrome	1280×800
Quantram Quadscreen	single/dual	monochrome	968×512
IBM Color/Graphics	single/dual	monochrome	640×200
IBM Color/Graphics	single/dual	4	320×200
Verticom H16	single/dual	16	1024×768
Cordata FastDraft 480	single/dual	16	640×480
Verticom M16	single/dual	16	640×480
STB XVI	single/dual	16	320×200
Hewlett-Packard 82960	single/dual	256	640×480
IBM Professional Graphics	single/dual	256	640×480
Verticom M256	single/dual	256	640×480
Cambridge-Micro-1024	dual screen	monochrome	1024×780
GraphAx 20/20 Graphics Card	dual screen	16	2048×1280
Ramtek	dual screen	16	1280×1024
BNW Graphics Adaptor	dual screen	16	1024×1024
Control Systems Artist I	dual screen	16	1024×1024
Vectrix PEPE	dual screen	16	1024×1024
Number 9 NNIOS Board	dual screen	16	1024×768
TAT Galaxy G-500	dual screen	16	1024×768
Quintar GrapPort	dual screen	16	832×630

Frontier CADGraph2	dual screen	16	640×480
Quintar GrapPort	dual screen	16	640×480
Quintar Model 1080	dual screen	16	640×480
Scion PC640	dual screen	16	640×480
Control Systems Artist II	dual screen	16	640×400
STB Super Res 400	dual screen	16	320×400
Vectrix VX384	dual screen	256	672×512
Vectrix Midas Card Set	dual screen	256	640×480
Number 9 Revolution Board	dual screen	256	512×512

If you want to put together a monochrome system that is economical and satisfactory, a Hercules Graphics Card is a good choice for a medium resolution board. This board has become the industry standard. It supports both graphics and text mode. If you already have a board that will support the text mode and still have space to add another board, the Profit Systems Multigraph I is a good choice for the graphics card. Either of these cards will give a resolution of 720 × 348.

For a color system, the choice is not as clear. The color systems are still being developed and sometimes software upgrades are not accompanied by hardware interface software upgrades. Your software may not support color. This may mean a color monitor being operated in monochrome mode, which really doesn't make much economic sense.

Appendix E

Input Devices

The following list gives an overview of various input devices.

Manufacturer	Input Device	Options
Calcomp 2000 series	Tablet	Stylus 4 button
Calcomp 2100 series	Tablet	Stylus 4 button 16 button
Calcomp 9000 series	Tablet	Stylus 4 button 12 button 16 button
Calcomp 9100 series	Tablet	Stylus 4 button 16 button
Geographics Drafting Board	Tablet	N/A
GTCO Digipad 5	Tablet	Stylus 5 button 16 button
GTCO Micro DIGI-PAD (type 7)	Tablet	stylus 4 button
Hitachi HICOMSCAN HD Series	Tablet	Stylus 4 button 4 button (color) 12 button
Hitachi Tiger	Tablet	Stylus 4 button 12 button
Houston Instrument Series 7000	Tablet	Stylus 1 button 12 button

Houston Instrument HIPAD DT11AA	Tablet	N/A
Kurta Series I and II	Tablet	Stylus
		3 button
Kurta Series III	Tablet	Stylus
		16 button
Mutoh CX3000 Drafting Machine	Tablet	3 button
Numonics 2200 Series	Tablet	Stylus
		1 button
		4 button
		16 button
Pencept Penpad 320	Tablet	N/A
SAC GP-7 Grafbar & GP-8	Tablet	Stylus
Scriptel SPD	Tablet	Stylus
		4 button
Seiko DT-3103	Tablet	Stylus
		2 button
Seiko DT-4103	Tablet	Stylus
		2 button
		4 button
Summagraphics Bit Pad One	Tablet	Stylus
		4 button
Summagraphics MM Series	Tablet	Stylus
		3 button
		4 button
Summagraphics Microgrid	Tablet	Stylus
		3 button
		4 button
		16 button
Sun-Flex Touch Pen	Touch Pen	Stylus
Logitech Logimouse R-5	Mouse	3 button
Microsoft Mouse	Mouse	3 button
Mouse Systems Mouse	Mouse	3 button
Summagraphics SummaMouse	Mouse	3 button
Torrington Mouse	Mouse	3 button
USI OptoMouse	Mouse	4 button
Koala Pad	Joystick (emulated)	2 button
Kraft Joystick	Joystick	2 button
Disc Instruments LYNX	Trackball	3 button

DIGITIZERS, MICE, AND TOUCH PENS

Although you can use the keyboard to create AutoCAD drawings, it's far more efficient to use a digitizing tablet, a mouse or a TouchPen. These are referred to as pointing devices. They control the location of the crosshairs on the screen. Any of these items can enhance the process of drawing by decreasing the drawing time and lowering operator fatigue. Each device operates differently.

Digitizing Tablets

A digitizing tablet is by far the most versatile piece of drawing input hardware. The operator controls the screen cursor by moving a stylus or puck over an electronically sensitive tablet. The tablet, that has a live area corresponding to locations on the screen, senses the position of the puck and passes that information to the computer.

A digitizer can be used as a pointing device to select screen menu items, to locate entities while drawing, or to input existing drawings by tracing (*digitizing*). It also allows entering AutoCAD commands with a tablet menu. Digitizer pucks with as many as 16 buttons are available. Button menus can be created allowing you to call macros by pressing the appropriate number on the puck. With this configuration, one button is always assigned as the pick button, which allows you to pick a command from the screen menu or place a point.

Digitizer Tablets—Cabling Information

Calcomp 2000 Tablet

Tablet Dimensions	-	11 × 11 inches
Transmission mode	-	9600 baud
		even parity
		7 data bits
		2 stop bits
		binary output
		run mode
		125 pairs per second
		English units
		PC format
		parity enabled
		fixed parity disabled

Interface - RS232C serial I/O port

Cabling

```
Digitizer                     Computer
    2 ---------------------------- 3
                                 — 4
                                 |
                                 — 5
    7 ---------------------------- 7
                                 — 6
                                 |
                                 — 20
```

Switch Settings

Switch	Open	Closed
S1	1,2,4,8,9	3,5,6,7
S2	7,8	1,2,3,4,5,6,9
S3	1,2,3,4,5,6,7,8	9

Button assignments

Input Device	"Pick" button	Menu button(s)
Stylus	stylus	n/a
4 button	0	1,2,3

Calcomp 2100 Tablet

Tablet Dimensions	-	11 × 8.5 inches
Transmission mode	-	9600 baud
		8 data bits

binary output
run mode
English units
parity disabled
parity check disabled
fixed parity disabled

Interface - RS232C serial I/O port

Cabling

```
Digitizer                    Computer
    2 -------------------------------- 3
    3 -------------------------------- 2
                                  — 4
                                  |
                                  — 5
    7 -------------------------------- 7
                                  — 6
                                  |
                                  — 20
```

Switch Settings

Switch	Open	Closed	Optional
B1	1,4,5,7,8	2,6	3
B2	1,5,8	2,4,6,7	3,9,10

Button assignments

Input Device	"Pick" button	button(s)	Menu item
Stylus	stylus	n/a	
4 button	0	1-3	1-3
16 button	1	2-9	1-8
		:	9
		<	11
		=	12
		>	13
		?	14

Calcomp 9000 Series Tablets

Models - 9120, 9240, 9360, 9480 and 9600

Interface - RS232C serial I/O port

Cabling

```
Digitizer                    Computer
    2 -------------------------------- 2
    3 -------------------------------- 3
                                  — 4
                                  |
                                  — 5
    7 -------------------------------- 7
                                  — 6
                                  |
                                  — 20
```

Switch Settings - model 9120

Switch	Up	Down
SW1	1,2,3,4,5,8	6,7
SW2	4,5	1,2,3,6,7,8
SW3	2,3,6	1,4,5,7,8

Switch Settings - model 9240

Switch	Up	Down
SW1	1,2,3,4,5,8	6,7
SW2	4,6	1,2,3,5,7,8
SW3	2,3,6	1,4,5,7,8

Switch Settings - model 9360

Switch	Up	Down
SW1	1,2,3,4,5,8	6,7
SW2	4,5,6	1,2,3,7,8
SW3	2,3,6	1,4,5,7,8

Switch Settings - model 9480

Switch	Up	Down
SW1	1,2,3,4,5,8	6,7
SW2	4,7	1,2,3,5,6,8
SW3	2,3,6	1,4,5,7,8

Switch Settings - model 9600

Switch	Up	Down
SW1	1,2,3,4,5,8	6,7
SW2	4,5,7	1,2,3,6,8
SW3	2,3,6	1,4,5,7,8

Button assignments

Input Device	"Pick" button	button(s)	Menu item
Stylus	stylus	n/a	
4 button	pick	1-3	1-3
12 button	0	1-9	1-9
		#	10
		*	11
16 button	0	1-9	1-9
		A-D	10-13
		#	14
		*	15

Calcomp 9100 Series Tablets
Models - 9136, 9148, 9160

Interface - RS232C serial I/O port

Cabling

```
 Digitizer                    Computer
    2 --------------------------------- 2
    3 --------------------------------- 3
                                       — 4
                                       |
                                       — 5
```

```
7 -------------------------------- 7
                                 — 6
                                 |
                                 — 20
```

Switch Settings - Digitizing Processor Board
                - Model 9136

Switch	Open	Closed
SW1	1,2,8	3,4,5,6,7

Switch Settings - Digitizing Processor Board
                - Model 9148

Switch	Open	Closed
SW1	1,2,7	3,4,5,6,8

Switch Settings - Digitizing Processor Board
                - Model 9160

Switch	Open	Closed
SW1	1,2,7,8	3,4,5,6

Switch Settings - Communications Interface Board
                - Models 9136, 9148, 9160

Switch	Open	Closed	Optional
SW1	2,3,8	1,4,5,6,7	
SW2	4	1,3,5,6,7,2	

Button assignments

Input Device	"Pick" button	button(s)	Menu item
Stylus	stylus	n/a	
4 button	pick	1-3	1-3
16 button	0	1-9	1-9
		A-F	10-15

Geographics Drafting Board
    Tablet Dimensions   -   30 × 30 inches
                         -   42 × 36 inches
    Interface - special card (fits in one expansion slot)

    Cabling - supplied with the unit

    Button Assignment - "pick" button is foot switch activated.

GTCO Digipad 5 Tablets
    Transmission mode   -   9600 baud
                              8 data bits
                              1 stop bit

    Interface - RS232C serial I/O port

    Cabling

Digitizer	Computer
3 -------------------------------- 3	

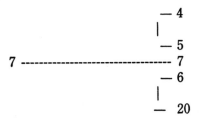

Digitizer cable end connects to port B on the tablet. A standard 25 wire straight connection cable can also be used.

Switch Settings - model 9600

Switch	On	Off	Optional
SW1	3,4,8	1,2,5,6,7	
SW2	5,7	6	1,2,3,4,8
SW3	3,4,7	1,2,6,8	

Button assignments

Input Device	"Pick" button	button(s)	Menu item
Stylus	stylus	n/a	
5 button	5	1-4	n/a
16 button	0	1-9	1-9
		A-F	10-15

GTCO Micro DIGI-PAD (type 7)

Tablet Dimensions	-	6 × 6 inches
	-	12 × 12 inches
Transmission mode	-	9600 baud
		2 stop bits
		binary output
		stream mode
		fastest sample rate
		0.005 inch resolution

Interface - RS232C serial I/O port

Cabling

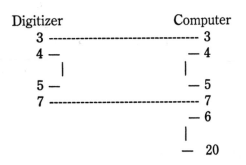

Button assignments

Input Device	"Pick" button	button(s)	Menu item

Stylus	stylus	n/a	
4 button	Red	Green	1
		Blue	2
		White	3

Hitachi HICOMSCAN HDG Series Tablets

Models -1111B (for 1111A see Hitachi Tiger Tablet)
      1216
      1515B
      2222
      4460

Interface - RS232C serial I/O port

Cabling

```
Digitizer                      Computer
    2 ----------------------------- 3
    3 ----------------------------- 2
    4 —                           — 4
        |                         |
    5 —                           — 5
        |
    8 —
    7 ----------------------------- 7
    6 —                           — 6
        |                         |
   20 —                           — 20
```

Switch Settings - models 1111B and 1515B

Switch	On	Off
DSW1	1,2,3	4,5,6,7,8
DSW2	3,5	1,2,4,6,7,8
DSW3		1,2,3,4,5,6,7,8

Switch Settings - models 1216,2222, 3648 and 4460

Switch	On	Off
MODE RATE	1,2,3,4	5,6,7,8
BAUD RATE	8	1,2,3,4,5,6,7

These settings assume the factory standard jumpers are installed.

Factory standard settings:

Item	Jumper Installed
1S	yes
RxC ASYNC	yes
TxC ASYNC	yes
SYNC	no
OP	no
F0	no
F1	no
RxC SYNC	no
TxC SYNC	no

Input Device	Button assignments		Menu item
	"Pick" button	button(s)	
Stylus	stylus	n/a	
4 button	1	2	1
		3	2
		4	3
4 button	Yellow	White	1
		Blue	2
		Green	3
12 button	0	1-9	1-9
		*	10
		#	11

Hitachi Tiger Tablet

Transmission mode	-	9600 baud
		Async
		Single port
		Port A
		7 data bits
		Even parity
		1 stop bit
		Test mode - off
		ASCII transmission
		Leading 0 suppression - off
		Function code output - on
		Buzzer - on (optional)
		Run mode
		Resolution - 0.001
		English units
		Incremental mode - off
		Rate 1
		Menu - disable

Interface - RS232C serial I/O port

Cabling

```
Digitizer                    Computer
   3 --------------------------- 3
   4 —                         — 4
     |                         |
   5 —                         — 5
   7 --------------------------- 7
                               — 6
                               |
                               — 20
```

Switch Settings - models 1111B and 1515B

Switch	On	Off
DSW1	6	remaining switches
DSW2	2,5	remaining switches
DSW4	1	remaining switches

Button assignments

Input Device	"Pick" button	button(s)	Menu item
Stylus	stylus	n/a	
4 button	1	2	1
		3	2
		4	3
12 button	0	1-9	1-9
		*	not used
		#	not used

Houston Instrument Series 7000 (COMPLOT)
Models - 7012, 7024, 7048 and 7060

Transmission mode -   9600 baud
7 data bits
even parity
2 stop bits
Stream mode

Interface - RS232C serial I/O port
Cabling

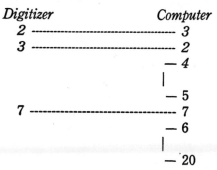

Cable connects to MODEM port on the digitizer.

Switch Settings - all models

Switch	Closed	Opened	Optional
SW1	1,6,7	2,3,5	4,8
SW2	7	1,2,3,4,5,6,8	
SW3		1,2,3,4,5,6,7,8	
SW4	1,3,4,5,6	2,7,8	
SW5	1,3,4,5,6,7	8	2
SW6	1,3		2,4

Button assignments

Input Device	"Pick" button	button(s)	Menu item
Stylus	stylus	n/a	
1 button	button	n/a	n/a
12 button	0	1-9	1-9
		*	10
		#	11

Houston Instrument HIPAD DT11AA Tablet
Transmission mode   -   4800 baud
                                  Stream mode

Interface - RS232C serial I/O port

Cabling

```
Digitizer              Computer
  9 —                    — 4
    |                      |
 10 -                    — 5
    |
 11 -                    — 6
    |                      |
 19 -                    — 20
    |
 20 ----------------------------- 7
 22 ----------------------------- 3
```

Kurta Tablets
Transmission mode   -   9600 baud
                                  binary
                                  8 data bits
                                  no parity
                                  1 stop bit (series II and III)
                                  2 stop bits (series I)

Interface - RS232C serial I/O port

Cabling

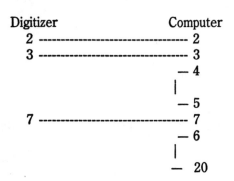

```
Digitizer              Computer
  2 ----------------------------- 2
  3 ----------------------------- 3
                         — 4
                           |
                         — 5
  7 ----------------------------- 7
                         — 6
                           |
                         — 20
```

Switch Settings - Series I

Switch	Up	Down
Program	1,5,6,7,8	2,3,4
Mode/Baud	4	1,2,3

Switch Settings - Series II

Switch	Up	Down
Program	1,8	2,3,4,5,6,7
Mode/Baud	4	1,2,3

Switch Settings - Series III

Switch	Up	Down
Program		1,2,3,4,5,6,7,8
Mode/Baud	1	2,3,4

Button assignments

Input Device	"Pick" button	button(s)	Menu item
Stylus	stylus	n/a	
3 button	Left button	Middle	1
		Right	2
16 button	1	2-16	1-15

Mutoh CX3000 Series Drafting/Digitizing Machine

Board Dimensions	-	900 × 1500 mm (model 12)
		1000 × 1500 mm (model 1015)
		955 × 1524 mm (model 3760)
		920 × 1500 mm (model 9015)

Transmission mode	-	9600 baud
		7 data bits
		even parity
		1 stop bit

Interface - RS232C serial I/O port

Cabling

```
Digitizer                          Computer
    2 --------------------------------- 3
    3 --------------------------------- 2
                                       — 4
                                        |
                                       — 5
    7 --------------------------------- 7
                                       — 6
                                        |
                                       — 20
```

Switch Settings - All Series

Switch No.	Function	Setting
1	Beeper	optional
2	X-axis parallel to bottom	on
3	Stream mode	on
4	Stream mode	on
5	9600 baud	on
6	9600 baud	on
7	9600 baud	on
8	Send (ignore CTS)	on

Button assignments

Button	Function
FW	"Pick" button
FE	first menu item
FS	second menu item
PS	Reset - absolute coordinates

Numonics 2200 Series Tablets
    Models - 1212 and 2020

    Transmission mode   -   9600 baud
                                        8 data bits
                                        1 stop bit

    Interface - RS232C serial I/O port

    Cabling

```
    Digitizer                  Computer
        3 ----------------------------- 3
                                      — 4
                                        |
                                      — 5
        7 ----------------------------- 7
                                      — 6
                                        |
                                      — 20
```

    Switch Settings - all models

Switch	Closed	Opened	Optional
A	1,8	2,5,7	3,4,6
B	3,5	-	1,2,4,6,7,8
C	2,3,4	1	-

    Button assignments

Input Device	"Pick" button	button(s)	Menu item
Stylus	stylus	n/a	
1 button	button	n/a	n/a
4 button	1	remaining	1-3
16 button	0	1-9	1-9
		A-F	10-15

Pencept Penpad 320
    Interface - special card (fits in one expansion slot).

    Hardware - PROM chips should be version C1 or higher.

    Cabling - supplied with hardware.

    Button assignment

Input Device	"Pick" button	button(s)	Menu item
Stylus	stylus	n/a	1-16*

    This device accesses a menu item by printing a number or letter on the digitizing tablet. See your local dealer for more information.

SAC GP-7 Grafbar and GP-8
    Transmission mode   -   9600 baud

```
                              7 data bits
                              odd parity
                              2 stop bits
```

Interface - RS232C serial I/O port

Cabling

```
    Digitizer                    Computer
        3 -------------------------------- 3
                                      — 4
                                      |
                                      — 5
        7 -------------------------------- 7
                                      — 6
                                      |
                                      —  20
```

Switch Settings - model GP-7 (serial numbers less than 31820).

	Closed (on)	Opened (off)
Switch	3	1,2,4,5,6,7,8

Switch Settings - model GP-7 (serial numbers 31820 and above).

	Closed (on)	Opened (off)
Switch	4	1,2,3,5,6,7,8

Switch Settings - model GP-8

	On	Off	Optional
Switch	1,5,6	2,3,4,10	7,8,9

Button assignment

Input Device	"Pick" button	button(s)	Menu item
Stylus	stylus	n/a	n/a

Scriptel SPD Tablet

Models - 1212, 1218, 2020 and 2436

Transmission mode   -   9600 baud
7 data bits
even parity
1 stop bit

Interface - RS232C serial I/O port

Cabling

```
    Digitizer                    Computer
        2 -------------------------------- 2
        3 -------------------------------- 3
                                      — 4
                                      |
                                      — 5
```

```
7 ------------------------------ 7
                                — 6
                                |
                                — 20
```

Button assignments

Input Device	"Pick" button	button(s)	Menu item
Stylus 4 button	stylus Left(extreme)	n/a remaining	1-3

Seiko DT-3103/4103 Tablets

Models - DT-3103 and DT-4103

Transmission mode   -   9600 baud
7 data bits
even parity
2 stop bits
BCD format

Interface - RS232C serial I/O port

Cabling

```
Digitizer                Computer
    2 ----------------------------- 3
    3 ----------------------------- 2
    4 —                          — 4
        |                        |
    5 —                          — 5
    7 ----------------------------- 7
    6 —                          — 6
        |                        |
   20 -                          — 20
```

Switch Settings - model DT-3103

Switch	On	Off
DSW1	1,2,3,7,8	4,5,6

Switch Settings - model DT-4103

Switch	On	Off
DSW1	6,7,8	1,2,3,4,5
DSW2	1,2,3	4,5,6,7,8
DSW3	2,4,8	1,3,5,6,7

Switch	Position
SW1	P
SW2	N

Button assignments

Input Device	"Pick" button	button(s)	Menu item
Stylus 2 Button	stylus White	n/a Blue	1

4 button	Switch 1	Switch 2	1
		Switch 3	2
		Switch 4	3

Summagraphics Bit Pad One

Transmission mode   -   9600 baud
even parity
2 stop bits
binary output
stream mode
fastest sample rate
0.005″ resolution

Interface - RS232C serial I/O port

Cabling

Digitizer	Computer
2 -------------------------------- 3	
4 —	— 4
5 —	— 5
7 -------------------------------- 7	
	— 6
	— 20

Switch Settings

All of the factory settings except for the following need to be corrected.

Switch	On
1	position 7

Button assignments

Input Device	"Pick" button	button(s)	Menu item
Stylus	stylus	n/a	
4 button	0	1	1
		2	2
		3	3

Summagraphics MM Series Tablets

Models - 961, 1201 and 1812

Tablet size   -   9 × 6 inches (model 961)
This tablet may also be oriented in the 6 × 9 direction.
12 × 12 inches (model 1201)
18 × 12 inches (model 1812)

These tablets have the option of being operated in either the normal digitizer mode or in a relative mouse type mode.

Interface - RS232C serial I/O port

Cabling - assumes factory set jumpers.

```
Digitizer                 Computer
    2 ------------------------------ 3
    3 ------------------------------ 2
                           — 4
                           |
                           — 5
    7 ------------------------------ 7
                           — 6
                           |
                           — 20
```

Button assignments

Input Device	"Pick" button	button(s)	Menu item
Stylus	stylus	n/a	
3 button	1 dot	2 dots	1
		3 dots	2
4 button	Yellow	White	1
		Blue	2
		Green	3

Summagraphics MicroGrid Tablets

Transmission mode	-	9600 baud even parity 7 data bits 2 stop bits
Interface	-	RS232C serial I/O port
	-	Two ports are supplied J4 (port 1) and J5 (port 2). Both are usable, but each is slightly different than the other.

Cabling - for connection to J4 (Port 1)

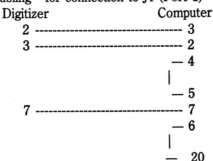

```
Digitizer                 Computer
    2 ------------------------------ 3
    3 ------------------------------ 2
                           — 4
                           |
                           — 5
    7 ------------------------------ 7
                           — 6
                           |
                           — 20
```

Cabling - for connection to J5 (Port 2)

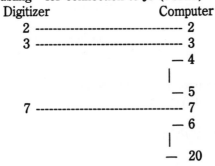

```
Digitizer                 Computer
    2 ------------------------------ 2
    3 ------------------------------ 3
                           — 4
                           |
                           — 5
    7 ------------------------------ 7
                           — 6
                           |
                           — 20
```

Button assignments

Input Device	"Pick" button	button(s)	Menu item
Stylus	stylus tip	stylus side	1
3 button	1	2	1
		3	2
4 button	1	2	1
		3	2
		4	3
16 button	1	2-9	1-8
		A-F	9-14
		0	15

Mice

A mouse provides some of the features of a digitizing tablet. A mouse also has a pick button and usually at least one other button that can be used with a screen menu. It doesn't, however, allow digitizing a drawing. This is because the mouse is a motion sensing device and it's the motion of the mouse itself that is registered on the screen, rather than a tablet's position response.

Some mice use optical sensors that require a special pad, while others use a ball that can be moved over any flat surface to detect the motion and position. In either case when you reach the edge of the pad or flat surface, you can simply lift the mouse and move it to a usable portion of the working surface to restore motion on the screen.

Mice—Cabling Information

Logitech Logimouse
      Models - R5, R7 and C7
      Interface - RS232C serial I/O port
      Transmission Rate - 9600 baud

As shipped from the manufacturer, the wiring for the R5 and R7 can be slightly different. Sometimes the unit can be hooked up right from the box. If that does not work, one of the two cabling arrangements will:

Cabling for models R5 and R7

Option 1

```
     Mouse                    Computer
       2 -------------------------- 3
       3 -------------------------- 2
                               — 4
                               |
                               — 5
       7 -------------------------- 7
                               — 6
                               |
                               — 20
```

Option 2

```
     Mouse                    Computer
       2 -------------------------- 2
       3 -------------------------- 3
                               — 4
                               |
                               — 5
```

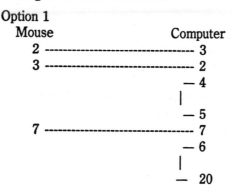

```
7 ------------------------------ 7
                               — 6
                              |
                              — 20
```

Model C7

The model C7 Logimouse may not work if it is hooked up to a hardware lock. This lock was on AutoCAD version 2.50. Updates have eliminated this piece of hardware. If you have this version of AutoCAD, then you might have to install the mouse on your second serial port.

Cabling for model C7

Mouse		Computer
2	----------------------------	2
3	----------------------------	3
4	----------------------------	4
5	----------------------------	5
6	----------------------------	6
7	----------------------------	7
20	----------------------------	20

In addition to the cabling changes for the model C7, you must either use the device driver MOUSE.SYS or the resident program MOUSE.COM. In either case one of the following statements must be added to one of your files. (This is not required for the R5 and R7 model mice.):

File	Statement
CONFIG.SYS	add device=MOUSE.SYS 9600 Re 2

or

| AUTOEXEC.BAT | add   device=MOUSE 9600 Re 2 |

Note: either one of these statements will set the mouse to be used on communications port 2.

Button Assignment
     Left - pick button
     Middle - first button menu item *
     Right - second button menu item *
        * regardless of mouse position

Cursor movement can be fast or slow, depending on the speed with which the mouse is moved. The speed at which the high-speed to low-speed cursor movement occurs can be changed in configuring the mouse.

Microsoft Mouse (For use on IBM PC only.)

The Microsoft Mouse is supplied with interface card and software. The interface card must be installed in an expansion slot inside the computer. The package comes complete with installation instructions.

Button Assignment
     Left - pick button
     Right - second button menu item *
        * regardless of mouse position

Cursor movement can be fast or slow, depending on the speed that the mouse is moved. The speed that the high-speed to low-speed cursor movement occurs can be changed in configuring the mouse.

Microsoft Serial Mouse
Interface - RS232C serial I/O port

Cabling

Mouse		Computer
2	------------------------------	2
3	------------------------------	3
4	------------------------------	4
5	------------------------------	5
6	------------------------------	6
7	------------------------------	7
20	------------------------------	20

Button Assignment
Left - pick button
Right - second button menu item *
* regardless of mouse position

Cursor movement can be fast or slow depending on the speed the mouse is moved. The speed that at which the high-speed to low-speed cursor movement occurs can be changed in configuring the mouse.

Mouse Systems Mouse
Interface   -   RS232C serial I/O port (direct hook-up)

To calibrate, move the mouse in large circles on the pad for about ten to fifteen seconds. Lift the mouse and look at its bottom. A red light should glow, indicating that it is ready for use. If a problem arises on a non-IBM unit, try another port if available.

Button Assignment
Left - pick button
Middle - first button menu item *
Right - second button menu item *
* regardless of mouse position

Summagraphics SummaMouse
Interface - RS232C serial I/O port

Transmission rate - 9600 baud

Cabling

Mouse	Computer	
2	------------------------------	3
3	------------------------------	2
		— 4
		|
		— 5
7	------------------------------	7
		— 6
		|
		— 20

Note: When using this device, AutoCAD will set it up for 9600 baud. If another program has set a different rate, the mouse must be turned off, then back on. At this point AutoCAD will request you to calibrate the mouse. This is done by moving the mouse diagonally across the pad.

Button Assignment
Left - pick button
Middle - first button menu item *
Right - second button menu item *
* regardless of mouse position

Cursor movement can be fast or slow depending on the speed at which the mouse is moved. The speed that the high-speed to low-speed cursor movement occurs can be changed in configuring the mouse.

TouchPens

A TouchPen™ can also be used for AutoCAD. A TouchPen consists of a fine, electrically charged mesh covering the screen and a pen or stylus with a special tip. You use the pen to point to the desired position on the screen and then close the circuit by placing your finger across a pair of metal rings on the pen to place or pick an item. The TouchPen is especially good for free hand sketching directly on the screen. It may make the operator a little tired if he or she has to hold the pen up for long periods.

TouchPen™—Installation Information

This device requires opening up the display console and installing an electronic screen covering the surface of the CRT. An adapter board on the CPU chassis is also required. This device is best handled by a knowledgeable technician. See a dealer who carries the Sun-Flex TouchPen for more information and installation.

Appendix F

Plotters

Plotters are the output devices that use pens to actually put the AutoCAD drawing on paper. As with all computer equipment, there's a tremendous variation in price and options.

PAPER SIZE

Probably the most important consideration is the size or sizes of paper you want for your final product. The list below gives the standard paper sizes.

Standard I		Standard II	
A	8.5″ × 11″	A	9″ × 12″
B	11″ × 17″	B	12″ × 18″
C	17″ × 22″	C	18″ × 24″
D	22″ × 34″	D	24″ × 36″
E	34″ × 44″	E	36″ × 48″

Be sure the plotter you choose can use the paper size(s) you need.

PLOTTER RESOLUTION

Plotter resolution, the precision with which the plotter can locate a given point, is very important. If the resolution is too coarse, the drawing might be produced with irregular lines instead of the clean, inked lines and text you want. The quality of the drawing is largely subjective, and sample plots are the best way to determine what you should buy. If the plotter resolution is too fine, speed can suffer.

PLOTTER SPEED

The speed of plotters varies widely. Plotter speed is normally specified in the diagonal direction. This will be the vector sum of the X-direction and Y-direction speeds, or about 1.4 times the axial speed. Speeds are usually measured in inches or centimeters per second.

Speed is not always the most important factor, and under certain conditions high speed can cause problems. The weak link in CAD is getting the ink on the paper. Too high a speed may not give the ink enough time to flow evenly onto the paper. Also, if you're plotting on a very smooth, heavy weight Mylar, a high-speed plotter can slip when drawing long lines. Slowing the plotter down can solve some of these problems.

PEN HANDLING

Pen changes are handled manually or automatically, depending on the plotter model. With the automatic pen changer, the drawing arm replaces the old pen and picks up the new one automatically. A manual changing system means you'll make the changes by hand during the appropriate pause in the plotting.

There are advantages and disadvantages to both systems. Automatic pen changers are faster, and, in theory, you don't have to watch them as closely. In practice, you'll have to keep an eye on the plot to make sure the ink doesn't dry out. Manual pen changers have fewer moving parts and generally cost less, but the hand changing can be annoying if you are plotting a large number of drawings at one time.

Replacement pens are also worth considering. Some plotters require special pens available only through the manufacturer. Others can use pens from several sources. Refillable pens cost less in the long run, but you might want to use disposables for their convenience and reliability.

The type of pen point is also important. The carbide tipped pen, if properly cared for, will give at least three times the service of a stainless steel pen.

The plotters listed below are currently supported by AutoCAD, that is, drivers are supplied by AutoCAD to operate them. Other plotters might work if the manufacturer provides the necessary driver files.

Manufacturer	Models supported
Alpha Metrics Alphaplot	I
	II
Amdek	AMPLOT II
Calcomp	81
	84
Gould Colorwrite	DS7
	DS10
	6120
	6310
	6320
Hewlett-Packard	7220
	7470
	7475
	7550
	7580
	7585
	7586
	ColorPro
Houston Instrument HI-PLOT	DMP-7
	DMP-8
	DMP-29
	DMP-40
	DMP-41
	DMP-42
	DMP-51

	DMP-51MP
	DMP-52
	DMP-52MP
	DMP-56
IBM	XY/749
	XY/750
	7371
	7372
	7374
	7375
Imagen Page Printers	Imagen Station
	8/300 Image Server
Ioline	LP 3700
Nicolet	ZETA 822
Penman Plotter	N/A
Roland DG	DXY-800
	DXY-101
Sweet-P	100
	600 (Six-Shooter)
Watanabe / Western Graphtec	MP1000

Plotters—Cabling Information

Alpha Metrics Alphaplot I and II

Automatic Pen Changer - Optional

Transmission mode -   9600 baud
                      even parity
                      7 data bits
                      1 stop bit

Interface - RS232C serial I/O port

Cabling

```
Plotter                        Computer
   2 ---------------------------- 3
   3 ---------------------------- 2
                                — 4
                                |
                                — 5
   7 ---------------------------- 7
                                — 6
                                |
                                — 20
```

Switch Settings Alphaplot I

Switch	Open	Closed	Optional
Internal	2,3,4,5,6,7		1,8
External	1,2,4,5,6,7	3,8	

Switch Settings Alphaplot II

Switch	Open	Closed	Optional
Internal	3,4,5,6,7	2	1,8
External	1,2,4,5,6,7	3,8	

Automatic pen changer option

WARNING - if you do not have an automatic pen changer and configure for one, damage to your plotter can result.

Plotting

Before plotting it is necessary to enter the following keystrokes:

With automatic pen changer
RESET, KEY E, KEY F, KEY A, KEY B, PEN UP.
Wait for pen carriage to stop cycling, then press REMOTE.

Without automatic pen changer
RESET, KEY 7, REMOTE

Amdek AMPLOT II

Transmission mode -   4800 baud
                          even parity
                          1 stop bit

Interface -   RS232C serial I/O port or Centronics
                          type parallel I/O port

Plotting speed -   100 mm per second or
                          200 mm per second (both are provided)

Serial operation

Switch Settings

Switch	On	Off
A	2,3	1,4,5,6,7,8
B	2,4	1,3,5,6,7,8

Cabling

```
Plotter                          Computer
  2  ------------------------------ 2
  7  ------------------------------ 7
 20  ------------------------------ 5
                                 — 6
                                 |
                                 — 20
```

Parallel operation

Switch Settings

Switch	On	Off
A	2,3	1,4,5,6,7,8
B	2	1,3,4,5,6,7,8

Cabling

A standard parallel printer cable is used.

Calcomp Model 81

    Transmission mode -   2400 baud
                                    even parity
                                    7 bits
                                    1 stop bit

Interface - RS232C serial I/O port

Switch setting
    Paper size switch - set at US for A size paper.

Cabling

```
Plotter                                  Computer
  2    -------------------------------     3
  3    -------------------------------     2
                                         — 4
                                         |
                                         — 5
  7    -------------------------------     7
                                         — 6
                                         |
                                         — 20
```

Set the correct baud rate with the XON or XOFF protocol.

Calcomp Model 84

    Transmission mode - 9600 baud
                              even parity
                              7 bits
                              1 stop bit

Interface - RS232C serial I/O port
Switch Settings

Switch	On	Off
	1,2,3,4,5,6,7,10	8,9

Paper size switch - set at US for A size paper.

Cabling

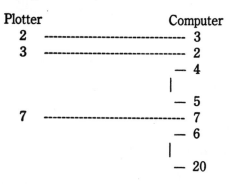

```
Plotter                                  Computer
  2    -------------------------------     3
  3    -------------------------------     2
                                         — 4
                                         |
                                         — 5
  7    -------------------------------     7
                                         — 6
                                         |
                                         — 20
```

Gould Colorwriter Models DS7 and DS10
    Transmission mode - 9600 baud
                              even parity
                              7 bits
                              1 stop bit

Interface - RS232C serial I/O port

Switch settings

	On	Off
Switch 3	1,3	2,4

Cabling

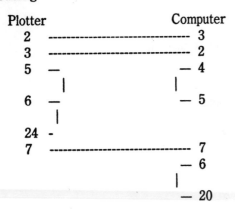

Plotter   Computer
2 ------------------------------ 3
3 ------------------------------ 2
5 —   — 4
        | |
6 —   — 5
        |
24 -
7 ------------------------------ 7
                                       — 6
                                       |
                                       — 20

Gould Colorwriter Model 6120

    Transmission mode - 9600 baud
                     even parity
                     7 bits
                     1 stop bit

Interface - Centronics - type parallel I/O port
Switch settings

Switch	On	Off	Options (paper size)	Not used
A	3,5,7	4,6,8	1,2	
B	1*			2,3,4

* normal plot

Cabling

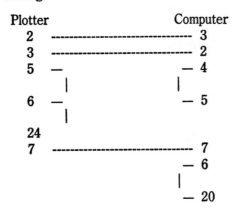

Plotter   Computer
2 ------------------------------ 3
3 ------------------------------ 2
5 —   — 4
        | |
6 —   — 5
        |
24
7 ------------------------------ 7
                                       — 6
                                       |
                                       — 20

Gould Colorwriter Models 6310 and 6320

    Transmission mode - 2400 baud
                     even parity
                     7 bits
                     1 stop bit

Interface - serial I/O port (male type)

Switch settings

Switch	On	Off	Options	Not used
2	1,3,7	2,4,5,6,8		
3	3,5,6	2	1,4	7,8

Cabling

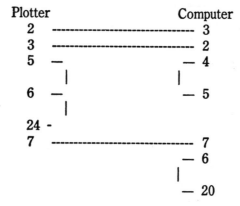

Plotter   Computer

```
Plotter                                Computer
  2   ----------------------------- 3
  3   ----------------------------- 2
  5   —                          — 4
         |                         |
  6   —                          — 5
         |
 24  -
  7   ----------------------------- 7
                                   — 6
                                      |
                                   — 20
```

Hewlett-Packard
  Models - 7470, 7475, 7550, 7580, 7585, 7586, and ColorPro.
    Transmission mode - 9600 baud
                            even parity
                            7 bits
                            1 stop bit
    Interface - serial I/O port

  Model - 7220
    Transmission mode - 2400 baud
                            even parity
                            7 bits
                            1 stop bit
    Interface - serial I/O port

Automatic roll-sheet feed option

Model	Option Available
7220	yes
7470	no
7475	no
7550	yes
7580	no
7585	no
7586	yes
ColorPro	no

Note: The model 7586 long plot capability is not supported.

Switch settings for models 7470, 7475, and ColorPro.

Switch	Setting
B1	0
B2	1
B3	0

```
B4          1
S1          1
S2          0
D-Y         D   (on models 7470 and 7475 only)
```

Switch settings for models 7580, 7585 and 7586

Function	Setting
RS232C speed selector	9600
Parity	on
Parity	even
Eavesdrop	off
Emulate	normal
Expand	normal

Cabling (all models)

```
Plotter                        Computer
  2 ------------------------------ 3
  3 ------------------------------ 2
  4 —                          — 4
       |                   |
  5 —                          — 5
  7 ------------------------------ 7
  6 —                          — 6
       |                   |
 20 -                          — 20
```

If you have a choice of hooking up the cable to either the *computer* connection or the *terminal* connection, the computer connection is preferred.

Houston Instrument DMP series
Transmission mode - 2400 baud
even parity
7 bits
1 stop bit
XON/XOFF protocol

Interface - RS232C serial I/O port

Cabling (all models except DMP 7 and 8)

```
Plotter                        Computer
  2 ----------------------------- 3
  3 ----------------------------- 2
                              — 4
                               |
                              — 5
  7 ----------------------------- 7
                              — 6
                               |
                              — 20
```

Cabling (models DMP 7 and 8)

```
Plotter                        Computer
  2 ----------------------------- 3
  3 ----------------------------- 2
```

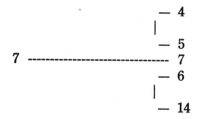

```
                              — 4
                              |
                              — 5
7  ------------------------- 7
                              — 6
                              |
                              — 14
```

DMP-29 Switch settings

	Open (1)	Closed (0)	Options
Switch	2,3,4,5	1,7,	6,8

For the DMP-29 the cable is connected to the plotter's modem port.

When using the DMP-40, DMP-41 and DMP-42 before a plot is begun, it is necessary to set the baud rate to 9600. This is done by pressing the "ENTER" then "up arrow" buttons.

To configure the DMP-51, DMP-52, DMP-51MP, DMP-52MP and the DMP-56 it is first necessary to press the "ENTER" then "SCALE UR" keys. This will put you in the menu mode for the plotter. Refer to the plotter's instruction manual for detailed configuring instructions. Once configured these plotters will retain these settings, until another configuration is done.

IBM MODEL XY/700 series
Model XY/749

Transmission mode - 9600 baud
even parity
7 bits
1 stop bit
XON/XOFF protocol

Interface - RS232C serial I/O port

Switch settings

	On	Off
Switch	1,2,3,4,5,6,7,10	8,9

The paper size switch should be set for "A" size. This setting is the "US" option.

Model XY/750
Transmission mode - 2400 baud
even parity
7 bits
1 stop bit
XON/XOFF protocol

Interface - RS232C serial I/O port

Cabling (both models)

Plotter		Computer
2	-------------------------	3
3	-------------------------	2

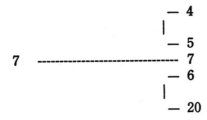

IBM MODEL 7300 series
Models 7371 and 7372

Transmission mode - 9600 baud
even parity

Interface - RS232C serial I/O port

Switch	Setting
B1	0
B2	1
B3	0
B4	1
S1	1
S2	0
D-Y	D

Models 7374 and 7375

Function	Setting
RS232C speed selector	9600
Parity	on
Parity	even
Eavesdrop	off
Emulate	normal
Expand	normal
Monitor mode	normal
Local	normal
Duplex	full
Direct connect	reserve
Dtr-Bypass	normal

Cabling (all models)

```
Plotter                    Computer
   2  ------------------------  3
   3  ------------------------  2
   4  —                       —  4
       |                       |
   5  —                       —  5
   7  ------------------------  7
   6  —                       —  6
       |                       |
  20  -                       —  20
```

Imagen Page Printers
Models - Imagen Station
         8/300 Image Server Printstations

Transmission mode - 9600 baud
                    no parity
                    8 data bits
                    1 stop bit

Interface - RS232C serial I/O port or Centronics type parallel I/O port

Parallel interface
    Requires a standard parallel printer cable.

Serial interface
    Cabling

```
    Plotter                            Computer
      2    ---------------------------    3
      3    ---------------------------    2
      4    ---------------------------    5
      7    ---------------------------    7
                                        — 6
                                        |
                                        — 20
```

Ioline LP 3700
    Transmission mode - 9600 baud
                        no parity
                        8 data bits
                        2 stop bits

Interface - RS232C serial I/O port

Cabling

```
    Plotter                            Computer
      2    ---------------------------    3
      3    ---------------------------    2
      4    —                            — 4
             |                            |
      5    —                            — 5
      7    ---------------------------    7
      6    —                            — 6
             |                            |
     20    —                            — 20
```

Nicolet ZETA 822
    Transmission mode - 9600 baud
                        even parity

Interface
-            RS232C serial I/O port
             (plotter hardware must include the ''MODE 6'' option—HPGL—
             RS232C format, version 5.4)

Cabling

```
    Plotter      Computer
      2    ---------------------------    3
      3    ---------------------------    2
```

```
4  —                           —  4
   |                           |
5  —                           —  5
7  ---------------------------  7
6  —-                          —  6
   |                           |
20 —                           —  20
```

Plotter end of cable connects to "TO MODEM" connection on the plotter.

Switch settings

Switch	On	Off	Options
SW01	2,3	1,4	
SW02	2	1,3,4,5,6,7	8
SW03	2,3,4	1,5	6,7,8

Variable switches
SW04A   8 pen speed - 80 percent of full speed
SW04B   5 pen pressure - medium

Penman Plotter

Transmission mode   9600 baud
-                    no parity
                     8 data bits
                     1 stop bit

Interface - RS232C serial I/O port

Cabling

```
Plotter      Computer
  2    ---------------------------  3
  3    ---------------------------  2
  4    ---------------------------  5
  7    ---------------------------  7
                                —  6
                                |
                                —  20
```

Roland DG Plotters

Models - DXY-101
       - DXY-800 (multipen unit)

Transmission mode - 9600 baud
                     even parity
                     1 stop bit

Interface - RS232C serial I/O port or Centronics
             type parallel I/O port

Parallel interface

Requires a standard parallel printer cable.

Serial interface

Cabling

```
Plotter                                    Computer
   2    ------------------------------      2
   3    ------------------------------      3
   4    ------------------------------      4
   5    ------------------------------      5
   6    ------------------------------      6
   7    ------------------------------      7
  20    ------------------------------     20
```

Switch settings
	On	Off
Switch	6,8,9,10	1,2,3,4,5,7

Sweet-P model 100
Interface - Centronics type parallel I/O port

Cabling - seek dealer or manufacturer's recommended cable for your particular application.

Sweet-P Six Shooter model 600
Interface - RS232C serial I/O port or Centronics type parallel I/O port

Parallel interface
Requires a standard parallel printer cable.

Interface - RS232C serial I/O port

Cabling

```
Plotter                                Computer
   3    --------------------------- 2
   7    --------------------------- 7
  20    --------------------------- 5
                                   — 6
                                   |
                                   — 20
```

Switch settings
	On	Option (paper size)
Switch	1,3,4,5,6,7,8	2

Watanbe / Western Graphtec MP1000
Transmission mode - 9600 baud
even parity
7 bits
1 stop bit
XON/XOFF protocol

Interface - RS232C serial I/O port

Cabling

```
Plotter    Computer
   2    --------------------------- 3
   3    --------------------------- 2
                                   — 4
                                   |
                                   — 5
```

```
7    ------------------------------- 7
                              — 6
                          |
                              — 20
```

Switch settings

	On	Off
Switch	2,3,5,6,8	1,4,7,9,10

Appendix G

Printers as Plotters

Some dot matrix printers can be used to plot drawings, but the quality of the drawing will not be as good as for a true plotter. The printed images from dot-matrix printers tend to be a little ragged, depending on the brand of printer.

Laser printers can provide a cost-effective printing alternative, particularly if you're using the laser printer for other applications as well.

Here is a list of printers supported by AutoCAD.

MANUFACTURER	MODEL	COLOR OPTIONS
Epson	FX80	Black/white
	LQ-1500	Black/white
Hewlett-Packard	LaserJet 2686A	Black/white
IBM	Color JetPrinter 3852-2	7 + white
JDL	750	7 + white (ribbon change)
Mitsubishi	G500-HI	7 + white
	G500-LO	7 + white
Okidata	84	N/A
	93	N/A
Printonix	4160	N/A
Texas Instruments	Omni 850	Black/white
	855	Black/white
	857	6 + white
	860	Black/white
	865	Black/white

Printer Plotters—Installation Information

Epson FX80

Transmission mode- 9600 baud
even parity
7 data bits
1 stop bit

Interface-parallel
Check owners manual for above settings
∿∿∿∿∿∿∿∿∿∿∿∿∿∿∿∿

Interface-serial
Epson main board switch settings

	On	Off
Dip switch 1	6,7,8	1,2,3,4,5
Dip switch 2	1,2	3,4

serial board above the main board (inside Epson)

	On	Off
Dip switch	1,2,5, 6,7,8	3,4

or, if your Epson has two Dip switches on the serial board.

	On	Off
Dip switch 1	1,2,3,6	4,5,7,8
Dip switch 2	1,2	3,4,5,6

Cabling
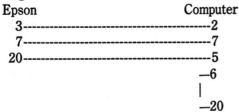

    Epson   Computer
     3---------------------------------------2
     7---------------------------------------7
    20---------------------------------------5
                              —6
                              |
                              —20

Hewlett-Packard LaserJet 2686A
Transmission mode—9600 baud
             no parity
             8 data bits
             1 stop bit

Interface - serial

Cabling
    Hewlett-Packard   Computer
     3 - - - - - - - - - - - - - 2
     7 - - - - - - - - - - - - - 7
    20 - - - - - - - - - - - - - 5
                          —6
                          |
                          —20

For plotting size limitations consult printer owner's manual.

Hewlett-Packard LaserJet Plus

Interface- serial
See data for Hewlett-Packard 2686A

Interface - parallel
Connect to Centronic type parallel port using standard printer cable.

For plotting size limitations consult printer owner's manual.

IBM   Color JetPrinter 3852-2
   Interface -   parallel
                      Connect to Centronic type parallel port using standard printer
                      cable.

JDL-750 and 750E

   Interface -   parallel
                      Connect to Centronic type parallel port using standard printer
                      cable.

If you have an E model, the E stands for extra wide. During the configuration, AutoCAD
will ask if you have an E model.

Mitsubishi G500
   Interface -   parallel
                 Connect to Centronic type parallel port using standard printer
                 cable.

Okidata 84
   This printer will not operate if any of the following options have been installed:
                      Plug 'n Play option
                      IBM-compatibility option
                      Apple compatibility option
                                 (Imagewriter)

   Transmission mode -   9600 baud
                         no parity
                         8 data bits
                         1 stop bit

   Interface - parallel and serial
               Regardless of port to be used the following front main board switch
               settings are required.

                              On   Off
               Dip switch   3   1,2,4,5,6,7,8

   Interface - serial
               On the serial board, jumper plugs numbered SP1, SP2, SP3, SP4,
               and SP5 all need to be set with the jumper on side A.

               Okidata main board switch settings

                              On   Off
               Dip switch 1   1,2,3,4,5,6,7   8
               Dip switch 2   2,3,4,5,6   1,7,8

Cabling
Okidata   Computer
   3   - 2
   4   -------------------------- 5
   7   -------------------------- 7
   6   —   —6
         | |
  20   —   —20

Okidata 93
This printer will not operate if any of the following options have been installed:

Plug 'n Play option
IBM-compatibility option
Apple compatibility option
(Imagewriter)

Interface - parallel and serial
Regardless of port to be used the following front main board switch settings are required.

	On	Off
SW-1	5,7	1,2,3,4,6,8
SW-2*	5,6	

* the remaining settings are factory set and should not be altered.

See cabling for Okidata 84. It is the same.

Printronix Model 4160
Interface - parallel
Connect to Centronic type parallel port using standard printer cable.

Options for this printer are set by jumpers. The following settings are required.

8 bit plot mode	W1	open
	W2	closed
	W3	open
Format least	W4	open
significant bit		
carriage return = no line	W5	open

To reach these jumpers the unit must be disassembled.

Texas Instruments Omni 800 series

Transmission mode - 9600 baud
no parity
8 data bits
1 stop bit

Automatic line feed - Off

Interface - parallel—requires Centronics type parallel interface.

- serial — requires a TI Serial to parallel adaptor (see TI representative).

Switch location: in bottom of printer under the printhead.

Model numbers 855, 857, 860 and 865

Switch	Position Parallel	Position Serial
SW 1	On	On
SW 2	On	On
SW 3	Off	Off

SW 4	On	On
SW 5	On	On
SW 6	On	On
SW 7	On	Off
SW 8	On	Off

Model number 850

Switch	Position Parallel	Position Serial
SW 1	On	On
SW 2	Off	Off
SW 3	Off	Off
SW 4	Off	Off
SW 5	Off	Off
SW 6	On	On
SW 7	On	On
SW 8	On	Off

Trackballs—Installation Information

Disc Instruments LYNZ Trackball
Model - LX200-192-A (found on bottom of device).

Interface - serial
- use modular to RS232C cable adaptor (in some cases it is also necessary to use a gender changer). All pieces are supplied with the unit.

Button Assignment
Left - pick button
Middle - first button menu item *
Right - second button menu item *
* regardless of mouse position

Joystick—Installation Information

A joystick can be used as a pointing device for AutoCAD. For a device such as the Kraft Joy stick to be used, an IBM Game Controller board such as "Joystick A" must be installed. The Koala Pad can also be used with this card.

Kraft button assignment
Red button on top - pick button
Black button on base - slow motion mode or first menu item

Koala Pad button assignment
Left - pick button
Right - slow motion or first menu item

H

Command Summary

APERTURE +2	Target box object snap size control.
ARC	Draws an arc.
AREA	Determines area and perimeter of a polygon.
ARRAY	Makes multiple copies, in a circular or rectangular pattern, of selected objects.
ATTDEF +2	Makes an Attribute Definition entity for the text information to go with a Block Definition.
ATTDISP +2	Globally toggles Attribute entity visibility.
ATTEXT +2	Gets drawing Attribute data.
AXIS +1	Puts ruler lines on the monitor.
BASE	Determines the basepoint for inserting the current drawing.
BLIPMODE	Toggles display of marker blips.
BLOCK	Combines a group of entities into a single, insertable object.
BREAK +1	Divides an object into two objects or erases part of an object.
CHAMFER +1	Draws a chamfer where two lines intersect.
CHANGE	Changes location, orientation, size, or other properties of an object or text string.
CIRCLE	Draws a circle.
COLOR	Sets the color for objects.
COPY	Copies objects.
DBLIST	Lists entity database information.
DELAY	Stops the execution of commands in scripts.
DIM +1	Allows dimension notations to be added to a drawing.
DIM1 +1	Allows a single dimension notation to be added to a drawing.
DIST	Displays the distance between two points.
DIVIDE +3	Puts a specified number of evenly-spaced dividing markers along an object.
DOUGHNUT +3	Draws doughnuts.
DONUT +3	Draws bagels.
DRAGMODE +2	Adds dragging ability to appropriate commands.
DTEXT +3	Dynamic text drawing.
DXBIN +3	A special purpose command for use with certain programs. Inserts binary files into a drawing.
DXFIN	Loads drawing interchange files.

274

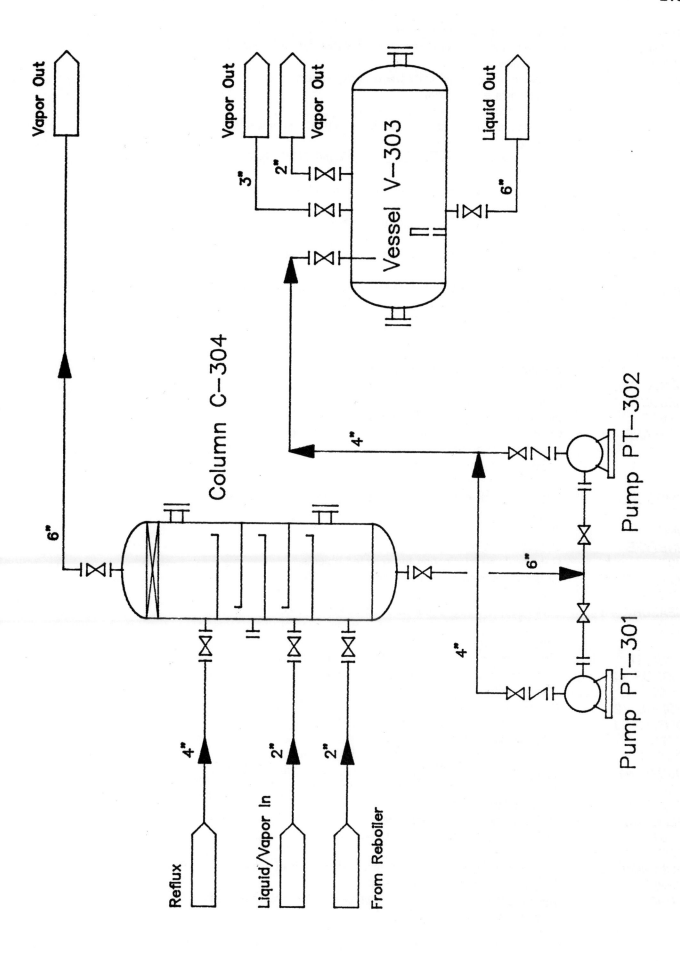

DXFOUT	Writes drawing interchange files.
ELEV +3	Determines extrusion thickness and elevation for entities in 3D.
ELLIPSE +3	Draws ellipses.
END	Saves the drawing and exits the drawing editor.
ERASE	Erases parts of a drawing.
EXPLODE +3	Breaks a block or polyline into its parts.
EXTEND +3	Causes a line, arc, or polyline to extend to meet another object.
FILES	Implements disk utilities.
FILL	Toggles automatic filling of solids, traces and wide polylines on and off.
FILLET +1	Connects two lines, arcs, or circles with a smooth arc of a specified or zero radius.
FILMROLL	A command in AutoCAD 2.6 for use with unreleased (as of July, 1987) 3D software.
'GRAPHSCR	Turns on the graphics display on single-screen systems; used in menus and scripts.
GRID	Toggles a grid of dots, at a specified spacing, off and on.
HATCH +1	Executes pattern-filling and cross-hatching.
'HELP OR '?	Lists valid command and data entry options and/or gets help for a specific command.
HIDE +3	Removes *hidden* lines and regenerates a 3D visualization.
ID	Identifies the coordinates of a specific point.
IGESIN +3	Loads an IGES file.
IGESOUT	Writes an IGES file.
INSERT	Inserts copy of an object block into drawing.
ISOPLANE +2	Chooses the plane of isometric axes to be the current plane in an orthogonal drawing.
LAYER	Creates and controls drawing layers and assigns linetype properties and color to layers.
LIMITS	Controls the checking of drawing boundaries and changes those boundaries.
LINE	Draws lines.
LINETYPE	Defines, loads and sets linetype.
LIST	Gets database information for selected objects.
LOAD	Gets user-defined shapes for use with SHAPE.
LTSCALE	Sets the linetype scaling factor.
MEASURE +3	Sets markers along an object at specified distances.
MENU	Puts command macro sets into the menu areas of the screen, tablet, and button.
MINSERT	Draws multiple copies of a block in a rectangular pattern.
MIRROR +2	Puts mirror image of entities around a specified axis.
MOVE	Moves entities to a new location.
MSLIDE +2	Creates a slide file from screen display.
OFFSET +3	Creates offset curves and parallel lines.
OOPS	Unerases last set of erased objects.
ORTHO	Forces lines to be either vertical or horizontal.
OSNAP +2	Allows precise location of object in reference to existing objects.
PAN	Moves the screen display along the drawing.
PEDIT +3	Allows polyline editing.
PLINE +3	Draws connected arcs and lines.
PLOT	Makes drawing hard copy on a plotter.
POINT	Draws single points.
POLYGON +3	Creates regular polygons with specified number of sides.
PRPLOT	Makes drawing hard copy on a printer.
PURGE	Removed unused blocks, layers, linetypes, and text styles if used as first command.

QTEXT	Displays text as boxes to avoid time spent in generating details.
QUIT	Exits the drawing without saving any changes.
REDO	Undoes an UNDO.
REDRAW	Cleans up the portion of the drawing on the screen.
REGEN	Recalculates and redraws entire drawing.
REGENAUTO	Lets other commands control automatic regeneration of drawing.
RENAME	Allows name changes for blocks, layers, linetypes, named views, and text styles.
'RESUME	Continues an interrupted command script.
ROTATE +3	Rotates an object.
RSCRIPT	Begins a command script again.
SAVE	Saves current drawing without leaving the Drawing Editor.
SCALE +3	Changes size of objects.
SCRIPT	Starts a command-sequence script.
SELECT	Creates a selection-set of objects for use in subsequent commands.
'SETVAR	Changes and/or displays system variable values.
SH +	3 Lets you use simple DOS commands.
SHAPE	Inserts pre-defined shapes.
SHELL +3	Lets you use other programs while still running AutoCAD . . . maybe.
SKETCH +1	Makes free-hand drawings.
SNAP	Forces points entered to lie only on grid points.$LF
SOLID	Makes filled-in polygons.
STATUS	Shows current drawing settings and data.
STRETCH +3	Stretches a portion of a drawing.
STYLE	Makes named text styles from the 4 or 5 basic AutoCAD fonts, with variations of horizontal scaling, mirroring, and obliquing.
TABLET	Lines up a blueprint or sketch to a digitizing tablet for accurate AutoCAD tracing. Tells AutoCAD where tablet menus are located on the tablet.
TEXT	Draws text according to selected size and style.
'TEXTSCR	Toggles to the text display. (For use in command scripts and menus.)
TIME	Displays time and date. Also provides elapsed timer.
TRACE	Creates solid lines of a specified width.
TRIM +	3 Erases entity parts that cross boundaries.
U	Undoes the previous command.
UNDO	Undoes multiple previous commands. Gives control of undo grouping facility.
UNITS +1	Chooses angle and coordinate display formats and precision.
VIEW +2	Returns a saved view to screen or saves and names the current screen display.
VIEWRES	Lets you set the precision and speed of drawing circles and arcs. "Fast ZOOM"
VPOINT +3	Chooses the 3D visualization point of view.
VSLIDE	Displays slide file.
WBLOCK	Writes entities to another drawing file.
ZOOM	Makes the drawing display larger or smaller.

I

Release 9

Version 2.6 was superseded by an upgrade called "Release 9," instead of "Version 2.7." The logic behind this nomenclature is that AutoCAD wanted to emphasize that this is their ninth major release in five years. (If you have paid for all eight upgrades, you probably didn't need to be reminded.)

In any case, "Release 9" includes more nifty features, among which is a customizable user interface, with pull-down menus, icon menus, and dialogue boxes, along with 15 more fonts, a few more commands, and more system variables.

COPROCESSOR REQUIRED

One not so nifty feature is that you now MUST have a coprocessor chip in your PC to run AutoCAD. This adds about $150 to $450 to your hardware costs, depending on whether you have a plain old PC or a new SuperWhiz/Bang 386. (As of this writing, some of the early 386 machines will not take a coprocessor chip at all, due to a hardware design fault, despite the fact that a socket is present. If you have one of these 386's, you had better stick with Version 2.6, it runs just fine and very fast without the 80387 chip.)

According to Autodesk, however, AutoCAD Release 9 will run much faster than earlier versions because it has been streamlined to operate ONLY with an 8087 or 80287 or 80387 chip present. (Only a masochist would try to do much AutoCAD without a coprocessor anyway; the zoom and pan times when a REGEN is required are three or four times longer without a coprocessor.)

USER INTERFACE

Release 9 has a new user interface. Portions of it will function only if the display driver for your system has been updated to accommodate it. Display drivers that have been revised in Release 9 to implement the new interface include: Hercules monochrome, IBM EGA, VGA, and CGA.

Some problems have been reported when running Release 9 with clone display boards. If Release 9 won't function on your system, try temporarily installing a "real" Herc board and see if the problem goes away.

PULL-DOWN MENU

The standard menu shipped with copies of Release 9 has a special section containing "pull down" menus (like Reflex and other software). You can customize this menu or create entirely new pull down menus of your own.

If you move your pointing device cursor to the top of the screen, where the coordinates are shown, a menu bar will appear. The options are:

Tools   Draw   Edit   Display   Modes   Options   File

Move your cursor to the desired item and push the select button. A window containing suboptions for that item will drop down into the graphics area. You can then point at and select any suboption. The suboptions for the standard pull down menu bar are as follows:

Tools. All of the various object snap modes can be selected transparently. (Remember, you may have more than one object snap mode in effect at one time.) You can also turn off *OSNAP* entirely. Other choices under the Tools menu are *Cancel, UNDO1, REDO,* and *REDRAW.*

Draw. Choices here are *LINE, ARC, CIRCLE, POLYLINE, INSERT, DTEXT,* and *HATCH.*

Edit. You can select *ERASE, MOVE, COPY, TRIM, EXTEND, STRETCH,* and *PEDIT* commands from this pull down menu.

Display. The available suboptions are *Window* (for a window ZOOM), *Previous (ZOOM P), Dynamic ZOOM, PAN,* and *3D VIEW.* (These are all done transparently and can be called during other commands.)

Modes. This allows selecting Drawing Aid Modes, Entity Creation Modes, or Layer Modification. Drawing Aid Modes include *SNAP, GRID, AXIS, ORTHO, ISOPLANE* and *BLIPMODE.* Entity Creation Modes include entity *COLOR, LINETYPE, and LAYER.* Layer Modification lets you create new layers, turn layers off and on, reset the current layer, and change layer *LINETYPE* and *COLOR.* (These are also done transparently.)

Options. Select from *AutoSHADE* (if you have it), *3D objects* for insertion, and *Fonts.*

File. The choices are *SAVE, END, QUIT, PLOT* and *PRPLOT.*

It should be noted that these pull down menus are not just another place to stash macros, but are a real productivity increaser. For one thing, the entity draw commands repeat automatically; that is, you will stay in that command until you hit [CTRL] C. This is ideal when you are doing the same type of operation over and over.

The standard AutoCAD pull down menus operate transparently, as much as possible, as noted above. For example, you can start to do a window *ZOOM* via the Display menu, pull down the Tools menu and turn off *OSNAP*'s, pull down the Modes "Drawing Aids" menu and turn off *SNAP*, and then continue the *ZOOM.*

Another difference is that, with ADE-3 present, the new pull down menus also contain "icons" (like those on the Macintosh) for certain suboptions, such as text fonts, hatch patterns, AutoShade parameters, and other items, letting you see what you are going to get without having to look in the book. Each hatch pattern is shown and there is a little box next to it to hit if you want to use that pattern.

CREATING PULL-DOWN MENUS

The best way to create your own pull-down menus is to clone the sample menu called "counter.mnu" and then take it apart using a text editor in nondocument mode. Modify the copy to suit your own needs after you have analyzed it line by line.

Some of the things you will discover are:

(1) The pull down sections of the menu are identified by headers of this form:

```
***POP1
***POP2
```

etc.

(2) The first line under POPx is the title that will appear on the pull down menu bar.

(3) If the menu title starts with a tilde (~), it will be displayed with reduced intensity. You can use this to flag menus that are deactivated, incomplete, or under development.

(4) A label like this: [—] will draw a horizontal line across the menu box.

(5) Don't put more items in a pull-down menu than your screen will handle, usually 20 or 21.

(6) Dollar sign ($) commands, to select other menus and submenus, can be placed in pull down menus. The pull down sections are identified for menu swapping by the names P1 through P10.

(7) $Px = * will cause the menu assigned to the POPx section to appear.

Note also that pull-down menus become inactive during *DTEXT, SKETCH, VPOINT,* and dynamic *ZOOM.*

You can create your own icons for custom applications as well. Icons can be drawn using AutoCAD, of course, and are managed for menu purposes by grouping them into libraries with the aid of the new *SLIDELIB* utility program.

SLIDE LIBRARIES

The new *SLIDELIB* utility program lets you collect slide (.sld) files into libraries (.slb files). To view a slide from a library in AutoCAD, enter *VSLIDE* and then the name of the library with the name of the slide in parentheses, thus: library(slide).

To make a slide library, first use EDLIN or a text editor to create an ASCII file consisting of a list of all the slide names. You don't need the extension .sld on the names; it will be understood by AutoCAD. For example, you might have a list of slides called *SLIDLIST.* To create a library called *NAMELIBR.SLB,* enter the command (from DOS):

SLIDELIB NAMELIBR SLIDLIST.

SLIDES FOR ICON MENUS

Here are a few rules for making slides that will be used for icon menus:

(1) Keep the icons simple for speed. Don't *HATCH* or *FILL* areas.

(2) Do a *ZOOM* Extents before using the *MSLIDE* command to make the .sld file.

(3) Icon menus display faster if you collect all the slides for that menu into a library.

ICON MENUS

The fastest way to construct your own icon menus is to study a renamed copy of the "counter.mnu." Note that:

(1) The icon sections start with ***ICON.*

(2) Not all display drivers support icon menus.

(3) The first line of the menu, below ***ICON,* is the title.

(4) The labels in an icon menu are the slide names.

(5) A blank as the first character in an icon label changes it to a regular text label, instead of a slide.

(6) $I = * in a menu item will display an icon menu.

(7) Icon menus can be nested, if desired.

An icon menu might look like this:

```
***ICON
**ISECTNA
[GOODIES]
[NAMELIBR(BLOCK1)]^Cinsert block1
[NAMELIBR(BLOCK2)]^Cinsert block2
```

```
[NAMELIBR(BLOCK3)]^Cinsert block3
[ CANCEL]^C
[ SECTNB]$I = ISECTNB $I = *


**ISECTNB
[DINGBATS]
[OTHERLIB(FIG1)]^Cinsert fig1
[OTHERLIB(FIG2)]^Cinsert fig2
[OTHERLIB(FIG3)]^Cinsert fig3
[ CANCEL]^C
[ SECTNA]$I = ISECTNA $I = *
```

In the icon menu above, there are two submenus called *SECTNA* and *SECTNB*. Each submenu has an item to call the other submenu. The slides for each submenu are grouped into separate libraries called *NAMELIBR* and *OTHERLIB*. Within those libraries are three slides each: *BLOCK1.SLD*, *BLOCK2.SLD*, *BLOCK3.SLD*, and *FIG1.SLD*, *FIG2.SLD*, *FIG3.SLD*.

DIALOGUE BOXES (ADE-3)

The pull down menus are only an inch or so wide at the suboption level. At the next level down, for sub-suboptions, you will find that some of them take up almost the entire screen. These windows are the new AutoCAD "Dialogue Boxes." The Modes "Modify Layer" macro, for example, contains a command ('DDLMODES) that calls up a dialogue box showing what layers are present, which layers are on or frozen, what colors and linetypes are used on those layers, and allows you to add new layers. This dialogue box has more than one page if you have a lot of layers in your drawing. You can see, and modify, your drawing layer structure by flipping through these pages and selecting items to change.

Similarly, you can see and modify all your drawing settings in one screen via the Modes "Drawing Aids" macro. This option issues the *'DDRMODES* command.

To change a toggle setting on a dialogue box, place the cursor in the check box and hit your select button. This will activate your choice and put a check mark in the box. To enter a value or a label in a box (such as the snap setting), pick that box and type the information in from the keyboard. Hit [Return] or the "OK" box next to the entry if the entry is what you intended; otherwise, edit it as needed. When all of the desired changes have been made to that screen, you can put it away by picking the "OK" box at the bottom. If you decide not to change anything, hit *"CANCEL"*.

It should be noted that field names displayed in dialogue boxes are limited to 24 characters. More characters can be present, but they won't be shown in the box. Attribute values created will be limited to 34 characters. Longer strings can be input by using ordinary INSERT (with ATTDIA turned off). Longer strings can be partially viewed in the dialogue box, but altering them will impose the 34 character limit.

For a list of new commands that include dialogue boxes, see below under "New Commands." A dialogue box has also been added to the *INSERT* command and can be activated by using the *SETVAR* command to set the *ATTDIA* system variable to 1. This dialogue box is used for entering the values for attributes associated with the block being *INSERT*ed. When this dialogue box is used, it replaces attribute verification.

NEW TEXT FONTS

The new text fonts include the following:

Romans: Roman Simplex
Romanc: Roman Complex
Romand: Roman Duplex
Romant: Roman Triplex

Scripts: Script Simplex
Scriptc: Script Complex
Greeks: Greek Simplex
Greekc: Greek Complex
Italicc: Italic Complex
Italict: Italic Triplex
Cyrillic: Alphabetical order (Alpha, Beta, Gamma . . .)
Cyriltlc: Transliteral order (A to Z order)
Gothice: Gothic English
Gothicg: Gothic German
Gothici: Gothic Italian

Besides text fonts, AutoCAD has provided symbol libraries for various fields:

Syastro: Astronomical Symbols
Symap: Map Symbols
Symath: Math Symbols
Symeteo: Meteorological Symbols
Symusic: Music Symbols

If you are going to use any of the symbol fonts, you should first make a character map showing which symbol corresponds to which English alphabet character. Each upper and lower case letter in a TEXT string will produce a different symbol. Additionally, the following keys stand for other symbols: [, \,], ^, __, ', {, |, }, ~, <, and >. This gives a total of 64 possible symbols per font.

To make a character map, first use the STYLE command to create a named text style containing the desired symbol font. (The STYLE command will automatically change the active text style to the newly defined style. You should manually change it back to "STANDARD" using the Style option under the TEXT command.)

Next, use the *TEXT* command to make lines of conventional text containing every letter (in alphabetical order, both upper and lower case) and the 12 characters listed above. Triple space between letters and divide the 64 total characters among four separate strings; otherwise AutoCAD's proportional spacing can cause enough misalignment to make it difficult to tell which symbol goes with which letter.

COPY each line of standard text directly below itself.

Use the *CHANGE* command to alter the style of the copy to the desired symbol style.

Do this for every symbol font you intend to use. It is probably a good idea to do this for the Greek and Cyrillic alphabets, too, if you are ever likely to use them.

Use *PRPLOT* to get hard copy of the character map(s).

NEW COMMANDS

Two of the new commands are *REDEFINE* and *UNDEFINE*. These will rarely be needed. *REDEFINE* allows you to replace AutoCAD commands with AutoLISP commands having the same name. *UNDEFINE* is used to deactivate the original definition of the command. You could, for example, define an AutoLISP *OFFSET* command that decurves polylines before creating the offset and then Splines both polyline frames. If you use the UNDEFINE command on the AutoCAD OFFSET command, the AutoLISP OFFSET command will take its place. To put things back the way they were, use the REDEFINE command on OFFSET to toggle back to the original AutoCAD form of the command. Very few users will find it necessary to do this.

The new "Dialogue Boxes" are called up by four added commands: *DDRMODES, DDEMODES, DDLMODES,* and *DDATTE.*

DDRMODES allows you to set *SNAP, GRID, AXIS, ORTHO, ISOPLANE* and *BLIPMODE.* You can toggle these functions on and off, and you can change the appropriate numerical settings for *SNAP,* etc. The X setting will be automatically used for the Y setting for *SNAP, GRID,* and *AXIS.* You can then set the Y value to another number if you wish.

DDEMODES is used to set the parameters that new entities will have when drawn, such as *COLOR, LINETYPE, LAYER,* and *ELEV.* The *LINETYPE* and *LAYER* options on this screen will call up secondary dialogue boxes to allow you to choose from *LAYER*s and *LINETYPE*s that have previously been created or loaded.

DDLMODES gives you a dialogue box for adding layers, changing layer settings, and renaming layers. It incorporates all of the LAYER command functions, as described above under User Interface.

All three of these commands above can be called transparently, while you are in the middle of another command, by putting an apostrophe in front of the command name.

DDATTE is used for editing attributes of a block. Pick any item you wish to change and enter the new information. When done, hit the "OK" box to complete the update. Hit "Cancel" if you change your mind.

INSERT COMMAND CHANGES

You can, under Release 9, set up the *INSERT* command so that the scale and angle are predefined *before* you drag a block into position. This is helpful if you are trying to place the block relative to other entities in the drawing. When asked for the insertion point you can enter any of these options:

Xscale	to preset the X scale factor
Yscale	to preset the Y scale factor
Zscale	to preset the Z scale factor
Scale	to preset X, Y, and Z scale factors to a common scale
Rotate	to preset the rotation angle
PXscale	to temporarily preset the X scale factor
PYscale	to temporarily preset the Y scale factor
PZscale	to temporarily preset the Z scale factor
PScale	to temporarily preset X, Y, and Z scale factors to a common scale
PRotate	to temporarily preset the rotation angle

For each of these selections, AutoCAD will prompt you for the appropriate data. You can then select another option, if desired, and drag the newly scaled block into position.

The last five options above will result in AutoCAD asking you for scale factors again after you have selected the insertion point. The first five will not; what you see is what you're going to get.

You can also turn off the attribute prompts during block insertion, if desired, by using *SETVAR* to set *ATTREQ* to zero.

Besides the Invisible, Constant, and Verify modes for attributes, there is now the "Preset" mode. Preset mode causes blocks to be inserted with the default attribute values, without asking.

MULTIPLE COMMANDS

Provision has been made for easier repetition of keyboard and menu commands for drawing and editing:

Keyboard repetitive commands. Normally, if you wanted to do a number of, for example, ID commands to determine the coordinates of certain items, you would have to enter ID, select the first point, hit [Return] to reinvoke the command, and so on. Release 9 added the *MULTIPLE* command modifier to keep you in any command until you hit [CTRL] C.

As soon as you type in *"MULTIPLE,"* AutoCAD will allow you to type in a space without taking it as a [Return]. You can then add the command you want to do repeatedly and hit [Return]. For the example above, you would enter *"MULTIPLE ID."* Then, every time you selected a point on the screen, the coordinates would be calculated and displayed on the command line. (You would probably be doing this with some form of object snap(s) active, and would flip to the text screen and do a Print Screen to record the points for later use.)

Menu repetitive commands. If you place *^C^C at the start of a menu macro (just after the macro label right bracket), AutoCAD will save the entire command, including any parameters set, and repeat it until you hit [CTRL] C. This eliminates the frustration of picking an item from a menu and then finding when you repeat the command with a [Return] that you have to re-enter all of the options selected.

An example of a menu repetitive command:

[CHG TEXT]^C^CCHANGE;\;;;;;;*

This macro will let you hit a series of text items where all you want to do is change the text string itself, not its height, angle, style, etc. This type of operation occurs fairly frequently.

SYSTEM VARIABLES

Certain system variables have been revised and others added. The following list gives the system variables affected under Release 9:

VARIABLE	TYPE	STATUS
ACADVER	STRING	Acad version number (Read-only)
ATTDIA	INT	ON: dialogue boxes are shown when entering attributes; OFF: prompts are used
ATTREQ	INT	1: AutoCAD prompts for attributes during insertions; O: AutoCAD takes the default values.
CHAMFERA	REAL	[saved with the drawing]
CHAMFERB	REAL	[saved with the drawing]
CMDECHO	INT	1: Turns off prompts if input is from an AutoLISP command; O: Prompts always ON.
DISTANCE	REAL	Set only by the DIST command.
MENUECHO	INT	Bit 2 = 1: Turns off prompts if input is from a menu item.
MENUNAME	STRING	Gives the name of the currently loaded menu.
POPUPS	INT	1: display driver supports the advanced user interface; O: popups, etc., not available
SPLFRAME	INT	Turns ON and OFF display of guide polygons in spline-fit polylines.
SPLINESEGS	INT	Allows calling for a specific number of segments for each spline patch.
TEXTSIZE	REAL	Specifies the default height for new text using the current font.

SPLINES

Release 9 also permits you to do "Splines." These are a smoother form of curve fitting during polyline editing with *PEDIT.* You can still "Fit" the polyline, as before. The "Fit" option produces a smooth series of connected arcs passing through all the vertices of the polyline. For a better fit, though, the Spline option under PEDIT will more closely match the polyline's contours.

VPOINT ROTATE

For 3D work, Release 9 lets you adjust your viewpoint under the VPOINT command by selecting the "Rotate" option. This gives a much easier way of determining the new viewpoint than specifying the X, Y, and Z coordinates. Instead, you specify the viewpoint by two angles, one relative to the X-axis and one relative to the XY-plane. This is a lot easier to visualize for most people than the coordinate method.

Object Selection

Some changes were made in object selection, too: A highlighted or dashed pickbox will be displayed during "Crossing" selections, if your display driver supports this feature. This will remind you that you are not doing an ordinary "Window" type selection.

A new selection option called "Box" lets you call up either the Window-type box or Crossing-type box, depending on the order in which you define the corners of the box. If you hit the left side of the box first, the "Window" selection box will be employed. If you define the right side of the box first, a "Crossing" selection box will be created. This is particularly handy in menu items where the type of selection box needed is not known in advance. Note that "box" can't be abbreviated.

The other new selection option is "Auto" (or *AU*). This does two things: first, it automatically switches to a window selection if the first selection point is not on an object. Second, it includes the "box" option feature as defined above. If you are writing a menu item where the type of selection needed could vary with the situation, use the Auto option for maximum flexibility.

Release 9 lets you temporarily turn off the repetitive object selection mode. After you have made a single type of object selection, the command you are in will proceed without asking for more objects. Turn off repetitive selection by entering "SI" at the select objects prompt.

FILE COMPATIBILITY

Another item of interest to some users is that files created on any computer under Release 9 can be transferred to another system without going through an intermediate *DXFOUT/DXFIN* double translation. This means that if you have networked several computers running both DOS and UNIX, the AutoCAD drawing files can be shared by all machines in the network.

MENU FILE COMPATIBILITY

You will find that menu files that have been compiled under earlier releases (.mnx files) will not work with Release 9. You must have the old, uncompiled .mnu file where AutoCAD can find it. You might have already found that Version 2.5 compiled menu files can't be moved from one PC to another. The best practice is to never delete the uncompiled .mnu files from the ACAD directory.

3-D EDITING CHANGE

In *3DLINE, 3DFACE,* or in commands that edit 3-D entities, you can use *OSNAP* modes to lock onto objects on the top face of an extruded object, if you are in a 3-D viewpoint.

ASSOCIATIVE DIMENSIONING

Associative dimensioning is now active for new drawings by default. To turn it off for new drawings, call up your prototype drawing and use the *SETVAR* command to set *DIMASO* to off (zero). Then *END* the drawing.

Other Bestsellers From TAB